interior design

interior design

a critical introduction

clive edwards

English edition
First published in 2011 by

Berg

Editorial offices:

First Floor, Angel Court, 81 St Clements Street, Oxford OX4 1AW, UK

175 Fifth Avenue, New York, NY 10010, USA

Berg is the imprint of Oxford International Publishers Ltd.

Library of Congress Cataloging-in-Publication Data

A catalogue record for this book is available from the Library of Congress.

British Library Cataloguing-in-Publication Data

A catalogue record for this book is available from the British Library.

ISBN   978 1 84788 313 1 (Cloth)
         978 1 84788 312 4 (Paper)

Typeset by JS Typesetting Ltd, Porthcawl, Mid Glamorgan

Printed in the UK by the MPG Books Group

www.bergpublishers.com

contents

———

Illustrations

Figures

Plates

acknowledgements

———

I would like to take this opportunity to thank the many individuals who have helped in various ways with this project. Firstly my editor at Berg, Tristan Palmer, who devised the original idea and has been so supportive throughout the whole process. Many practitioners were generous with their time and assistance, especially in the sourcing and supply of images of their work. I therefore thank Lena Anderson, Adrian Avram, Anna Autio, Lena Chin-Katz, John Davis, Jennifer Demaio, JoAnne Dugas, Susan Ginesi, James Harvey, Nakagone Ikuku, Alison Jones, Bolam·Lee, Barbara McFall, Tarlyn Mead, Giles Miller, Jodie O'Connor, Toshinori Okino of ILYA Corp, Claudia Oliva, Leena Pallasoja, Sandy Patience, Neil Pearson, Sarah Roberts, Marilyn Sturgeon, Dimitrios Tsigos, Natasha Webb, Lesley Whitworth and Ben and Oscar Wilson. Korenna Cline and Stuart Perkins of the ASID graciously assisted me in my searches.

My colleagues Jan Bowman, Tina Frank and Jill Wells offered valuable help and advice. Finally, I thank Lynne Edwards for her caring and constant support as well as her continuing interest in my work.

chapter 1

---

introduction

The subtitle of this work uses the word 'critical' to reflect its meaning as careful judging and observation, reflection and the application of objective approaches to the study of interiors. A critical evaluation includes analysis, identification and explanation. This introduction will therefore offer some definitions and explain the methodology of the work, and so will include aspects of theoretical positions derived from psychology, semiotics, social science, philosophy, gender studies, history, politics and technology as they relate to interiors. This allows a degree of abstraction from the daily practice of interior design.

In addition, considerations including issues of dwelling, location, the public and private, ideology, archetypes and ethics will allow interior design to be understood as being integrative of a number of disciplines, so influencing its development. This approach should give the reader the chance to see interior design as something more than compositional techniques, colour schemes and design solutions, without denying their importance in actual practice. Indeed, I consider these in depth further on. The transdisciplinary approach therefore adapts and adopts theories and methods from several disciplines and applies them to create a set of knowledges for interior designers.

However, the particular characteristics of interior design are crucial, and to balance the conceptual aspects, the introduction will consider the distinctiveness of interior design practice as a way of creating places that may have a very long-lasting or transient impact; that may be in old buildings or new; domestic or corporate; public or private. This approach allows for the discussion of the essential and fundamental practices of the profession, while later chapters will develop the study and practice of the planning and design of interior architectural spaces, their furnishings and equipment, as undertaken by interior designers.

definitions

What Is Interior Design?

Interior design is a professionally conducted, practice-based process of the planning and realization of interior spaces and all the elements within. Interior design is concerned with the function and operation of the space, its safety and efficiency, its aesthetics and its sustainability. The work of an interior designer draws upon many other disciplines, such as environmental psychology, architecture, product design and aesthetics, in relation to a wide range of building spaces including hotels, corporate and public spaces, schools, hospitals, private residences, shopping malls, restaurants, theatres and airport terminals. Put another way: 'The interior is a contextualized backdrop for all human engagement and is much more than just the sum of its parts' (Taylor and Preston 2006: 9).

This emphasis on the human aspects is all-important as it can be easy to become involved in abstractions of space, design and decoration or in overemphasizing particular aspects of the space to the detriment of the well-being of human occupants and users. It is clear that a holistic approach is essential.

Popular (Mis)perceptions

Interior design has suffered from an 'identity crisis' that now shows signs of being overthrown. Compared disparagingly with architecture, it has actually been an integral part of many architectural practices for many years. Some consider that interior design is about being creative but not necessarily professional, with a lack of rigour and consistency within itself. A growth in university level educational provision and the development of professional associations over recent decades has altered this situation dramatically. Popular culture sees interior design as having a residential focus, and apparent connections to the role of women, domesticity and home-making exacerbate this. Lastly, some are of the opinion that interior design has little in the way of any design theory related to its practice, in the sense that what it provides are simply 'add-ons' to existing work.

A variety of different though overlapping practices relate to interiors at various levels. These range from large-scale architectural projects to home decorating. Therefore, a comprehensive range of activities and approaches has to come under the umbrella of the term 'interior design'.

Mark Taylor and Julieanna Preston express this range by suggesting that interior design can be 'a decorative craft, an architectural speciality, a spatial art or a physical articulation of social interaction' (2006: 9). This wide-ranging definition allows the introduction of a whole array of interior design concepts.

Interior Architecture

We may define interior architecture as the design of structurally created interiors, for domestic, recreational and business usage, which apply some architectural processes. The knowledge base would include aspects of architecture, the design of structural systems, HAVC systems, interior design, knowledge of recognized standards for occupational and safety matters, and professional responsibilities. Graeme Brooker and Sally Stone posit that 'interior architecture is concerned with the remodelling of existing buildings and attitudes towards existing spaces and structures, building reuse and organisational principles. It bridges the practice of interior design and architecture …' (2007b: 126). In mainland Europe, the interior architect generally undertakes the type of work that in North America would be recognized as interior design.

Interior Decoration

A simple definition suggests that interior decoration is the planned co-ordination, for artistic effect, of colours and furniture, etc., in a room or building. Brooker and Stone again give a fuller and more comprehensive definition: 'Interior decoration is the art of decorating interior spaces or rooms to impart a particular character that fits well with existing architecture. Interior decoration is concerned with such issues as surface pattern, ornament, furniture, soft furnishings, lighting and materials' (2007b: 126).

The interior decorator has had a bad press over the years. Architect and critic Christian Norberg-Schulz was dismissive of anyone other than the architect being involved with interior spaces:

> We may ... mention the meaningless profession of the "interior decorator". The interior evidently is a primary aspect of the architectural totality. It therefore necessarily belongs directly to the task of the architect. The possibility for teamwork does not exist, as teamwork has to be based upon a meaningful division of the architectural totality. The division in exterior and interior is not meaningful in this context. What we need are "designers" who create artefacts which the architect may choose between. (1965: 204)

Christian Norberg-Schulz (1926–2000)
Norberg-Schulz was a Norwegian architect who developed theories of architecture. Initially influenced by Gestalt psychology, Piaget's educational theories and structuralism, he moved from these analytical and psychological concerns towards issues surrounding the phenomenology of place. His ideas, including analysis of the *genius loci*, have a resonance for interior designers (despite his comments above) because human responses to their environment are poetic as well as analytic. He encouraged the elevation of the idea of 'place' over space.

Tom Loveday explored the distinctions between interior decoration and design and pointed out that interior decorators usually deal with surfaces and objects placed in space. He suggests that 'their main form of activity is *selection* and *purchase*, according to assemblies of *taste*'. On the other hand, he suggests that interior designers determine three-dimensional space, using geometry, by manipulating representations of material substances or 'building work'. At the same time, interior designers use sample boards to represent materials as part of the representation of their design, often to a 'client'. This causes a certain degree of connection to interior decoration at the same time as to architecture. For the interior designer, it is the reflective, critical and theoretical practices, especially the concept of critical distance, that marks them out. (Loveday 2003) It is this issue of critical rigour that I use to distinguish interior decoration from interior design.

Interior Design

A limited definition suggests that interior design is the design of the interior of a building, including its furniture, fittings, finishes, etc., according to artistic and architectural criteria. Brooker and Stone's more encompassing definition suggests that: 'Interior design is an interdisciplinary practice that is concerned with the creation of a range of interior environments that articulate identity and atmosphere, through the manipulation of spatial volume, placement of specific elements and furniture and treatment of surfaces' (2007b: 126). This definition, which stresses interdisciplinarity, also reinforces the connections to the user, the space and the materials employed in the creative process.

The knowledge base of interior design requires a critical understanding of the designing, equipping and furnishing of residential and commercial interior spaces, within a sustainable framework. It includes a knowledge of design theories and practices; computer applications for drafting and graphic techniques; principles of interior lighting, acoustics, systems integration and colour co-ordination; furniture and furnishings; textiles and their application; the history of interior design and period styles; basic structural design; and building codes and inspection regulations, and the application of these to interiors, including offices, hotels, factories, restaurants and housing. In certain circumstances, a working knowledge of business practices is essential.

Professional Definitions

The BIDA (British Interior Design Association) defines interior designers as persons qualified by education, experience and recognized skills who identify, research and creatively solve problems pertaining to the function and quality of the interior environment. They perform services relevant to interior spaces that include programming, design analysis, space planning, aesthetic evaluation and inspection of work on site, using specialized knowledge of interior construction, building systems and components, building regulations, equipment, materials and furnishings. In addition, they prepare drawings and documents relative to the design of the interior space. In comparison, an interior decorator can give advice on entire decorative schemes, including furnishing and furniture, but will not enter into building contracts or supervisory contracts.

The IIDA (International Interior Design Association) definition follows:

For the purpose of improving the quality of life, increasing productivity, and protecting the health, safety, and welfare of the public, the Professional Interior Designer:

- Analyses the client's needs, goals, and life and safety requirements.
- Integrates findings with knowledge of interior design.
- Formulates preliminary design concepts that are appropriate, functional, and aesthetic.
- Develops and presents final design recommendations through appropriate presentation media.
- Prepares working drawings and specifications for non load-bearing interior construction, materials, finishes, space planning, furnishings, fixtures, and equipment.
- Collaborates with professional services of other licensed practitioners in the technical areas of mechanical, electrical, and load-bearing design as required for regulatory approval.
- Prepares and administers bids and contract documents as the client's agent.
- Reviews and evaluates design solutions during implementation and upon completion.

(IIDA)

Beyond Definitions

Despite definitions, bodies of knowledge and business and professional practice, interior design is also about the intangible aspects of interior spaces such as atmosphere and performance. The French philosopher Jean Baudrillard considers that the term 'interior design' sums up the 'organizational aspect of the domestic environment, but it does not cover the entire system of the modern living space which is based on a counterpoint between DESIGN and ATMOSPHERE'. He suggests that 'both mobilize the value of play and of calculation – calculation of function in the case of design, calculation of materials, forms and space in the case of atmosphere' (1996 [1968]: 30). In other words, there must be a relationship between the technical design and the culturally based atmosphere or sense of place. This idea clearly links interior design to human needs.

The designer Shashi Caan has identified a number of qualities of interior design that make these connections. Firstly, she identifies the essential need for shelter, and its concomitant aspects of habitation and occupation, and then develops the need to manipulate the space. As interior design is transformative of spaces, it is tangible and experiential through the senses, and is therefore emotive and evocative about human activity, well-being etc. It interprets spaces through a relationship to context and site. It is about the reality of place more than a concept of abstract space. Interior design has the potential to be the catalyst for sensual, magical, efficient and/or aspirational spaces (Caan 2007: 52).

Interior design, then, must incorporate the decorative, know itself and have a conviction about its role and legitimacy. Ideally, interior design should touch the soul, stimulate the senses and inspire people; it should create delight, and make manifest people's dreams and aspirations. Interior design needs to develop itself as a discipline, but this is not without problems. Lynn Chalmers has suggested that 'interior design, as a discipline, is caught between the structure and self-importance of architecture and the laissez-faire and self-indulgence of interior decoration' (2007: 78).

Finally, we need to tease out the distinction between the discipline and the profession. It is not absolute by any means, so it is best to see these two on a continuum, based on their particular support systems. For example, universities and learned societies often underpin disciplines in a spirit of unity, whereas a broadly defined 'marketplace', operating in a spirit of difference, generally supports professions.

the discipline of interior design

Discipline, in the academic sense, refers to the configuration of ideas and knowledge in particular combinations and within particular constraints. An academic discipline is a branch of knowledge, taught or researched at degree level. What characterizes disciplines are the academic journals that publish research, the activities of professional or learned societies, and the academic departments or faculties in which their practitioners operate.

Both scholarly and practical activities underpin the discipline of interior design. Over 2,000 years ago, the Roman architect Vitruvius wrote in his *Ten Books of Architecture*: 'The arts are each composed of two things, the actual work and the theory of it. One of these, the doing of the work, is proper to men trained in the subject, whilst the other, the theory [liberal arts] is common to all scholars' (1960: 11). To maintain, identify and support a discipline, a body of theory, a research base for both theory and practice and an education support system are required in addition to the actual activities the discipline undertakes. Therefore, it is important for interior designers to continue their professional education by keeping up with developments in these fields as they affect interiors.

In addition, various other branches of learning impact on interiors and these have, in turn, had an effect on creating a body of theory. These include humanities subjects (e.g. aesthetics, history, philosophy, visual art, architecture and design); social sciences (e.g. sociology, psychology, gender and sexuality, ethnic studies and anthropology); and applied sciences, (e.g. business, education, technology and environmental studies).

The Influence of the Humanities

The humanities, which encompass the applied arts of architecture and design, the visual arts, philosophy (including aesthetics), history and geography, will all influence interior design theory and practice. These fields of study offer some answers to the contextualizing of the past and the present, considerations of where we have come from and why we build, furnish and decorate our spaces as we do. The chapters on history, decoration and design will be informed by these influences and reinforce their importance.

The Influence of Visual Culture

Visual culture can be a catch-all term for any visual manifestation from 'Old Masters' to the World Wide Web. It particularly relates to visual events that offer knowledge, explanation or gratification to the viewer. The media related to visual culture includes such examples as digital multi-media, film, fashion, art & design and graphics. It is clear that architecture and interior design are part of the world of visual culture as they have connections with most of the fields associated with visual culture and the theories attached to them. The crossover between the catwalk and the interior is also increasingly in evidence, as well-known couture brands enter the interior market. Visual literacy is crucial to interior designers in terms of critical thinking, as well as in the reception and deployment of things visual. An understanding of the visual codes, dialogues and theories of visual culture will assist this process (see Elkins 2003). Like material culture, the influence of the contemporary visual culture will be direct and potent on the practice of interior design.

The Influence of Material Culture

Material culture is the study of the values and attitudes of a particular community or society at a given time through the evaluation of their objects. The direct link between object and use tends to make the past more accessible and often more interesting as it relates to the everyday when possible. Material culture can explore the minutiae of living and thus provide insights into the lives of ordinary people who often fall below the documented histories. In this sense, interior design represents some of the values of a culture through its particular objects. Contemporary material culture will also influence the designer through a process of osmosis as well as deliberate engagement.

The Influence of Social Sciences

Since interior design is as much about people as it is about the visual and practical, it is no wonder that many issues arising from studies in sociology, psychology, gender and sexuality, ethnic studies and anthropology (human groups and individuals) have illuminated developments in interiors. By using concept-based methodology, we can examine the links between the principles of interior design and theoretical concepts as 'scenarios' that explore and explain. Cultural theorist and critic Mieke Bal points out that: 'Concepts are not fixed. They travel – between disciplines, between individual scholars, between historical periods, and between geographically dispersed academic communities. In addition, between disciplines, their meanings, reach and operational value differ. These processes of differing need be assessed before, during, and after each "trip"' (2002: 24).

This is a valuable reminder that theoretical concepts often do not directly transfer but need adjusting to each new situation. The chapters on human needs and space will address a number of issues associated with this field.

The Influence of Applied Sciences

We often use the applied sciences in interiors on an intuitive basis rather than through detached experiment or analysis. The role of business and economics, education, technology, light and colour, materials science, environmental studies and psychology have increasingly influenced the work and practices of interior designers. The chapters associated with light, colour, business, interior elements and environment will explore some of these influences.

theory and interior design

Theories are not intended to be prescriptive but should inform the thought processes of design and assist in asking questions, predicting plans and developing thinking tools. 'Theories are like toolboxes' (Tilley 2006: 10), they are particular and limited, but can point us in a direction and conversely they can limit or blind us. They represent presence and absence. Although 'blunt tools', they do have a role in reflecting upon the world, helping to make sense of it.

Engagement with theory is therefore crucial as it allows designers to reflect, articulate and engage in discourse within their own and other disciplines with intellectual rigour. Indeed, it is essential for designers to recognize the theory that they already have (although they may not recognize it as such) in terms of, say, concepts of form, perception, creativity, etc. An understanding of these concept-based methodologies, along with critical thinking about the creative design process, amongst other things, is part of the well-educated designer. Susan Close points out: 'there is a logical connection between theory and practice in interior design that involves content, context and narrative … Pertinent issues such as: space, place, globalization, gender identity, branding, migration, performativity and privacy that are significant areas of theoretical study are all transferable to the more revisionist study of interior design being constructed in the twenty-first century' (Chalmers and Close 2007: 79). Later chapters consider some of these aspects.

The role of theory is to cultivate, develop and support the advancement of interior design as a discipline through interaction, mediation and discourse. The value of theory is not so much that it will assist the interior designer directly in their work (although this may be a by-product); rather it will improve their position and power. At this point it is worth summarizing some important theories, as follows:

Perception Theory

J.J. Gibson considered that perception was only understandable in terms of the environment and the natural conditions found there. Three characteristics were involved: the medium (atmosphere), the substance (materials) and the surface (border) between material and atmosphere. Therefore, for example, colours, shapes, forms and illumination will influence individual

---

James Jerome Gibson (1904–1979)

James Jerome Gibson was one of the most important twentieth-century psychologists in the area of visual perception. In his standard work, *The Perception of the Visual World* (1950), Gibson developed the idea that animals tested information from their surroundings. He used the word 'affordance' to refer to the active opportunities that an object or environment provided. Affordances are the qualities of an entity, or a situation, that lets people act appropriately. This idea has been widely adopted in the work of designers and ergonomists.

---

perceptions and consciousness. This reflects the idea of cognitive affordances where substance, surface and texture are arranged so as to make recognizable the object or space. Perceptions are not just visual – they involve all the senses, as well as formal aesthetics, colour relations, space syntax and so on. Perception theory talks about the 'stimulus information' that is selected by an individual to make responses (rather than the stimulus being inherent), thus creating ambiguity in particular responses to designs. Understanding this recognizes the individual nature of perception and avoids blanket assumptions.

Gestalt

Gestalt means 'organized whole' and refers to the form or shape-forming ability of our senses. Developed by psychologists in the early twentieth century, it particularly relates to the way we recognize figures and whole forms rather than simply perceiving a mass of lines and curves. One of the important points made by the Gestalt theorists is that humans do not respond to individual sensations but to a range of interconnected information that enables a person to structure their environment as opposed to reacting to it. We identify characteristics of the whole differently to the individual components. For example, a chair has its parts – legs, back, seat cushion, etc. – but when one sees a chair, one is not conscious of these separate parts; one is simply aware of the chair. Even though we see the components, they are of less significance. These responses to potential visual overload enable people to make sense of their surroundings through 'laws' relating to proximity, similarity, closure and continuation. Although by no means the only perception tool, the 'organization in terms of Gestalt Laws makes for economy in the encoding of information, and allows us to grasp maximum information through a relative minimum of means and effort' (Kreitler 1972: 89).

Narrative

Although often associated with literature and communications, narrative has some analytical uses in interior design. In this context, narrative is a process used to identify meaning for people within an interior (Ganoe 1999: 1–15).

Discussions and interaction between designer and client are valuable in creating a 'narrative' that will allow the designer insights into lifestyles and approaches to particular conditions. The particular value of narrative, especially in a culturally diverse industry such as interior design, is that it enables designers to begin to relate to alternative interpretations of space and place, and explores choices. This avoids formulaic or 'one size fits all' approaches and allows for interactions on both sides. If interior design is partly about creating meaning in spaces, designers need to understand the attitudes and feelings of their clients and user-groups. Although 'universal design' may address some practical issues, there are many subtle differences in attitudes to, and use of, interiors that we can discover through narrative. Cathy Ganoe argues that the development of new 'cultural-environmental meanings', based on the diversity of cultures that converge in the contemporary world and through new technologies, indicates that narrative will be increasingly useful in developing design solutions (1999: 1–15).

theory, practice, discourse

Interior designers need to relate theories to the 'how' and the 'why' of actual practice. Terence Love develops the conjunction of theory, practice and discourse. In his system, 'the levels of abstraction or meta-theory are based on a hierarchical form. The lowest level of abstraction [1] refers to an individual's direct, sensual interaction with the world. They then progress through objects, to the design process and finally to a philosophy, where the highest level [10] is concerned with human values, assumptions about existence and the implications of those assumptions' (2000: 293–313). This is a potentially useful framework for evaluating various theories, so we now explore what that framework might help us to understand.

Level 1. Direct Perception of Realities

In this initial level of thinking about interior design, perception refers to the use of the senses to perceive what is around us. The sensory aspects of interior design are clearly crucial to the core human-centred mission of the profession. An approach that refers to subjective experiences examined through the senses is pertinent to the designer's approach. However, the subjective experiences of the individual are those that are generally not directly observable by others. An often-quoted example is the concept of 'redness'. How do we know how other people experience the quality of redness? These subjective perceptions or experiences will often also include emotional, cognitive or conative experiences, thus making the perception process even more complex.

Level 2. Description of Objects

To communicate our understanding of surroundings we describe things with adjectives to distinguish them from similar others. These descriptions are important conveyors of meaning and have cultural and sociological influences. When discussing objects it is important to be aware of the distinction between emotive, pragmatic and analytical language. The nature of perception is crucial to this process. Designers (amongst others) have recognized the importance of accurate description, for example. The development of colour notation, which can offer an analytic approach rather than an emotive one, recognizes this. The opposite is also true where we express the emotive values of colours over the physical.

Level 3. Behaviour of Elements

The idea of a relationship between parts is the key to understanding how a component interacts with other elements of a design and external situations. 'Although elements have intrinsic characteristics, their properties are more commonly defined by other elements and external influences' (Love 2000: 311). A simple example would be to say 'the room is divided by a screen'. In other words, we perceive things in relation to how they interact with other things.

Level 4. Mechanisms of Choice

How are decisions about choice made? Our hierarchy of needs influences choices based on feelings and values (see further below). According to psychologist William Glasser's choice theory, we base our choices on human needs of survival, belonging and connecting, power and significance, freedom and responsibility, and fun and learning.

Glasser suggests that there is an internal 'quality world' in which, starting at birth and continuing throughout our lives, we place those things that we value highly. Glasser also talks of a 'comparing place', in which we measure the world we experience with our inner 'quality world'. We attempt to behave so that we can try to achieve a real world experience consistent with our imagined 'quality world' (Glasser 1999). Understanding how this process might work will assist interior designers to programme designs based on research that asks why as well as how, so that design decisions might go some way towards creating the quality worlds people aim for.

Level 5. Design Methods

Design methods reflect the process of design (see Chapter 4) where designers devise strategies and tactics, where methods such as synectics, brainstorming and 'thinking outside of the box' occur. A number of approaches to design methods can add up to a complete solution to meet the needs of all involved. Firstly, there is the application of critical thinking and various research methods to create new insights and improved design solutions to existing and new problems. Secondly, there needs to be an assessment of the visual relationship between the parts and the whole in a design scheme. Thirdly, the redefining of specifications of design solutions leads to better guidelines for traditional and contemporary design activities and encourages multidisciplinary or team solutions. Fourthly, there is the virtual planning or prototyping of a design to make comparisons between possible outcomes before producing it. Lastly, there is the issue of sustainability, which allows development and improvement of design solutions incrementally. This area also uses design elements (see Chapter 5) such as balance, form, scale, proportion, harmony and symmetry/asymmetry to generate ideas that will derive directly from the designer's experience to create interior spaces.

Level 6. Design Process Structure

In interior design, a sequential process of concepts, programming, developing, implementing and evaluating forms an underlying structure (see Chapter 5). The apparently codified approach that uses information, selection and management methods needs to work in conjunction with the particular creative aspects of interior design. As this process may not always connect to others, linear models of the design process need to ensure continual appraisal, evaluation and feedback between the practice and the process.

Level 7. Theories about the Internal Processes of Designers and Collaboration

Love says that 'this level includes the descriptions of theories about the reasoning and cognition of individual designers, of negotiated design in collaborative design teams, and of cultural design effects on designers' output' (2000: 306). The influences of the humanities, sciences and material and visual culture, mentioned earlier, clearly have a role in this context.

Cognitive theory asserts that solutions to problems take two forms. Solutions come either through a planned problem-solving procedure (e.g. flow charts) or through the intuitive judgements that are informal but clearly understood. This dichotomy was considered by Christopher Alexander, who in 1964 wrote: 'enormous re-

sistance to the idea of systematic processes of design is coming from people who recognize correctly the importance of intuition, but then make a fetish of it which excludes the possibility of asking reasonable questions' (1971: 9). In other words, designers work best through the internal processes of logic and intuition combined.

> **Christopher Alexander (1936–)**
> Alexander is interesting for interior designers as he developed a 'pattern language' that 'describes a problem which occurs over and over again in our environment and then described the core of the solution to that problem, in such a way that you can use this solution a million times over, without ever doing it the same way twice' (Alexander 1977: x). Pattern language follows a process of defining the general design problems in a particular field. It then expresses the key features of successful solutions to achieve a particular aim. The designer then moves from one issue to another in a logical sequence, but the process still allows numerous differing ways through the design process. Alexander's method is applicable to any level of design, and being based on empirical studies and anthropological data, appears to be a human-centred approach.

Level 8. General Design Theories

This level of abstraction raises issues around the notion of designing itself. For example, interior design is a creative activity, but what do we mean by creativity? Rob Pope has written eloquently on this topic. He raises a number of matters around creativity that can affect interiors. The initial stages of design planning should revolve around a 'sensitivity to initial conditions' that entails 'creating "from the beginning", with a full awareness that this is the continuation of other things and will bring yet other things into being'. The development of the design should reflect 'emergence rather than imposition of order', which entails 'feeling for and thinking about an appropriate shape, form, design – "fitting" for your immediate aim and need but capable of fulfilling a broader, even if initially obscure purpose' (2005: 132–133).

This will only be successful if the designer is 'open to the apparently chance or accidental event, including "mistakes" that in the event may turn out to be crucial in avoiding mere repetition of the predictable and help usher in the freshly different, singular and arresting'. This is further considered by Pope as 'being prepared to "tolerate ambiguities", "suspend disbelief", sport with both "negative" and "positive capabilities", and to look for closure without foreclosure'. One of the essential qualities of creativity for Pope is the recognition of 'non-linearity', which entails 'going with the flow – but only as far as it brings you back transformed and enriched; holding to a line – yet appreciating how it bends and flexes' (132–133).

Finally, Pope offers 'Irreversibility as a principle of formation', which entails 'making something (of yourself for and with others), going for provisional completion (but not absolute conclusion), [and] making a difference (by expressing a preference)' (132). This creative approach is much more human-centred than prescriptive design methods might be.

Level 9. Epistemology of Interior Design Theory

This aspect considers the theory of knowledge and the issue around questions such as what is (design) knowledge, how do we acquire (design) knowledge, and what do we know? Love suggests that 'Assessment of the validity or coherency of design information, methods and theories is seen to be part of the intrinsic creative activity of the designer or design theorist' (2000: 311). Engaging in this level of debate allows the interior designer to develop the discipline's body of knowledge, both critically and actively.

Level 10. Ontology of Design

Ontology is the study of the groups of things that exist or may exist in some domain. Love's final philosophical point argues that design is not mechanistic, but rooted in human lives and is associated with the assumptions and beliefs of human values that structure a view of what human existence is. Therefore design has a direct influence on individuals' 'being' in the world and thus on their actions.

research and the interior designer

Although I have argued that practice is rooted in theory, research and experience clearly inform it directly. We can categorize research in interior design as (a) research that aims to develop knowledge and understanding of how designers work and how they have worked in the past; (b) research conducted through practice and (c) research that goes towards developing a demonstrable knowledge base that other designers will use. Whatever approach we use, a key point to remember is the variability of people and places. Boundaries change, viewpoints are varied, spaces differ and people grow, fall ill, work and play. Therefore, the interior designer or researcher has to think critically and creatively to respond to the physical needs of people and meet their social, aesthetic, cultural and psychological needs. A tall order indeed!

The chapters that follow this introduction develop the ideas introduced here. It will be clear now that the knowledge required by an interior designer is a continuing, contextual, growing, global and challenging process that cannot be limited to a set of components. Seeing it in relation to the wider knowledge bases, both in design and beyond, is important as we now enter the world of interior design.

chapter 2

the development of the interior

CHAPTER OVERVIEW

The history of interiors and their design is part of culture. It may cover the visual and material culture associated with the history of architecture, design, interiors, furniture and accessories used in civilizations all over the world, from ancient times to now. When discussing the history of the interior, we could start with the first found spaces such as prehistoric caves and their decoration; we might begin with the Ancient Greeks and Romans or in the Renaissance. This particular chapter has its primary focus on the period from the nineteenth century to the twenty-first. The reason for this follows Charles Rice, who argues that the '[interior] emerged as a new and distinct concept at the beginning of the nineteenth century' (2007: 177). Chronologies, thematic approaches and analyses of the influences of one culture on others are ways of presenting the histories of interiors. This chapter follows a conventional chronology informed by social and cultural issues that influenced the interior. In any event, designers need to develop an appreciation of the past to develop a sense of the present and to inspire their future design work.

introduction

The values of studying the histories of interior design are many: it may be simply for pleasure, for inspiration or for borrowing, but at root, it is an intellectual training, since the writing of history is as much designed as the interiors themselves. Katerina Rüedi explains: 'For me, history is theory is ideology and cannot be separated from design; it forms a complicit and compromised interpretative framework that extracts specific forms of consciousness from the apparently "natural"

realm of creativity and directs it toward changes in the collective and necessarily barbaric cultural domain' (1996: 109–125).

This intellectual challenge that links history and theory to ideology makes the point that interior designers need to engage with social and intellectual enquiry and critically address their own and other people's ideologies. More specifically, histories of interior design show how people have solved similar problems to our own within the context of their own cultures. Finally, professional interior designers should be able to develop their own ideology and not rely on received wisdom. Understanding that history is not 'the past' is a first step. All history writing and interpretation is 'situated' through choices, pre-judgements and methodological preferences, so there are no 'correct' interpretations of the past to rely on (see Jenkins and Munslow 2002: xiv).

Contemporary thinkers also see history more as a series of disruptions than as a continuum. Discussing design history, Abigail Harrison-Moore further points out that 'A history of style is as problematic as one based on specifically named designers. An aesthetic reading proposes that design is autonomous, but an object cannot be divorced from its context and a building is more than a set of facades' (2006: 35). With these provisos, discussions of generic styles and individual personalities can help in locating a framework for the wider contextual issues. In addition to these points, there is the issue of the canon of work. Writings on much of the history of interior design are from a perspective of western white cultures, with little reflection or consideration of communities, diversity in terms of culture, gender and sexuality and issues of 'real living'. Indeed, in some senses every interior is unique so a canon can be meaningless. However, there have been important historical trends or styles that have influenced individual interiors and these have formed the groundwork from which other styles and tastes have developed and changed. They have become the collective memories that are histories.

Although history is a partial account informed by a particular cultural emphasis, it is also heart and memory; and the drawing upon memory is the basis of most design decisions. History

therefore can serve as a source of possibilities for present situations, filtered through the mesh of contemporary cultures, technologies, social conditions and ecologies as a translation process. Adrian Snodgrass and Richard Coyne succinctly explain that 'History, the past, memory continue as they always have, and always will, to pervade every single thought and action that takes place in the design studio' (2006: 144).

In addition, although the interior is often a cultural form that is short-lived, fragmentary and discontinuous as a form of structure, it is not fully separate from architecture. That is why there is much reference to architecture in this work. In any event, readers must be cognisant of the challenges, strains and omissions that arise from such a complex set of situations.

the nineteenth century

The reasons we can start a consideration of the interior in the nineteenth century are numerous. The importance of the pace of change, the nature of industrialization and the changes that it wrought meant that the concept of 'dwelling' and the use of spaces in other contexts became altogether different issues, away from the production and distribution of goods. The growth of nationalism and liberalism, in part stemming from the French Revolution, provided the background for the changes that were to make this the century of transition. The gradual reforms in education and representation of the people, and the developments in industrialization and communication, were all part of a tendency towards improvement, growth and material gain. Other changes, such as the development of electrification, personal communications and the mechanization of many parts of industry, all helped to develop and improve the infrastructure that was necessary for a burgeoning economy.

There is no doubt that, during the nineteenth century, a redistribution of wealth encouraged more spending on consumer goods. However, overall there was an ongoing change in most people's approaches to their spaces. Living conditions gradually improved, assisted by medical improvements, and this in turn laid stress on the notions of comfort and well-being, certainly for the burgeoning middle classes.

According to Walter Benjamin, 'we must understand dwelling in its most extreme form as a condition of nineteenth century existence' (1999: 220). He went on to say:

> The original form of dwelling is existence not in the house but in the shell. The shell bears the impression of its occupant. In the extreme instance, the dwelling becomes a shell. The nineteenth century, like no other century, was addicted to dwelling. It conceived the residence as a receptacle for the person, and it encased him with all his appurtenances so deeply in the dwelling's interior that one might be reminded of the inside of a compass case. (256)

The *Oxford English Dictionary* defines the interior as 'the inside of a building or room, esp. in reference to the artistic effect …', with the earliest example of this use being from 1829. Although this conscious 'artistic effect' had clearly been in evidence before the nineteenth century, it was in

Walter Benjamin (1892–1940)

Walter Benjamin was a German–Jewish Marxist philosopher–sociologist, literary critic, translator and essayist. He was a key theorist of urban modernity and his major work, *The Arcades Project*, explores many aspects of it. He was critical of nineteenth-century patterns of family life and the 'cluttered' interiors that supported them. He thought that, as society took on the role of warmth and security associated with the home, there would only be a need for sparse living spaces so that material things became less important than a social spirit.

this period that the most important social change, the usurpation of the aristocracy as arbiters of taste in favour of a prosperous middle class, developed rapidly. The employment of an architect (in limited cases), a retailer or upholsterer, or the perusal of contemporary journals and writings, were the main ways by which people could develop their interiors until the advance of professional interior decorators/ designers in the late nineteenth century.

Architecturally, the search for a style for the nineteenth century was confounded by the demands of the new age. Railway stations, hospitals, courts, museums, factories and warehouses all made demands on architecture and interior design and planning that it was ill-equipped to handle. The search for, and the subsequent battle of, styles led to an eclectic approach to architecture, and consequently furniture and furnishing design, which resulted in a series of revivals and other configurations. In contrast, there were the industrialized building changes of Joseph Paxton, Henri Labrouste and Gustave Eiffel, who employed iron and glass in their work. This meant that an alternative visual ethos developed in parallel, one that would only be fully recognized in the early twentieth century. However, this was certainly, in terms of interiors, a minority taste, and eclecticism actually better reflected the varying tastes of the wide range of consumers.

directoire/empire 1795–1820

In early-nineteenth-century French interiors, the Directoire and later the Empire style continued the taste for classical influences. In their famous design book, *Receuil de décorations intérieures* (1801, 1812, 1827), Charles Percier and Pierre Fontaine wrote in support of this approach: 'It is a delusion to believe that there are shapes preferable to those which the Ancients have handed down to us' (in Groër 1986: 10). High-style interiors were characterized by a masculinity and formality relieved by particular decoration based on classical motifs. The symbols adopted for the style included motifs such as the bee, the laurel wreath, the imperial eagle and the letter N that was associated with Napoleon.

In 1804, Baron Denon published the results of his exploration in Egypt following Napoleon's campaign, and the newly discovered archaeological remains provided authentic sources for copying models for the Egyptian craze that followed. In addition to this style, there was a taste for the Oriental and for the Chinese in particular. To achieve these exotic effects, the use of beech, turned and painted to imitate bamboo, was common.

The use of original lacquered or japanned panels in carcase furniture was also part of the taste. In contrast, Georges Jacob's furniture of polished mahogany and ormolu mounts depicted a subdued luxury, while features such as military-style versions of classicism with tents, draperies and accoutrements of warfare and militaria became fashionable. The Empire style loosely translated into the Biedermeier in Germany, the Regency in Britain and the late Federal or Classical style in America.

biedermeier 1815–1848

The Biedermeier label refers to the products of literature, music, the visual arts and interior design in the period roughly between the years 1815 and 1848. Although stylistically there were considerable similarities with the French Empire style, the Biedermeier, particularly associated with Germany and Austria, refers to a more middle-class taste and as such demonstrates the development of designs intended for their interiors as opposed to those of wealthy patrons. The style epitomized the change from aristocratic grand gestures to more modest bourgeois interiors that placed an emphasis on privacy and comfort. Indeed, Biedermeier was a term coined later to critique the materialistic but limited aspect of life for the bourgeoisie.

Interiors using warm blond woods, natural flowers, planting and lighting, all in well-furnished room spaces, reflected this particular lifestyle. Manufacturers employed new techniques of production to achieve these developments; in terms of furniture, for example, machines were used to cut veneers, stained pear wood substituted ebony and stamped brass replaced cast bronze. Simulation was common in many aspects of interior design work. In addition to the issues of comfort, the need to economize on space meant that designers often produced furniture to be dual purpose or small scale and created stunning visual effects with textiles, upholstery and drapery. The numerous watercolours and paintings that depict such interiors indicate the apparent significance of the interior as a family space and refuge from the outside world throughout this period.[1]

US greek revival *c*.1820–1850

Classical imagery was ideal for the newly formed United States of America as it seemed to represent the new nation and the dream of a model democracy based on ancient Roman, then Greek, ideals. Although few Americans visited the archaeological sites, plenty of pattern books were available and many immigrants were familiar with European versions of classicism. Thomas Jefferson was important in developing the Greek ideals of republicanism that were represented in both politics and design. The trend was towards an adaptation rather than a rigorous following of rules, often resulting in elegant simplicity.

regency britain 1790–1830

The Regency period spanned much more than the technical Regency (1811–1820) and generally refers to the period *c*.1790 to 1830. The taste for classical purity was reintroduced from France by

Henry Holland. Thomas Hope developed it in his *Household Furniture and Interior Decoration* of 1807. The publication of George Smith's *Collection of Designs for Household Furniture* of 1808 (Plate 1) popularized it in the trade. The growth of design and pattern books such as these above reflects the emergent importance of upholsterers who continued to develop the business of interior decoration, while individual consumers began to use reference books to explore possible imagery for their interiors. The important periodical *Ackermann's Repository of Arts, Literature, Fashions, Manufactures, etc.* covers the period 1809–1829 and is an important milestone in demonstrating the connections between fashion and furnishings. Ackermann's publication was a trendsetter that encouraged a taste for Greco-Roman styles and lavish window treatments. Designers also used a range of eclectic styles including those derived from Egyptian, Italian Renaissance, Norman, Gothic, Tudor, Chinese, Turkish and Indian imagery. The influence of the Romantic and Picturesque movements are also evident here.

The impact of the Industrial Revolution made itself felt on interiors in terms of the introduction of lighting by oil and gas and the use of cast iron for railings, balustrades and fixtures, as well as a wider and more sophisticated range of textile products. There were also developments in the manufacture of metal bedsteads and campaign furniture (furniture intended to be readily dismantled and reassembled when required) and a craze for adaptable or so-called patent furniture. In some cases, designers completely hid the technology within a decorative effect, whilst in others it remained exposed. For the most part though, there was a defined hierarchy of materials and styles that commentators considered appropriate for particular interiors/rooms. These developed (with minor adjustments) over the nineteenth century.

mid-century developments

For much of the nineteenth century, a range of possibilities developed and overlapped. It was recognized at the time that there was considerable borrowing from the past in terms of style. H.W. and A. Arrowsmith, in their *House Decorator and Painter's Guide* (1840), claimed that 'The present age is distinguished from all others in having no style that can properly be called its own.' However, they continue by saying that: 'The productions of the ancient and modern masters are now to be found in the houses of the people, and the elegant arrangements of domestic decoration are no longer confined to the palaces of princes and places of public amusement, but we have them around us by our own fireside' (1840: 111–112).

Writing in 1864, Robert Kerr commented in the Preface to his *The Gentleman's House*, 'it is well known that there are few good things so good—and therefore so well worth describing—as a good English house' (1864). This sentiment reflected much of the attitudes of the burgeoning middle classes in England, Europe and increasingly North America towards the house as a home.

Indeed as the century progressed, there was an increased emphasis on the social and economic infrastructure to support the growth of society. In terms of architecture and interior design, public buildings, business premises, leisure facilities and shops, all of which required appropriate designs, reflected this change. Interesting crossovers in the connections between shop displays and hotel furnishings and their impact on the domestic interior are evident. As visual exemplars, they gave consumers ideas of what was fashionable. Katherine Grier has highlighted this aspect of the dissemination of taste for interiors in her work on American middle-class interiors. She points out that those public spaces such as Pullman railcars, steamboats, hotels and photographers' studios all served as models for private parlour-making and design (1988).

The Victorian period witnessed a massive growth in the business of advice in relation to the home, whether in terms of etiquette or furnishing, rearing children or dealing with servants. Although men wrote many architectural tracts, many women wrote books and published articles, aimed at other women, especially in relation to the decoration and organization of the domestic interior. Advice books provided the recipes and blueprints for the rapid expansion of middle-class homes, especially in Britain and North America. John Claudius Loudon's *Encyclopaedia of Cottage, Farm and Villa Architecture and Furniture* (1833) was one of the most influential. With over 2,000 illustrations, it offered readers designs for small Grecian villas, villas in the 'Old Scotch style', 'Old English' houses, castellated Gothic, Italian Gothic and even a Swiss chalet style. Works such as T. Webster and F. Parkes's *Encyclopaedia of Domestic Economy* (1844), A.J. Downing's *The Architecture of Country Houses* (1850), Gervase Wheeler's *Rural Homes, or Sketches of Houses*

Suited to American Life (1851) and Catherine and Harriet Beecher Stowe's *The American Woman's Home* (1864) were all very influential in developing an ethos of home and its correct decoration.

gothic revival 1830s–1880s

The stimulation of the Gothic revivals that developed across Europe occurred through a range of factors including romantic views of history, nationalism, antiquarian interests and a style that was not as rigid and fixed as classicism, thus offering a range of decorative opportunities. A number of highly influential architects and critics developed a framework for discussing and analysing the Gothic, which gave it credence not only as a religious style but also as one appropriate for public and private buildings.

A.W.N. Pugin (1812–1852)

Augustus Welby Northmore Pugin was an English architect, designer and theorist of design, particularly known for his work in the Gothic Revival style. Pugin published two important books, *Contrasts* and the *True Principles of Pointed or Christian Architecture*, to support his ideas of a Gothic revival. He thought that Christian traditions, both architectural and moral, played an important role in changing and developing society. Pugin and his writings were influential among later critics and designers, including Ruskin, Morris and the Arts and Crafts movement.

Foremost among these were A.W.N. Pugin and his work *True Principles of Pointed or Christian Architecture*, published in 1841, John Ruskin's writings, especially his *Stones of Venice*, and Viollet Le Duc's work in France. These examples illustrate the connections between ideology and design. They reinforced the search for stability, continuity and a sense of history through a rise in religion and the all-important notion of the sanctity of home. Architects and designers employed Gothic styles for public buildings and interiors and for some domestic spaces. However, in many cases the decorators employed the style to provide decorative details often used only in particular rooms.

reformed gothic 1835–1860s

This style, based on an interpretation of Pugin's work, utilized principles of revealed construction, honest use of materials and a limited vocabulary of ornament, and was developed to adapt to nineteenth-century living conditions a little more. It also began to address concerns about the general standard of taste in designed products.

Bruce Talbert's publication *Gothic Forms Applied to Furniture, Metal Work and Decoration for Domestic Purposes* (1868) popularized the Reformed Gothic style. It was characterized by, for example, simpler use of woollen textiles as opposed to Pugin's rich, patterned wallpapers, and thus reflected a change of clients from aristocrats to the middle classes, and a nod to the beginning of Arts and Crafts. However, there was still reliance upon architectural ornament and polychromy for interior effects that imitated the Gothic.

One of the most influential works on interiors on both sides of the Atlantic was Charles East-lake's *Hints on Household Taste,* first published in 1868. It was a very successful primer for those involved in the furnishing and decoration of an interior. The style he advocated, known as 'Eastlake' or 'Modern Gothic', reflected a more artistic environment. Eastlake explained one of his reasons for writing his book: 'I have never met with a class of men who were so hopelessly confirmed in artistic error as ordinary decorators' (1868: 198). Many later publications echoed this cry.

Charles Eastlake (1836–1906)
Charles Locke Eastlake was a British architect and furniture designer. Eastlake was particularly significant in the establishment of canons of taste concerning domestic furnishings. His *Hints on Household Taste* (1868) advocated simplicity in shapes combined with honest craftsmanship. Eastlake urged that people furnished their houses 'picturesquely', but in conjunction with the latest technologies. In the United States, his ideas influenced design so much that people attached the 'Eastlake' label to a whole style genre.

In the United States, Alexander Jackson Davis's *Rural Residences* was to develop the picturesque taste in the USA, while A.J. Downing, in his *Architecture of Country Houses*, developed a filtered version of European Gothic that was apparently more suited to the modest taste of Americans.

italian renaissance revival 1830s–1870s

Widely employed in Europe and North America, the Italian Renaissance revival was an eclectic style that borrowed motifs and features from a generic idea of Renaissance architecture and interiors. The combination of apparent luxuriousness, its infinite adaptability to plans, scale and site and its commercial potential made it a successful revival style. A.J. Downing described its value in 1850: he said that the Italian style suited contemporary culture because it 'addresses itself more to the feelings and the senses, and less to reason and judgment, than the Grecian style, and it is also capable of a variety of expression quite unknown to the architecture of the five orders' (1850: 380). The culture Downing mentions was particularly manifest in the interiors of public buildings, gentlemen's clubs, hotels and grand residences that employed this style. Architects trained in the Beaux-Arts tradition often designed them.

rococo revival or neo-rococo 1830s–1880s

The Rococo Revival is probably more representative of nineteenth-century taste than the more recognized styles. Linked as it was to gilded carving, antique French furniture and boiseries, it reflected wealth rather than 'good taste'. Originating in England, through the availability of *ancien régime* furnishings purchased from Revolutionary France, the style gradually filtered down the scale and ended as a 'tous les Louis' style that remained commercially popular, though reformers found it ridiculous. Details of furniture such as the cabriole leg and the balloon back became standard fare for interior furnishings, along with upholstery featuring crapauds, confidantes, ottomans, bornes, tête-à-têtes; all suited to the theatre of the nineteenth-century interior.

In France itself, 'the style Pompadour' developed during the reign of Louis Philippe (1830–1848) and continued into the 1870s. Its apparent connections with aristocracy made it attractive for the creation of elegant spaces. Inevitably, there were detractors.

Jacob von Falke (1825–1897)

Jacob von Falke was a German curator, historian and critic. He considered art and design as objects, which he saw through the lens of industrialism, and the ambitions of the middle classes. Falke thought that an object's purpose was the basis for correct design. In his *Art in the House*, he stated that by using the considerations of function, material and appropriate production processes the best products would occur. In terms of interiors, he believed in an emphasis on colour and form as opposed to slavish style-following.

German critic Jacob von Falke derided the misuse of historic revivals. Writing on the International Exhibition in Vienna in 1873, Falke made an amusing commentary. 'In so far as style is concerned the modern Frenchman dwells in the eighteenth century, he sleeps in that century likewise, but he dines in the sixteenth, then on occasion he smokes his cigar and enjoys his coffee in the Orient while he takes his bath in Pompeii' (in Thornton 1984: 308). A little later, von Falke, writing in his important work, *Art in the House: Historical, Critical, and Aesthetical Studies on the Decoration and Furnishing of the Dwelling*, explored the counter position. He said: 'A design, a form of decoration, a piece of furniture may have style without belonging in style to any one of the famous art epochs, either as original or copy …' (1878: 171). He continued by discussing furniture design. Furniture had style, he said, 'when it is exactly what it ought to be, when it is suited to the purpose for which it is intended, and it has the purpose unmistakeably inscribed upon it' (171). His position sometimes sounds like a call to Modernism.

It is important to remember that, although the key figures of the history of interiors are associated with stylistic tendencies, it was actually the manufacturers and suppliers of products that influenced the majority of interiors. Important retail and contract furnishing businesses in many major cities offered full house furnishing and decorating services and were responsible for many private and commercial interiors during this period. An example of this is in the catalogue of the London retailers Shoolbred, of Tottenham Court Road (Figure 2.1). The image is one of a number that depict an interior in a complete historical style. During the second half of the century, department stores began to offer similar services to a less affluent group of consumers.

This process was manifest in another feature of nineteenth-century interiors found in a study of trade catalogues. It is clear that there was a hierarchy of designs designated as appropriate

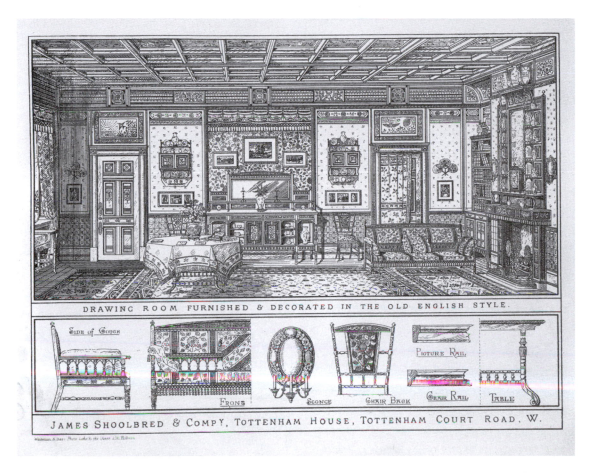

Figure 2.1 Illustration from a catalogue by James Shoolbred & Co., London, England showing a drawing room furnished and decorated in the Old English Style, 1876.

to particular rooms; for example, the Rococo revival for parlours, Gothic style for dining rooms, Renaissance for libraries, and so on. What is also interesting about the various company estimates is that they show a considerable homogeneity of styles across financially varying levels and house sizes that were deemed appropriate for typical lifestyles, thus endorsing the idea of a common understanding of an established taste.

exoticism 1870s–1890s

The impact of foreign travel often associated with colonial activity meant that the visual culture of other societies was adapted for some interiors. This of course was not a new phenomenon but was one that touched many in a variety of forms during the nineteenth century. Owen Jones encouraged this taste in his *Grammar of Ornament*.

Owen Jones (1809–1874)

Architect and designer Owen Jones was a major force in attempts to move away from the existing aesthetic sensibility. His attempts to develop a new visual language for the nineteenth century were rooted in his studies of other cultures, in particular Islamic. His theories, explained in his masterwork *The Grammar of Ornament* (1856), demonstrated the possibilities of flat patterning, geometry and the use of abstraction in ornament and pattern. His influence extended through his associations with design schools as well as high-profile patrons.

In addition, exhibitions and retail displays of non-western goods fuelled the taste. Whether it was Egyptian, Moorish, Turkish, Arab or Indian, the motifs were adapted to western lifestyles often without reference to the original applications. An example is the project of King Wilhelm I of Württemberg: the King contracted Karl Ludwig von Zanth to design villa buildings in the Moorish style (Plate 2). Although this example was intended for a whole palace, in reality it was often specific spaces such as billiard or smoking rooms or artists' studios that used these styles.

The effect of these stylistic influences often served to provide selective pattern and decorative imagery as opposed to wholesale borrowings. The influential designers Owen Jones and Christopher Dresser used these non-western inspirations to move away from naturalistic representations to stylized, two-dimensional designs that led design reform from the mid-nineteenth century. In 1874–76, Christopher Dresser wrote in his *Studies in Design*:

> Those effects that are "subtle" – which are not commonplace – which are attained by the expenditure of special skill or knowledge, are the best, provided that the end which is most desired is attained by them. … By our decorations we must ever seek to achieve repose, but we must always remember that repose is compatible with richness, subtlety, and radiance of effect. (1874–76: 11–12)

This commentary on interiors combines something of an ideal in combining the human need for 'repose' with the visual stimulus of the surroundings.

Christopher Dresser (1834–1904)

Christopher Dresser was an important designer and author who was instrumental in contributing to the Anglo-Japanese and Aesthetic movements in design. One of the first independent industrial designers, Dresser often advocated design through new materials and production techniques. His publications on design and decoration include *The Art of Decorative Design* (1862) and *Principles of Design* (1871–72). His major publication, *Japan, Its Architecture, Art and Art-Manufactures* (1876), documented his influences. His particular aesthetic was simple and spartan to a degree that appears to be at odds with his own time.

arts and crafts 1860s–1910

The Arts and Crafts movement and the works of those associated with it often appear to combine an interest in humans needs with decorative functions. The perceived confusion over the role and nature of applied arts design of all kinds led to some attempts at combining reforms of a social nature with design reforms. This resulted in the formation of the Arts and Crafts movement. Developed in England, partly as a response to the poor standards of design, its main protagonist was William Morris.

William Morris (1834–1896)

William Morris was an English architect, furniture and textile designer, artist, writer, socialist and Marxist. A seminal character in craft and design history, he is associated with both the Pre-Raphaelite Brotherhood and the English Arts and Crafts movement. Morris was a polymath interested in the relationships between work and the worker as much as Gothic architecture and flat pattern design. His company, Morris Marshal Faulkner and Co., sold his products from 1861. This firm covered most of the decorative arts and supplied a number of important interior schemes. Morris's works remain fashionable to this day. Although his famous dictum 'Have nothing in your houses that you do not know to be useful or believe to be beautiful' had a resonance with many architects and designers that followed, his personal desire to link the artistic and the political in order to reform society never materialized.

William Morris founded his business in 1860, and he and his associates developed a particular idea of interior design that incorporated pattern, symbolism, fine art and the vernacular. Walter Crane perceptively wrote in 1891 that:

> The great advantage and charm of the Morrisian method is that it lends itself to either simplicity or splendour. You might almost be as plain as Thoreau, with a rush bottomed chair, a piece of matting and oaken trestle table; or you might have gold and lustre … gleaming from the sideboard, and jewelled light in the windows, and walls hung with arras tapestry. (1911: 54)

The polemical basis of Arts and Crafts was far more than stylish patterns and useful furniture. It was a call for a return to simplicity, truth to materials, recognition of the vernacular and a sense of place, all informed by the consideration of the past linked by a harmonic conjunction of the arts and crafts through the value of work. The interiors of Holly Mount, Beaconsfield by Charles Voysey (Figure 2.2) perfectly illustrate his view that conventions were stifling and interiors should reflect 'repose, cheerfulness, simplicity, breadth, warmth … harmony with surroundings, absence of dark passages or places, evenness of temperature' (1911). Morris's dilemma was in producing handcrafted products that were expensive and time-consuming to make. Morris's own well-known concerns about his work recognized this issue: 'it is only that I spend my life ministering to the swinish luxury of the rich' (in Thompson 1988: 250).

Despite Morris's concerns, the linking of progressive architects and designers with the general

Figure 2.2 Interior of Holly Mount, Knotty Green, Beaconsfield, Buckinghamshire, by C.A. Voysey, 1905.

ideals of the Arts and Crafts movement was one of the foundations for the modern movement that was to come in the twentieth century. For example, Hermann Muthesius, who published his *Das Englische Haus* in 1904–5, was to be an important influence on approaches to house design, decoration and furnishing, with wide impact in Germany and Scandinavia.

Morris's ideas were also to make an impression in the USA in particular areas. The influences ranged from individual architects and designers, such as Frank Lloyd Wright and the Greene

brothers, to the mail-order products of Sears Roebuck and others, who sold Arts and Crafts-inspired buildings and their furnishings to anyone who could afford them.

Again, journals were influential in spreading the ideals. The magazine *House Beautiful*, founded in 1898, and Gustav Stickley's journal *The Craftsman,* published between 1901 and 1916, showed plans, articles and ideas for complete house furnishings in an Arts and Crafts style. Stickley definitely had a didactic purpose in his work and publications. Aiming at the burgeoning moderate and modest American middle classes who were in search of an identity, he stated: 'A simple democratic art should provide them with material surroundings conducive to plain living and high thinking, to the development of the sense of order, symmetry and proportion' (1905: 53). This link, between human needs and particular decorative interior design solutions, suggested a reformist agenda (Plate 3).

'queen anne' revival 1870–1890s

Alongside the Arts and Crafts movement was the development of the so-called Queen Anne Revival style. Architects who tried to respond to some of the excesses of mid-Victorian taste led this eclectic style. It considered urban design and looked back to a simpler, more elegant period such as the early eighteenth century. This was just a starting point and the style soon developed links with Aestheticism and the vernacular. It was especially appropriate for the middle-class domestic house as it had little relation to the religious Gothic or the foreignness of the Classical. With connections to bohemian lifestyles, the interiors did not necessarily reflect the exterior. The use of eclectic collections of objects, art furniture and decoration, and subtle colour schemes based upon tertiary colours, created a very particular effect. It straddled the moralist Arts and Crafts and the eccentric Aesthetic movement and as such was quite successful for particular consumer groups.

The German historian and critic Robert Dohme wrote in his *The English House* (1888), in praise of the Queen Anne style, 'One no longer finds in present day English architecture those academically correct villas striving towards monumentality, conventionally laid out inside, developed as canons of classical periods, whereas with us they are indeed still the fashion. Less monumentality and more comfort, less classicism and more individuality – this can be the motto of modern English domestic architecture in contrast to our German counterpart' (in Mallgrave and Contandriopoulos 2008: 28). Again, the emphasis on comfort and individuality as two of the main roles of the interior was to be crucial. The American Queen Anne style, based on a range of picturesque approaches that included the Stick, Shingle and Eastlake styles, can cause confusion.

aesthetic movement

The Aesthetic movement was a particular approach to art and design that was not really a style, more a philosophy of 'art for art's sake' that eschewed hierarchies or distinctions between the fine and decorative arts. It defined beauty as an independent vital force that transcended religious, historical and geographic boundaries. For aesthetes, the idea that 'art is for art's sake' alone meant that any attempt to use art to serve other ends lessened its value. This contrasts with the ideas of some Victorian reformers who saw that art had a moral, narrative and didactic role to play.

Flourishing in the 1870s and 1880s, the interiors associated with the Aesthetic movement had a particular mix of eclecticism, a taste for collecting and evidence of an artistic eye. The scheme devised by architect George Aitchison for 44 Belgrave Square, London gives a flavour of the taste (Plate 4). Followers believed that decorative art should be equal in status with the fine arts and that surface decoration was a force for good. Designers and architects should see themselves as artists, and indeed artists should return to the realm of design. William Morris himself was popular with Aesthetic designers and clients. This declared need for beauty in everyday life encouraged an 'Art in the Home' movement. The movement advocated the cultivation of good taste, informed enjoyment of one's surroundings and the use of artfully embellished domestic goods.

At the extremes, decadent self-indulgence in the form of attempts to make one's own life a 'work of art' resulted in claims of triviality and self-absorption. Oscar Wilde was the epitome of this approach. He was, however, capable of interesting critiques on interiors. Here he talks of the use of tertiary colours: 'the aesthetic movement produced certain curious colours, subtle in their loveliness and fascinating in their almost mystical tone. They were, and are, our reaction against the crude primaries of a doubtless more respectable but certainly less cultivated age' (Wilde 1890).

Apart from a muted colour palette, the aesthetic interiors used their collections and displays, and the layering of patterns, textures and objects, to create artistic effects. Above all was the influence of Japanese art and design on interiors. Elegant simplicity, refined beauty, asymmetry, precision and delicacy of colour were the key ideas adopted from Japanese approaches to design.

From the 1870s, attempts by the Aesthetic movement to influence furniture design were successful. Ideas again taken from Japanese art and design produced a lighter and more delicate range of furniture. The 'art furniture-makers' were particularly responsible for this sort of work. E.W. Godwin was the most important designer in this field, his productions using carefully balanced components combined with Japanese materials such as stamped leather and netsuke. This furniture was fitted with silver components and often ebonized. The 'Japanese taste' also extended to poor copies of art furniture, often comprising standard designs embellished with fretwork. Far more successful, though on a less elite level, was the use of bamboo and other Japanese products such as grass cloth, lacquer panels and leather papers. Interiors that combined Japanese matting, blue-and-white porcelain, etchings and decorative motifs ranging from peacock feathers to sunflowers all epitomized this approach.

The last quarter of the century also saw a taste for Moorish and Middle Eastern styles characterized by pierced and carved fretwork (sometimes imported from Cairo and named Cairene), inlay, carpets and cushions and potted palms. These developments ran alongside the other survivals and revivals.

colonial revival 1880s–1930s

The need for a particularly American style, as a response to the rapid changes that occurred economically and politically between 1880 and 1930, seemed to demand a return to a more settled time, which would relocate America through its historic interiors. In combination with an arts and crafts sensibility and an artisan's approach to design through purity and morality, the colonial revival touched the hearts of many Americans. The colonial heritage was posed against the excesses of Victorian design so there was also a didactic element in visiting restored colonial designs as well as employing features such as open fireplaces, tall case clocks and spinning wheels in interiors.

The development of an historic preservation movement, concerned with national history and the artistic value of old buildings and their interiors, resulted in groups taking more care of historic sites and buildings. The Society for the Protection of New England Antiquities and the later Colonial Williamsburg venture demonstrate this approach, which continues to this day. Indeed, the re-creation of Colonial Williamsburg as a tourist attraction in the 1930s, along with the facsimile products linked to it, continued a demand for colonial style homes and furnishings. In 1936, Nancy McClelland wrote that 'within the last decade, however, there has been an increasingly noticeable swing back to American furniture and American styles. This is partly due to the revival of nationalism that came after the world war and to a widespread desire to build into our surroundings the qualities that we consider purely "American"' (5).

spanish revival 1880s–1930s

The Spanish Revival was a particular style generally associated with American states that have Hispanic connections. In 1927, the Spanish-influenced interior was compared favourably with contemporary American interiors: 'The floors, ceilings, and wainscots, while colourful, are subdued by the large area of simple plastered wall; hangings, while rich, are used with discrimination;

> **Nancy McClelland (1877–1959)**
> Nancy McClelland began her career in Wanamaker's department store in New York in 1913, establishing a decorating section there. In 1922, she set up a firm specializing in re-creating historic interiors. As well as interior work, she was a respected lecturer and authority on wallpapers and antiques. McClelland realized the value of training and education if interior design was to professionalize itself. To this end, she advocated the establishment of standards that included licensing for practitioners. She was the first woman national president of the American Institute of Interior Decorators, now the American Society of Interior Designers. She published widely in the field of antiques and period homes.

and the furniture, often of the richest ornamentation, preserves in its main line a sane architectural mass; nothing is overdone. This is the stumbling block of most Americans; they will get too many things into the room' (Newcomb 1927: 114). The Mexican manner, the Mission revival and the general borrowing of Mediterranean influences made this an eclectic and popular design approach, especially in Florida and California.

Whatever the style employed, the importance of the interior influenced British and American homes in the second half of the nineteenth century at all levels of society. Women had particular roles in the interior. These included the ability to create homes as artful refuges for men folk, to refine children's minds, enhance the work of servants and elevate national culture. A growing infrastructure of book and magazine publications, named designers, window and in-store displays and the gradual development of the interior design profession further supported the commercial development of interior decoration. (See further Chapter 3).

Whether the interior was a full-scale reproduction of a past style or just had some hints that referred; whether the products were imitation or the 'real thing'; whether the furniture was antique or a copy; it did not seem to matter, as long as one reflected a lifestyle and taste appropriately. The reality of many interiors was that they were not in any way 'pure' stylistically. The individual nature of domestic interiors at least meant that elements of eclecticism were nearly always evident.

art nouveau 1890–1905

The decorative style loosely called Art Nouveau developed around the period 1880–1910, especially in Paris and Brussels to start with, but then with many other manifestations across Europe and North America. Various sources influenced the movement including the Arts and Crafts and the Rococo Revival styles, though it was as varied as the designers chose to make it. Although it has been defined as two types, the sinuous organic (France, Belgium, Holland) or the geometric rectilinear (Scotland, Scandinavia, Germany, Austria), the range of designs was wide. However, the style has some recurring themes, the most well known being that of nature. Abstracted designs based on plant life are the most identifiable and recognizable. Writing in 1897 about the Belgian designer Victor Horta, contemporary commentator

Thiébault-Sisson explained: 'the point of departure of these innovations is the observation of nature. But although the artist [Horta] observes nature and is inspired by her for this or that motif, and seizes from plants the secret of the delicate undulations or graceful curves of their stems, nevertheless, his ambition has never been to do anything which might directly resemble nature' (in Benton, Benton and Sharp 1975: 17).

Rejecting Classicism in the main, designers also borrowed extensively from other historical or geographical models. Shapes based on the vernacular designs of the Middle East, Far East and Africa, for example, were interspersed by the application of motifs from ancient Celtic and Viking examples. Thirdly, they derived imagery from the metaphysical and emotional facets of the Symbolist movement. Art Nouveau was a paradigmatic eclectic style. Art Nouveau in Hungary was different from that in Glasgow, which was different again from that found in Turin.

In the USA, the work of Associated Artists (Louis Comfort Tiffany and Candace Wheeler) linked arts and crafts skills and values to the creation of interiors, whilst in Scotland Charles Rennie Mackintosh and the Glasgow School were to have a major influence on European developments, although largely ignored in the rest of the United Kingdom. The style associated with Mackintosh began as an elongated and florid version of Art Nouveau combined with a variety of imagery, and later developed into a rectilinear style, familiar in his chair designs and interiors. The example of the competition entry drawing by Mackintosh for the dining room of a proposed 'House For an Art Lover', produced in 1901, illustrates both these tendencies (Plate 5).

vienna secession and wiener werkstatte *c*.1897–1930

The importance of the relationship between art and design and contemporary life was the driving force for the Viennese-based Secession moment. The concept of the creation of a total work of art as the ideal often meant ignoring the issue of expense. In 1903, the establishment of the 'art and design guild', the Wiener Werkstatte, ensured a supply of highly crafted and designed objects for interiors. They developed a design language that related to new approaches to shapes, materials, colours and an idea of simplicity in the applied arts. To avoid repeating historic styles, geometric formulation became the basis for designs. Architects and designers worked together to create some seminal interiors. Otto Wagner's Post Office Savings Bank in Vienna is a classic, as is Josef Hoffman's Palais Stoclet near Brussels. The latter project is a great example of the concept of the total work of art that integrates building, interior, artworks and accessories with a common visual language.

industry and industrialization

Whilst these revivals, styles and fashions had varying degrees of impact on interiors ranging from the most exclusive designs to 'high street' commerce, other developments in interior design for commercial use were taking shape. Two particular strands of interior design practice epitomize this period: the rise of the hotel and the public spaces associated with it and the planning of buildings, especially tall buildings, designed for corporate activities.

Towards the end of the nineteenth century, in the cities of the industrial north of the United States, progressive architects built the first commercial offices. New technologies such as telephones, electric lighting and the typewriter meant that the centralization and processing of a wide range of office tasks was now possible. Initially, the layout of these buildings included suites of separate rooms opening into corridors. This plan would then be stacked to the height of the building. However, over time, improving construction techniques, which allowed for large, open areas, negated the need for divided small offices, so American clerical office workers sat in rows in large, open spaces. The adoption of Frederick Winslow Taylor's principles of scientific management, through, for example, work-study and division of labour (based on factory layouts), ensured a continuous flow of work and simple but effective supervision. However, in contrast, supervisors and managers remained in small offices furnished more like domestic interiors than businesses.

One of the first purpose-designed business environments for a specific company use was the Larkin Company Administration Building of 1904 in Buffalo, New York. Designed by Frank Lloyd Wright for a successful mail-order soap company, the innovative design of the space included the positioning of the main services in the corners, allowing the creation of a large atrium in the body of the building. To maintain indoor air quality, the building had one of the first rudimentary air-conditioning systems. The workforce laboured together in the open galleries that surrounded the central top-lit atrium space. Wright's concern for a total design concept that addressed itself to the

Frank Lloyd Wright (1867–1959)

Frank Lloyd Wright was one of the pioneers of modern architecture and design in North America. He welcomed the new technologies, materials and engineering systems but linked these to a sensitive understanding of their relation with people. This emotional appeal, along with sensitivity to surroundings, makes his work very approachable. He was particularly concerned that the spaces within a building were the essence of architecture and was keen to design the total building, including interiors. This concept of 'the total work of art' has been a source of contention between architects and interior designers, including Wright, who was also a designer of furniture, furnishings and equipment.

clients' needs meant that he designed custom-made steel office furniture and the first 'system' furniture and built-in cabinets around the walls. Designers were beginning to notice previously ignored issues. Ideas about operating efficiency, function and services all began to come together. The famous Scheepvaarthuis in Amsterdam, built to house various shipping companies in 1916, was not only functional but was also elegantly fitted out with stained glass, ironwork and high-quality materials. The Art Deco imagery is evident (Figure 2.3).

Otto Wagner's students made some perceptive comments on the future of interiors. Discussing hotel design, they summarized his teachings by saying:

The building must function like a perfectly constructed machine; it must in its installation be on the level of wagons-lit; and it must in matters of hygiene and cleanliness, of all objects for use, be up to clinical demands. What is needed is a synthesis of hospital, sleeping-car and machine. Perhaps in fifty years we shall reach such excellent hotels, always assuming that progress increases with today's tempo. (In Pevsner, Richards and Sharp 2000: 95)

This apparent synthesis was not long in coming.

modernism

Complexity reflects and characterizes Modernism. In terms of interiors, Modernism includes a number of issues: the gradual professionalization of the business of interior design; the address to issues of urbanization, technology and new materials; a consciousness of living in the present; an understanding of the nature of mass markets, media and consuming patterns; and the importance of the individual and the self and the expression of this through matters of taste (see Sparke et al. 2009: 4–6). However, there were particular attempts to link modern art and design, to enhance the aesthetics of spaces.

One example is the London-based Omega Workshops founded by artist and critic Roger Fry. He, like William Morris, desired the union of the fine and decorative arts in building and design. Post-Impressionist influences meant that designers applied features such as bright colours and bold, simplified forms to their works, but, inevitably,

Figure 2.3 (Facing page) Interior staircase of the Scheepvaarthuis, Amsterdam, 1916.

the venture was limited and rather amateurish. Commercial outlets run by lady decorators noticed these ideas. For example, Lady Sackville opened a decorating shop called Spealls in 1911. Her Post-Impressionist influences are seen in this scheme designed in 1913–14 for her daughter Vita: 'Her walls are of shiny emerald green paper, floor green; doors and furniture sapphire blue; ceiling apricot colour. Curtains blue and inside-curtains yellowish. The decoration of the furniture mainly beads of all colours painted on the blue ground; even the doorplates are treated the same' (in Calloway 1988: 63). Although these approaches were modern, this 'decorator' approach to the integration of art with design was in contrast to other approaches, such as the work of De Stijl.

de stijl 1917–1931

To achieve the housing improvements and hygiene goals of the Modernist agenda, the benefits of standardization and technology were extolled. One way of achieving these was to develop the Open Plan ideal. Theo Van Doesburg, one of the key members of the Dutch De Stijl group, said: 'The new architecture has broken through the wall, thus destroying the separateness of inside and outside ... This gives rise to a new, open plan, very different from the classical one, in that interior and exterior spaces interpenetrate' (in Padovan 2002: 4).

The group considered spatial relations above all, and wanted no reference to history or nature. They saw interior surfaces as canvasses that created a seamless blend of objects and build-

ing. Achieving social goals through simplicity in design via the universal was more important than any individual demands. Like many Modernist manifestos, this plan went against the grain of self-expression, and ignored the relation of the individual to their spaces and the desire for decoration in interiors. Theo Van Doesburg again: 'The New architecture is anti-decorative. Instead of dramatizing a two-dimensional surface or serving as superficial ornament, colour like light becomes an elementary means for pure architectural expression. This is literally what we must master in the new process of creating architecture' (Baljeu 1974: 204).

Gerrit Rietveld's Schroeder House, built in Utrecht in 1924, clearly shows the interior as manifesto. The plan of the first floor is completely open, the walls are moveable and much of the furniture is built-in, so allowing the interior spaces to be contemplated and lived in (Heynen, in Sparke et al. 2009: 126–128). Although the house was a success for the client, it was not destined to be a blueprint for many others.

the bauhaus 1919–1933

The Bauhaus experiment was instrumental in bringing together many of the disciplines of practical art under the umbrella of architecture to create the total work of art or *Gesamtkunstwerk*. De Stijl, Expressionism and Constructivism, along with the embracement of efficiency, the democratic design ideal and, importantly, links between academic and craft skills, formed the bases of the Bauhaus idea. The goal of systematic experimentation, in both theory and practice, was the key to the

Walter Gropius (1883–1969)

Walter Gropius was a German architect and founder of the Bauhaus School in 1919 who, along with Ludwig Mies van der Rohe and Le Corbusier, is widely regarded as one of the pioneering masters of modern architecture. One of his main beliefs was that well-designed places/spaces could integrate the individual with society. The Bauhaus School curriculum put various materials-based craft exercises at the foundation of student work. Formal design and fine art work followed at later stages. Gropius and others took their ideas to England and America, following closure of the school in the 1930s.The influence of this practice-based approach to design has been formidable in the teaching of art and design.

vision of Walter Gropius. This ideal of seamless integration of theories and practice to create critically thinking designers is still an agenda today.

The interiors associated with the Bauhaus revolve more around individual commissions and particular furniture objects, although standardization of components was a goal. In 1927, the important Werkbund-sponsored architectural exhibition (entitled the Weissenhof Siedlung) of workers' housing reflected the new thinking. It was comprised of twenty-one white-painted buildings that only varied slightly in form, and all had the features that were linked with what later would be known as the 'International Style'. These included basic façades, flat roof terraces, long, horizontal windows and open-plan interiors.

The influence of the Bauhaus crossed the Atlantic in the early 1930s. The 1932 International Style exhibition at the Museum of Modern Art in New York created a wider awareness of their approach to design.

international style

Derived from the 1932 exhibition staged in the Museum of Modern Art in New York, entitled 'Modern Architecture: An International Exhibition', the style was a challenge to tradition. Although it had a number of variants, its key features included an emphasis on volumes of space not mass, regularity not symmetry and the obvious use of materials and techniques as opposed to applied ornament. The influence of functionalism, new factory layouts, new materials and scientific management all impacted on the development of the house as 'a machine for living', as termed by Le Corbusier. If the house were to be a machine, then this would influence its furnishing and decoration.

In 1925, Le Corbusier wrote about the furniture of these interiors and made connections with functionalism and office technology: 'Bring office furniture into the apartment, but according to a different aesthetic plan. After all, a house is only fitments on the one hand, and chairs and tables on the other. The rest is clutter … (in Benton, Benton and Sharp 1975: 137). By 1929, Corbusier had taken this thought further and suggested that pigeon holes based on a module would suffice for all storage, and even make a wall. This approach to furnishings was, however, completely at odds with human needs and desires generally. What was appropriate in an office environment did not

(Charles Edouard Jenneret) Le Corbusier (1887–1965)

Le Corbusier was a Swiss–French architect, urban planner and designer, often seen as one of the founders of the Modern Movement. His villas, which he designated as 'machines for living', usually included particular features that he called the five points of architecture. These were pilotis to support the main building over a service area, a flat roof with garden, a free floor plan, strip ribbon windows and a free façade. Corbusier's writings were influential. His work *Vers une architecture* (1923), translated as *Towards a New Architecture* (1927), explored his thinking about architecture and design, and is essential to the understanding of the Modern Movement.

translate to domestic interiors and how people surrounded themselves when at home.

The efforts of these architects and designers received accolades from the design establishment but were often less than popular with the intended clients. In 1926, Le Corbusier designed standardized houses, as perfect objets-types, in the Pessac residential complex near Bordeaux. He intended these to satisfy essential and typical human requirements. Unfortunately, they completely ignored the human need to express itself. In fact, in subsequent years, the residents transformed the buildings into 'homes' by the addition of personalizing details to humanize the spaces. As Phillipe Boudon nicely points out: 'It seems that everybody has now converted his

"machine for living" into a "chez soi"' (in Malnar and Vodvarka 2004: 68).

scandinavian modernism

In another part of Europe, however, designers were more in tune with the links between humans' needs and their environments. In 1919, the art historian and critic Gregor Paulsson defined the democratic design ideal in his influential book, *More Beautiful Everyday Things.* Here he expressed the idea that well-designed and well-made goods should be available more widely. Although Paulsson promoted the benefits of standardization and design as a better way to meet society's needs, he also saw that changes in social attitudes were the real key to providing a better everyday life for the majority. Commentators soon noticed these attitudes. According to the English critic P. Morton Shand: 'The Gothenburg Exhibition of 1923 revealed Sweden to an astonished world, not merely as an artistic nation but as almost the only one that really counted as far as design and craftsmanship was concerned' (Naylor, in Greenhalgh 1990: 171).

By 1930, the Stockholm Exhibition showed the world what Swedish design in particular meant – a restrained Modernism linked to a variety of functionalism. Morton Shand also wrote a review of this exhibition, extolling the virtues of Swedish grace. For him it meant '… austere, ice-clear neo-classical chastity … simple charm … elegant … a line characterized by its slender, almost elfin grace … the very Swedish sweetness and light' (Howe 1999: 99). In the same journal, Sir Harold Werner wrote: 'Two vigorous trends could now

Figure 2.4 (Facing page) Finnish Pavilion for the New York World's Fair by Alvar Aalto, 1939.

be seen in Swedish industrial art, which were to some extent in opposition to each other – one more traditional, emphasizing handwork ... The other a more modern style related to functionalism which concerned itself chiefly in the creation of quite new and good designs suitable for mass production and intended for a wider public ...' (Naylor, in Greenhalgh 1990: 182).

The 1939 World's Fair in New York introduced the style to the USA. Alongside their exhibit at the fair, the Royal Swedish Commission published a catalogue entitled *Movement Towards Sanity in Design*, clearly demonstrating their particular approach to products. The temporary interior for the Finnish Pavilion, erected for the New York World's Fair in 1939, was a '52-ft high Pavilion [that] consisted of four stories in all. The uppermost series of photographs showed the Country; the next, the People; the third, somewhat lower down, Work, and finally the bottom series depicted the results of the above three factors—the Products' (Aalto and Fleig 1963: 124–130) (Figure 2.4). Finnish architect Alvar Aalto's use of wood – a feature of Finnish life and landscape – was part of the structure, the exhibits and the decoration:

> The interior finish was of wood with different profiles so formed as to create an harmonic rhythm of materials and photographic presentations. The materials used in the construction of the wall surfaces were also treated as objects on exhibit. ... The roof, too, was used as exhibit area: aeroplane propellers of pressed wood, a Finnish specialty, churned the air both as objects on display and as a source of ventilation. (Aalto and Fleig 1963: 124–130)

During the post-war period, in particular the 1950s, Scandinavian design reached wider popularity in the home furnishings market. Indeed, as a style, it provided inspiration to many mass-production furniture designers in the USA and it established a furniture aesthetic that fashion-conscious consumers embraced most enthusiastically. Whether called Danish Modern, Swedish Modern or Scandinavian Modern, the style became familiar to many American and European families who lived with it throughout the 1950s to 1970s. It was no coincidence that this ideal became quickly recognized. The Scandinavian ideal often reflected the 'good design' characteristics defined by the then current thinking.

Based on humanitarian and social practices, and the engagement with the vernacular tradition and sensitivity to materials, this approach was different to expressions of particular theoretical considerations. It seemed to recognize the importance of designing with people in mind, hence the emphasis on appropriate size, cost and quality. Recent interior designers still pick up on this tradition. In 2002, Lena Anderson used classic Swedish-designed chairs and a rug depicting the Swedish flag in a contemporary office breakout space (Plate 6).

art deco 1910–1940

Whilst Modernism strove for some intellectual purity and anonymity in architecture and interior design, the period 1910–1940 also saw a style initially developed by luxury French *ensembliers* that was later to touch the popular imagination. This heady mix of influences from Art Nouveau,

Wiener Werkstatte, Bauhaus and Modernism was peppered with imagery from technology and non-western cultures, and thus offered interior decorators a magnificent toolbox from which to draw. Forms, materials and colour imagery derived from an astonishing array of influences, including eighteenth-century French, Egyptian, Cubist, Mayan, African and Oceanic forms as well as those mentioned above. Its showcase was the 'Exposition Internationale des Arts Décoratifs et Industriels Modernes', held in Paris in 1925 as a 'world's fair' for decorative arts. With the absence of Germany for political reasons, and America for their own reasons regarding costs and a perceived lack of quality work, the exhibition emphasized the lead of the French in the decorative arts. Pavilions expressed the luxury and quality of French products, especially those of the members of the Société des Artistes Décorateurs.

However, 'Art Deco' soon reached America through exhibitions and magazines and, before long, objects ranging from cigarette lighters to skyscrapers used the style. The skyscraper lobbies in particular lent themselves to lavish interior decoration and the examples of the Chrysler Building, Empire State Building and the Chanin Building all demonstrate the combination of fine materials, craft skills and Art Deco motifs that are still familiar.

Architect and furniture designer Paul T. Frankl expressed the conviction of the time in terms of interior design: 'Ours is the era of the machine. Machinery is creating our style. It is imposing a new tempo and a new mode of life. With shameful sentimentality we still cling to the outgrown "styles" of the past – to houses designed in period styles ridiculously alien to their settings; to gilded gewgaws and polished marbles, to pseudo-period furniture' (1972 [1930]: 25).

By the 1930s, American companies began to consider developing not only efficient working environments but also buildings and interior spaces that expressed their corporate ethos. For example, in the Johnson Wax Co. building, Frank Lloyd Wright developed his notion of the company as an organism. As the outlook from the building was not pleasant, Wright located the employees in a large, open, top-lit space elegantly supported by slender 'mushroom' columns. The *St Louis Dispatch* reported in 1937 during construction: 'The 250 workers will occupy a single great room, only those machines which are noisy being segregated, and cork ceilings will absorb the sound rising from the heated rubber floor, blend[ing] it into a placid hum.' This concern for the working environment was exemplary; however, the paternalistic nature of the company was emphasized by the penthouse location of directors and managers at the top of the building.

The escapist mode of Art Deco design, with its shades of exoticism, luxury and glamour, was well adapted to cinemas, hotels and other commercial buildings throughout the 1930s. The rooms of Eltham Palace, London, illustrate the ideal of sumptuous luxury. Built in 1936 for Stephen and Virginia Courtauld, the dining room contrasts precious woods with a silvered ceiling, and fashionable pink leather upholstered dining chairs with black-and-silver doors portraying animals and birds from London Zoo (Figure 2.5).

Ocean liners offered another interior space for the decorators' imagination to run wild. Styles ranged from Tudor country houses through Italian

Figure 2.5 Dining room, Eltham Palace, designed by Seeley and Paget, 1936.

Renaissance to Pompeiian interiors and the Art Deco. Often, these interior designs linked to the nationality of the shipping company. Commercial manufacturers successfully introduced versions of Art Deco into the mass market and influenced products such as textiles, furniture, wallpaper and accessories. These products particularly reflected the imagery of zigzags, sunbursts and jazz patterns, allowing a large number of people to enjoy a modern interior.

eclecticism and the rise of the decorator 1880s–1940s

Classicism, historicism and programmed designs based on traditional examples had suited the luxury requirements of the newly wealthy entrepreneurs, industrialists and bankers and reflected their taste in architecture. Imitative designs based on past styles were particularly successful in America, where there was little in the way of a national history upon which to draw. However, there was a growing demand for interesting and tasteful interiors that exhibited more individuality. Indeed the demands of eclectic architecture and their interiors encouraged a new breed of decorators, antique dealers and agents to meet that demand. One strand of this development continued the tradition of the eighteenth-century Parisian *marchands-merciers*. Businesses such as Lenygon and Morant in London, Charles Alavoine and Jeanselme in Paris and Herter Brothers (from 1864) in New York were good examples that were able to combine the services of antique dealer, furnisher, decorator and stylist.

A particularly interesting development was the publication of Edith Wharton and Ogden Codman's *The Decoration of Houses* in 1897. Although it urged a return to classic French models for schemes and furnishings that began a lasting relationship between the French interior and the USA, its professed concern with 'house decoration as a branch of architecture' and not with 'superficial application of ornament totally independent of structure', was a major change (Wharton and Codman 1978 [1897]: Introduction). Despite this emphasis on connections between architecture and interior design, the rise of the 'decorator' was to be an important milestone in this history.

Edith Wharton (1862–1937)

Edith Wharton was an American novelist, short story writer and designer. In *The Decoration of Houses* (1897), Wharton and co-author Ogden Codman sought to move away from the design failures of their time and improve interior design and taste. Wharton and Codman offered both theoretical and practical advice about interior design. They contended that room decoration was an important part of architectural practice, with interior architectural elements as important as the exterior of a house. Arguing that interiors should be governed by classical canons of good taste based on French and Italian styles of the eighteenth century, often with an emphasis on simplicity, proportion, fitness and balance, the book has chapters that explain these ideas and explore how they could be used in particular rooms.

Elsie de Wolfe (1865–1950)

Elsie de Wolfe was an American interior decorator, nominal author of the influential 1913 book *The House in Good Taste*, and a prominent figure in New York, Paris and London society. Her interior design philosophy, based on lightening and removing clutter and opening up spaces, reflected a growing twentieth-century or modern identity. She achieved this through the use of opened-up spaces decorated in light, refreshing colours and employed objects such as potted palms, Persian rugs, mirrors and faux finishes. The architectural establishment frowned upon all this as they considered the links between fashion, feminism and commerce to be frivolous. Nevertheless, de Wolfe developed a trend that has become part of the decorator's approach to interiors.

The gendered approach to discussing interiors is evident in two proximate publications. In Elsie de Wolfe's *The House in Good Taste* of 1913, she says:

> We take it for granted that every woman is interested in houses—that she either has a house in course of construction, or dreams of having one, or has had a house long enough wrong to wish it right. And we take it for granted that this American home is always the woman's home: a man may build and decorate a beautiful house, but it remains for a woman to make a home of it for him. It is the personality of the mistress that the home expresses. Men are forever guests in our homes, no matter how much happiness they may find there. (6)

In complete contrast, the designer Frank Parsons, in his *Interior Decoration, Its Principles and Practice* of 1915, says: 'The house is but the externalized man; himself expressed in colour, form, line and texture. To be sure, he is usually limited in means, hampered by a contrary and penurious landlord or by family heirlooms, and often he cannot find just what he wants in the trade; but still the house is his house. It is he' (1920: vii). For Parsons, the business of furnishing and decorating the modern home of 1915 was a vital profession. Here he stresses the importance of environments in society: '[The modern house] furnishes the environment in which are born and nurtured the early impressions of those who are to set the taste standards in the generations that follow. This consideration dignifies interior decoration by placing it among the serious professions'

(1920: 225). Parsons saw the role of the domestic interior as an influential tool in improving human life through the education process.

The rise of the female decorators who started by 'putting a room together' for a friend and then soon developed their work into serious business ventures demonstrated a less didactic approach. These included Rose Cumming (1887–1968), a decorator who employed period elements with strong colour, draperies and imposing accessories. There was also Ruby Ross Wood (1880–1950), who assisted Elsie de Wolfe initially, then established herself as a decorator who employed common sense and simplicity in her planning. She had a well-known mantra: 'The final judgement in decorating is not the logic of the mind, but the logic of the eye.' Thirdly, there was Eleanor McMillen (1890–1991), who established McMillen Inc. in 1924 and had a trademark of styles mixed around French period furniture.

To some, this eclecticism was simply dilettante work and therefore lacked the seriousness of architectural design and planning. In her 1934 autobiography, *A Backward Glance*, Edith Wharton wrote: 'Architects of that day looked down on house decoration as a branch of dressmaking, and left the field to the upholsterers, who crammed every room with curtains, lambrequins, jardinières of artificial plants, wobbly velvet covered tables littered with silver gew-gaws and festoons of lace on mantle piece and dressing tables' (106–107). For architects, this reputation issue continued, especially in relation to interior decorators. Talking about the Plaza Hotel in New York, Frank Lloyd Wright commented disparagingly: 'There were Ravenna mosaics on the floor, but they covered them up with rugs. A lot of it has been spoiled by inferior desecrators' (Wright 1954b).

An important factor in the development of the interior decorator/designer derived from the development of the anonymous residential apartment block. It was in these spaces, whether in London, Paris or New York, that the decorator could create 'interiors'. These spaces (in many cases large in scale and grandeur) did not warrant the services of an architect, so were empty canvasses for a range of decorators to wield their influence (see Reed in Sparke et al. 2009: 79–93). It was for these clients that the lady decorators of the 1920s and '30s in particular rose to meet the challenge of creating identities for their clients. For example, in 1938, Sibyl Colefax started a successful business, later joined by John Fowler. Between them, they developed the idea of 'humble elegance' associated with the slightly faded grand interiors of the aristocracy. Mrs Guy Bethell and Mrs Dryden ran another well-known interior decorating firm and shop in Duke Street, Mayfair, known as E. Elden. Near there, Somerset Maugham's wife Syrie established Syrie Ltd, 'where her estranged husband once uncharitably imagined her as "on her knees to an American m-m-millionairess trying to sell her a chamber-p-p-pot"' (see 'The Architecture of the Estate'). Beverley Nichols, in his novel *For Adults Only* (1932), lampooned these businesses. As always with satire, there is an element of truth lurking:

A small furniture shop not far from Berkeley Square. In the window is a piece of incredibly expensive and astonishingly dirty brocade, hanging over a 'pickled' chair.

A Provençal dix-huitième commode, also pickled, looms forbiddingly in the background. There is little else save a few cushions and a Sheraton desk. (In Calloway1988: 215)

Additionally, in London, and no doubt elsewhere, department stores like Harrods, Fortnum and Mason, Waring and Gillow and Maples also supplied a full service for interior decoration, often employing well-known architects and designers to those unable to reach the social heights of Mayfair.

In the USA, interior decorators who had an 'eye' and were able to mix eclectic groupings of objects and colours together serviced a similar market. These included Dorothy Draper, who became a specialist in bright-coloured versions of neo-Baroque interiors, Nancy McClelland, a specialist in period styles, and Mrs Henry 'Sister' Parish, who developed the English country house look.

mid-twentieth century 1940s–1960s

Post-war interior design reflected not only a revision of Modernism but also an embracement of pluralism aided by the growth in visual media and culture. The post-war developments in interior design were also marked by the rise in the corporate market. People made distinctions between those who worked as space planners and interior designers and those whose work concentrated on the domestic as stylists or interior decorators. In the UK, reformers who wanted to introduce modern design into the domestic sphere influenced post-war homes. The Council of Industrial Design was a key player in this development and sponsored many exhibitions, such as the examples seen at Hatfield New Town from 1953, which include a Modernist-influenced approach where more traditional accessories enhance simple contemporary furnishings (Figure 2.6).

Post-war Modernism developed in two ways – geometric and organic. For many, the key words were efficiency and new technology. The geometric, based on Bauhaus teaching, developed particularly in the USA, where many of the Bauhaus faculty established themselves. The style seemed to represent a new start in the west led by the USA, especially in terms of commercial development, the office block and the factory. Geometric Modernism was a flagship for the brave new world of technologies, standardization and production, along with the application of new materials.

In the 1950s and '60s, the International Style skyscraper or hermetically sealed 'glass boxes' became the symbol of commercial and cultural success. With the development of successful air-conditioning and fluorescent lighting, these buildings could be laid out in any way required. There was no need to have natural lighting or ventilation since the suspended ceilings allowed for artificial lighting and air supply. Interior design firms such as the Knoll Planning Unit epitomized the elegantly furnished interiors, complete with collections of artworks. In fact, Florence Knoll gave a spurt to the change from interior decorator to interior designer whereby the designer becomes responsible for the space planning, services and equipment, as well as the furnishing and fittings and aesthetic input (Tigerman 2007: 63). Commercial interior design became bigger business as work, environment and the brand or public face of companies become even more important. Architectural practices began to consider these aspects more, and firms such as Skidmore Owens Merrill and the Knoll Planning Unit took the lead in this work.

Florence Knoll (1917–)

Florence Knoll Bassett is an American furniture designer and architect who trained in the Miesian Modernist tradition. She and Hans Knoll founded Knoll Associates to develop ranges of architect-designed furniture. Although she designed furniture in a strict Modernist style, it was her work for corporate offices that best demonstrated her American interpretation of the International Style rationalist design theories. She applied the principles of design to solving space problems. Her ideas for offices were for a fresh, orderly interior, based on open plan layouts in conjunction with iconic Modernist designers' furniture. Her concept of the 'total design' that included the architecture, the interior design and graphics were important pointers to later developments in the business of interiors.

During the 1950s in Europe, there was a radical change in ideas about office layout. The German management consultants Quickborner developed the idea of a *Bürolandschaft* or 'office-landscape'. Rather than treat workers as part of a Taylorist system of production control, this

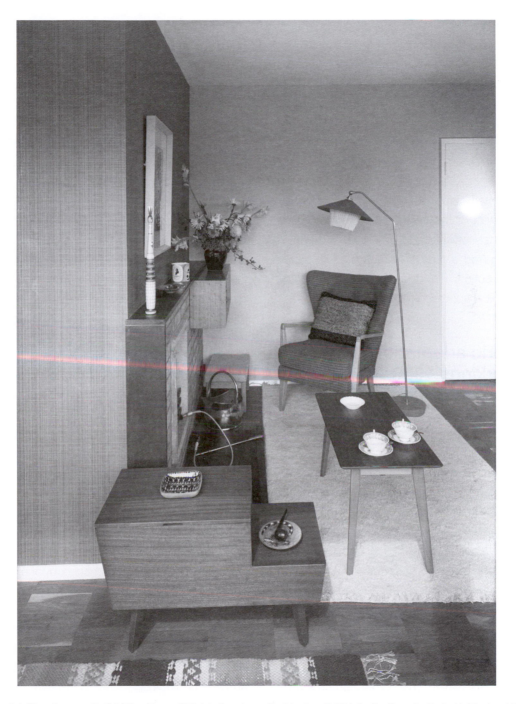

Figure 2.6 Show house at Hatfield New Town, 1953. Interiors planned by Mrs Joan Pattrick for the Council of Industrial Design, 1953.

plan considered people as individuals through a sociological examination of human relations at work. The plan allowed for some freedom in the layout of furniture in large, open-plan spaces. Although it used similar mechanical services to American examples, the employment of moveable partitions and organic planting created a degree of delineation and privacy. The use of fitted carpets and noise-absorbing ceiling panels partially tempered the sounds of a large office. The benefit of this layout was the acknowledgement that 'office work' was very wide-ranging and required a flexible approach to its planning and execution. This developed further in the non-hierarchical approach to planning.

historic adaptations and reworkings 1930s–2000s

The continuation of eclectic approaches that were often rooted in past designs has been a constant feature of interiors during the twentieth century. This practice developed in various ways, ranging from academic reconstructions and replicas to re-creations of an imaginary past or adaptations based loosely on historic styles. The twentieth century also saw the rise of the conservation movement, whereby rehabilitation and adaptation of buildings and spaces were developed.

Conservation is generally taken to mean conserving an existing space/building in its current form, however that may be, at the very least to make it safe but with minimal intrusion. The next level is preservation, which also maintains a minimally invasive ethos but may update systems and buildings to current quality standards, if appropriate.

Rehabilitation maintains the essential character of a building and its interior spaces but allows for some reconstruction using original parts, replacing missing elements etc. Restoration can have different meanings: it may be that anything added to the spaces since initial building is removed to try to re-create the original look, or it may be more sympathetic in that it follows the rehabilitation path and brings the space back to life.

Adaption is the reuse of a building and its spaces. It is also referred to as adaptive reuse or remodelling and is often associated with interior architectural practices. At its most extreme, the façade is kept, whilst the rest of the building is demolished and entirely reconstructed.

Finally, there is the revival or reconstruction of historical styles. These incorporate new-builds based either on the plan of an original space or on a new site. Approaches may be fanciful, such as Disneyland, or be more faithful to original patterns. The reworking of historical precedents, in terms of interiors particularly, will take many forms. These may relate to the furnishing of historic houses using documented fabrics, wallpapers and furniture; they may draw on the past for inspiration and create an eclectic mix; or they may create an updated effect, loosely based on historic styles. John Fowler and his work for the interiors of houses managed by the English National Trust defined the English country house look. In conjunction with Sibyl Colefax, they established a decorating business that built on these traditions and became a recognized name in this type of decoration (see Ward in McKellar and Sparke 2004).

The American decorator Billy Baldwin created an American style of interior decoration that used the following, all judiciously located: strong silhouettes; deep, glossy walls; tailored Louis XVI armchairs and deep, low, boxy sofas; fitted carpets with small repeat patterns; bulbous white plaster lamps; Chinese lacquer screens; printed cottons; rattan; crisp colours; and objets d'art. He is reputed to have said: 'No matter how taste may change, the basics of good decorating remain the same: We're talking about some place people live in, surrounded by things they like and that make them comfortable. It's as simple as that' (in Gray 2004: 103).

Designers such as Dorothy Draper, Sarah Lee and Rita St Clair, who produced eclectic interior styles based on an interpretation of the buildings, though often with dramatic interventions of scale, pattern and material, undertook the restoration and renovation of important historic interiors. Designers such as John Saladino and David Hicks have also taken classical principles and adapted them with a mixture of antique and new furnishing. Hicks was particularly well known for dramatic colour schemes, often with clashing accessories, symmetry and roomscapes.

All of these period styles or revivals are subject to the vagaries of fashion and taste, and may reflect cultural changes as the underlying ethos of particular styles may chime with particular issues of nostalgia, power play or simply reactions to previous styles.

pop design *c.*1960–1975

If design reflects cultural values and uses the symbols of that culture to reflect itself, then Pop design is a classic example of this process. This was a truly popular style, particularly linked to the post-war youth explosion, which embraced life and exuded confidence through a number of common features. These included bright colours, reworked Art Nouveau and Deco patterns, the influence of Pop Art and the dichotomous use of throwaway materials, along with a renewed interest in natural materials and craft skills.

The 'Pop aesthetic' found favour in restaurant design, boutiques and products such as wallpaper, textiles and furniture. All of these new approaches to design upset the old order, built on ideals of purism, good taste and simplistic functionalism. Market forces were the new arbiters of taste. In addition, Pop design avoided the dictatorial approaches of Modernism and embraced variety, difference and attitude. This 'Postmodern' approach recognized a pluralistic society, which did not want to have a particular set of values linked with the general taste imposed upon it. An idea for a 'House of the Future', displayed at the London Ideal Home Exhibition in 1956, showed the potential of plastics. Designed by British architects Alison and Peter Smithson, and intended to be a mass-produced plastic structure, it included revolutionary features such as a self-cleaning bath, easy-to-clean corners and remote controls. In the dressing area there was a plastic, fabricated built-in vanity/storage unit to fit the wall (Plate 7).

high-tech 1970s–

The ideas about harnessing new technologies for architecture and interiors have a long history, but those developed by Buckminster Fuller in his

Dymaxion houses from 1929 onwards were important. A later development in attempts to create economical and speedy production of houses were the California Case Study Houses (1945–1966). These adapted Modernist principles, often using industrial materials. A famous example of engineering products used to create a house is the California home of Charles and Ray Eames. However, in this case, the industrial shell held a quite contrasting interior: 'In contrast to the starkness of many international style interiors, Eames's interiors were increasingly filled with distinctive arrangements of furniture, rugs, flowers, pillows, toys, candles, shells and other collectibles that approached a high Victorian clutter' (Dunster).

This 'functioning ornament' idea was clearly not the same as high-tech style, but the aesthetic of 1970s and 1980s interior design, based on the products intended for industrial use such as heavy-duty flooring, scaffolding and office equipment, etc., introduced their own decorative surfaces and finishes. A good example of the style is the Hopkins House in Hampstead, London. Built in 1976 with similarities to the Eames House in California, this steel and glass building, based on a simple structural grid, uses prefabricated industrial materials in an uncompromising way (Figure 2.7).The irony is that these interiors often celebrated the industrial through the hand-made or assembled, employing sophisticated joints, expensive materials and finishes.

minimalism

The use of simple geometric shapes in as many as possible of the design components defines Minimalism. Minimal colours, defined by textures and simple finishes, are another hallmark of the style. Minimalism is partly rooted in the simplicity of the rationalist designers of the early twentieth century. It also connects to other ideals of pure form and the fundamental elements of design and space planning. The oft-quoted mantra of Mies van der Rohe, 'Less is more', but with close attention to detail, also reflects the aims of the Minimalists. The work of John Pawson, for example, 'focuses on the quality of the spatial sequence and on the refinement of the smallest details of junction, light and surface' (see Pawson). The Minimalist approach suited a particular type of exclusive retail store, but in domestic interiors it is often softened by textures and interesting shapes. However, pure Minimalism and the imposition of strict order and regulation is a limited taste. The opposite is often more popular.

postmodern

First applied to architecture and design in the 1940s, the term Postmodern is, in one sense, anything that comes after Modern, and then on to the pluralism of Pop in the 1960s (see above). It rejected the absolutist approach of the Modern movement. Postmodern describes a general cultural mood, expressed in such diverse disciplines as literature, philosophy, critical theory, politics, architecture and design. The underpinning idea of Postmodernism recognizes that life is a problem of organized complexity. This is the opposite of the ideal of elegance and simplicity often associated with Modernism.

Figure 2.7 Hopkins House, Hampstead, showing study corner of the living area, Designed by Sir Michael Hopkins, 1976.

In 1966, American architect Robert Venturi published his seminal book *Complexity and Contradiction in Architecture*, which effectively gave the Postmodern movement a manifesto. Venturi proposed an architecture, and by extension a form of interior design, that was all things that Modernism was not, i.e. complex, ambiguous, eclectic, symbolic and historical. The architecture

Robert Venturi (1925–)

A controversial American architect and critic of mainstream modern architecture, Venturi published his 'gentle manifesto', *Complexity and Contradiction in Architecture*, in 1966, in which he argued for a vitality that used 'conventions unconventionally'. In 1972, Venturi wrote *Learning From Las Vegas*, which developed the argument for architecture and design that had some symbolic meaning, as opposed to elitist and elegant Modernist work. These works influenced the Postmodern approach to design where popular culture, colour and pattern were positively encouraged as a reaction to pure-white mainstream Modernism.

that Venturi produced in the 1960s had close affinities with the contemporary Pop painting movement, and he sought his imagery within mass culture. These buildings' features included an emphasis on content over form, symbolism over rationality and multiple meanings over single meanings.

Style or not, Postmodernism has a number of features that identify it and that can be summarized. It aims to be deliberately challenging and complex. The celebration of 'otherness', difference and heterogeneity found in society accounts for the pluralist approach to architecture and design since the 1970s. Radical eclecticism, or the mixing of different 'languages' to engage different tastes and cultures and describe different functions, has been a defining aspect of Postmodern architecture and design.

One of the clearest demands of Postmodernist theory in architecture and design is that the buildings and interiors speak on two levels at once, through their dual coding. Firstly, they speak to those who care about the specifically designerly or architectural meanings, and secondly, to the public at large or the local inhabitants who care about issues concerned with comfort, traditional building uses and ways of life. This dual coding therefore demands the extension of the language of design in a number of different ways. This then intends to lessen the disjunction that occurs between the elites who create environments and the public who use them. The juxtaposition of new and old, amusing inversions of the old, and the employment of colour, ornament and so on, achieve this.

All these constitute a return to 'content' and in many cases, decoration. In addition, they result in a building or object that is not self-referential but reaches out to the rest of us by many associations and references. The furniture of Robert Venturi with historical references to the eighteenth century, Michael Graves using elemental silhouettes of basic forms, and interiors by Hans Hollein that referred to Art Deco forms provide just some examples.

office/corporate

A particular manifestation of Postmodern planning and design was the linking of functions with human needs. A fascinating development was the concept of a 'workers' village' developed by the Dutch architect Herman Herzberger. Herzberger designed his Centraal Beheer insurance company project, built in Apeldoorn, Holland in 1974, so that the occupants 'would have the feeling of being part of a working community without being lost in the crowd' (Caruso St John). The unfinished concrete building, with its repetitive small platforms, allowed small groups of people to congregate, and they were encouraged to personalize and decorate the space. The arrangement was apparently less efficient though much more attractive to work in than other contemporary Modernist offices.

New office buildings often still followed the general pattern of narrow runs of cellular offices arranged along a central corridor. The ambition for each employee to work in their own office or amongst a small group was the new formula that seemed to contradict all the claims of Bürolandschaft. To deal with this, the Swedish design practice Tengbom invented the 'combi-office' idea. This combined cellular offices on the exterior of a building, leaving a common space for employees and services in the centre.

Many new developments in out-of-town sites or peripheral settings have used the increased amount of open space to build shallower-plan offices that have more contact with the outside, as the old-style deep, artificially lit and air-conditioned layout has been linked to 'sick building syndrome', higher employee absenteeism and dissatisfaction. The extensive use of the web, and portable devices such as laptops and mobile phones, has created situations where workers undertake tasks in a variety of locations. The development of concepts such as 'hot-desking' and more team-based working meant that the bland and standardized open-plan office was outdated. Work patterns and attitudes to the office changed as well. The 'dress code' became more relaxed and many companies have now started to open 24 hours to facilitate flexible operational patterns.

Another interior design-led change is in the planning of medical facilities. In the 1970s, hospitals began to exchange their sterile, functional image for a friendlier model, to meet the new challenges of the marketplace and to adapt to the changing attitudes to illness and death. The hospital model, designed to treat patients and families more as guests than as clients, provides public spaces to act as community meeting places and accommodations that are more hotel-like. These changes attempt to reduce the apparent gulf between patient, community and the hospital experience.

sustainable design

Sustainable design is a crucial response to the needs of the planet in terms of the impact of design on all levels of the building, its site, equipment and furnishing. Known as Green design, Eco design, Environmental design, they all have the common goal of conserving, renewing and controlling the resources of the Earth. The outward appearance of projects may reflect this concern or the designer will conceal them in the work. The use of aluminium is one example. Although often having a higher initial cost, it has a range of properties that include formability, flexibility, light weight and, of course, superb recyclability. The material's excellent durability, very low maintenance costs, high scrap value and energy-efficient recycling not only represents a sustainable approach but is also economic (Figure 2.8).

Figure 2.8 Aluminium kitchen demonstrating both Modernist design principles and use of sustainable material, Schiffini, 2010.

Design has become increasingly internationalized over the last one hundred years and now, finally, a sustainable approach is also gathering pace across many countries. It is not just a one-way street though: interest in traditional and vernacular solutions from various cultures, not simply as a source of decorative motifs to borrow, but as potential solutions to particular problems, has grown. The need for an understanding of the cultural/contextual relationship between building work and the site, use and sustainability is also important. Therefore, modern technology is not always the answer, even if it appears to be. We now recognize much more the importance of local solutions to neighbourhood and regional issues, particularly where they relate to climatic conditions or cultural habits. (See further Chapter 11.)

chapter 3

history and structure of the profession

CHAPTER OVERVIEW

This chapter considers the history and structure of the discipline and profession of interior design. Although considered a relatively new discipline, the skills and approaches linked to interior design work have a long history. Whilst there are common components in the discipline, various countries and regions have developed particular approaches to their own professional practice, so this introduction is necessarily general.

The chapter gives a broad overview of the development of professional practice in interior designing with an emphasis on the changes that occurred in the twentieth century, as they were the most important. It also emphasizes the changes that occurred in the later nineteenth century that encouraged women to enter the business and the subsequent attempts to professionalize their work. The structure of the design profession in general terms is considered by briefly noting developments in trade associations and registration issues. The chapter then introduces the crucial role of education and continuing learning. The chapter ends with a brief consideration of the business and industry that supports and supplies interior designers.

origins and history

From the early sixteenth century, following publication of various treatises on architectural practice, architects became more involved in interior decoration, as did artists. Raphael, for example, developed schemes to create the idea of a total ensemble. The establishment of the Gobelins Workshops in Paris, under the artistic direction of Le Brun, assisted the creation of integrated and highly crafted interiors. In England, during the 1620s and 1630s, architect Inigo Jones designed components for his interiors. One highly successful designer was Daniel Marot (1661–1752), who worked both in Holland and in England. He worked on the architectural shell, producing designs for upholstery, textile window treatments and interior woodwork. William Kent (1685–1748) was one of the first professionals in England to work as an architect while also designing furniture and decoration.

It soon became commonplace for architects to produce proposals for entire interiors as well as the building itself. Plans, perspective watercolours and cross-sections, in addition to exploded views of rooms, were all part of the visualization process. British architects who represent this include the Adam brothers, William Chambers and James Wyatt. A little later, Karl Friedrich Schinkel in Germany and Charles Percier and Pierre Fontaine in France also established themselves as overseers of whole building schemes, often right down to the final detail.

During the eighteenth century, upholsterers also worked on interiors, especially if the work was mainly refurbishment. In conjunction with the architects and clients, craftsmen-led businesses orchestrated and co-ordinated sub-contractors and their own workers in most aspects of the interior decoration and design processes. In France, the *marchands-merciers* took an important role as connoisseurs, importers, designers, patrons and co-ordinators of interior schemes, liaising with clients and makers as well as having their own shops.

In an attempt to differentiate themselves as professionals, architects established the Institute of British Architects in 1834 to develop and uphold professional standards, and to distinguish themselves from the 'trade'. By the mid to late nineteenth century, architects were still planning total design concepts, especially in the new design tastes of Arts and Crafts, the Aesthetic movement and Art Nouveau, as well as in public and commercial buildings. In contrast, the upholsterers and retailers were dealing with the growing middle-class market for the design and supply of domestic middle-class interior decorations,

in addition to commissions for public buildings. The German applied arts author Julius Lessing, writing in 1878, noted the 'project management' role where the decorator 'manages to link the individual trades together in a unified achievement' (Muthesius 2009: 39).

Reformers challenged the notion of the retailer as an arbiter of taste in interiors, as the distinctions between the 'trade' and the profession were important to those who made their living from it. The well-known design reformer Christopher Dresser pointed out that interior decoration was a skilled profession and decorators should advise their clients as to how rooms should be decorated and furnished, much as doctors or solicitors would advise in their own fields: 'The decoration of a room is as much bound by laws and by knowledge as the treatment of disease' (Dresser 1988 [1879]: 39).

Although the design 'profession' was initially generally male-dominated, there were notable exceptions. Indeed, women's involvement in the domestic sphere during the nineteenth century had ensured an interest in the decoration of the interior.

The cousins Agnes and Rhoda Garrett certainly expressed a similar attitude to Dresser's comments above with regard to professional approaches. The Garretts had trained in an architect's office, and then went into business as interior decorators with serious and professional attitudes. Echoing Christopher Dresser, they wrote that 'Decorators may be compared to doctors. It is useless to put yourself under their direction unless you mean to carry out their regime' (in Ferry 2003: 18).

The American Candace Wheeler was 'the mother' of the profession, as she was one of the first women to run a successful interior design business. She founded the Society of Decorative Art in New York in 1877, an organization devoted to helping American women artists and artisans to gain training in the applied arts. Wheeler also found success as a professional textile artist and in 1879, with the designer Louis Comfort Tiffany, co-founded the interior-decorating firm of Tiffany & Wheeler, serving as the partner specializing in textiles. The firm of Associated Artists followed. Wheeler left the partnership with Tiffany in 1883 to form her own textile design firm. During the late 1880s, Wheeler became one of the first women to work professionally in a field dominated by male upholsterers, architects and cabinet-makers. The professionalization issue continued in the United States when in 1895, Candace Wheeler wrote about 'Interior decoration as a profession for women' in *The Outlook* magazine (see Peck and Irish 2001).

Soon after this, in 1897, Edith Wharton and Ogden Codman published *The Decoration of Houses*, which remained an influential book for over forty years. Codman and Wharton advocated that the true basis of interior design was the European tradition of robust architecture accentuated by furniture and furnishings that suited the space. Rooms based on simple, classical design principles, such as symmetry and proportion, were the most successful. They go on to say:

> House decoration has come to be regarded as a black art by those who have seen their rooms subjected to the manipulations of the modern upholsterer. Now, in the hands of decorators who understand the funda-

mental principles of their art, the surest effects are produced, not at the expense of simplicity and common sense, but by observing the requirements of both. (Wharton and Codman 1897: Introduction)

In Europe, the concept of the *Gesamtkunstwerk* or 'total work of art' continued to make connections between architecture and the interior. It was this concept that Baillie Scott was addressing in 1895 when he said: 'It is difficult for the architect to draw a fixed line between architecture of the house and the furniture. The conception of an interior must necessarily include the furniture which is to be used in it, and this naturally leads to the conclusion that the architect should design the chairs and tables as well as the house itself' (Baillie Scott 1895). This approach of course ignored the majority of interiors that existed in extant buildings. It was in these spaces that the interior designers would come into their own. There were soon additions to the pioneering works of the Garretts, Candace Wheeler and Edith Wharton.

In 1913, Elsie de Wolfe (1865–1950) published her influential *The House in Good Taste* (Sparke 2005). She was in demand to 'make over' the interiors of wealthy homes, changing them from the late Victorian style into more modern schemes featuring light, fresh colours and displaying her penchant for antique or reproduction eighteenth-century French furniture. She was amongst the first 'decorators' to receive a fee for her design services rather than a commission on the sale of furniture purchased via a retailer. This change in the payment process signified a revision of perceptions from the dilettante to the professional.

Career guidance for women published in 1924 in the USA pointed out the nature of the changing situation:

> As a distinct occupation, interior decoration is not yet clearly defined, but it may be said that it is developing into a profession. It is true that the upholsterer, the retailer of furniture and hangings, and the gift shop-keeper frequently advise their patrons on a whole scheme of decoration. On the other hand the architect may assume responsibility for the interior decoration as well as the construction of a building. The professional decorator, however, is equipped with skill in design and with a knowledge of architecture and historic ornament, of textiles, woods, paint, fixtures, furniture, draperies and rugs. In addition to this training she must have high ethical standards, business ability, and an intimate knowledge of the trades with which she comes in contact. (Bureau of Vocational Information 1924: 108)

The passage presciently continues by stating that: 'The future holds promise in this occupation, however, only for those qualified persons who will secure thorough training and practical business experience' (108). The emphasis on training and business was important, and it is revealing to see that a number of famous names started their careers in the trade working for department stores as advisors and sales people.

Nancy McClelland (1877–1959) was also an important figure in the professionalizing of interior decoration. Through her own business, established in 1922, through publishing, through advocating education and training and the establishment of processional organizations, she encouraged the professional development of interior decoration and design. McClelland was a major force in the business, being a founder member of the American Institute of Interior Decorators and the first woman to be national president of that association. In *An Outline of Careers for Women: A Practical Guide to Achievement*, published in 1929, McClelland wrote:

> I should recommend, as preparation, a course in a school of fine and applied arts. Such a course, which covers two or three years' work, should include drawing, both freehand and mechanical; some training in architecture; and a technical knowledge of colour. A working idea of the technique of lighting is necessary, and some acquaintance with rugs and materials must be acquired. A broad historical background also is necessary in understanding periods and the manner of life of the people of various countries. A more intimate acquaintance with good architecture through travel is of enormous value in treating wall decorations, in planning and designing panelling, and in getting the best effects in badly proportioned rooms. Travel is also one of the most delightful ways to acquire knowledge of the furniture, tapestries, paintings, and garden ornaments of foreign countries, as well as of the characteristic furniture of our own country. (In Fleischman 1928: 246)

As a preparation for a career in interior design, this was a good start. Other women were high-profile decorators. Dorothy Draper, well known for her neo-baroque interiors, was the epitome of the wealthy elitist decorator-socialite. She had a great success decorating for her friends and clients in America during the early to mid twentieth century (Varney 1988). Interestingly, she also specialized in designing commercial interiors. Eleanor McMillen founded her business, McMillen Inc., in 1924, and called it 'the first professional full-service interior decorating firm in America' (Massey 1990: 129). Considered a pioneer in her field, she built her reputation on her ability to combine great style with a keen sense of business. She went to both business and secretarial school after having studied design for three years at the Parsons School in New York and Paris. 'I thought if I was going to do it at all, I'd better do it professionally', she once said. 'That's why it's McMillen Inc. and not Eleanor McMillen. I wasn't one of the "ladies"' (in Vogel 1991). This pointed distinction marks a serious change in approach.

It was not only in the USA that the interior design business was flourishing in the early years of the twentieth century. In France, *ensembliers* who specifically created works in an 'Art Deco style', such as Jules Leleu, Sue et Mare and J.M. Frank, undertook interior decoration projects. In England, Syrie Maugham established Syrie Ltd in London in 1922, and as her reputation grew, so did her business. She later opened shops in New York and Chicago. Although her fame rested on her 'white decors', by the mid-1930s she had moved to create interiors with baroque accessories and striking colour schemes. A little later, Sybil Colefax founded Colefax and Co. In 1938, John Fowler joined her, and became responsible for the development of a grand and elegant ap-

proach to design, mixed with understatement and comfort, that has become known as the 'English country house' style (see Wood 2007).

After World War II, a new breed of designer emerged specializing in commercial projects, which became an increasingly important part of the business. Interior planners and consultants became the new professionals as they took advantage of the opportunities offered by the development of large corporate building works. A fine example of this is the work of Florence Knoll and the Knoll Planning Unit. Bobbye Tigerman explains:

> [Florence] Knoll's self-conscious identification as both architect and interior designer suggested something more radical and destabilizing to the clean distinction between the professions—namely, that the time-honoured hierarchy of architect over interior designer was bankrupt. The work of architects and interior designers differed only in the area of the building assigned, not in process or method. And if this equivalence was true, the architect and interior designer required the same intellectual capacity and creative talent, and the interior of the building deserved the same attention as the exterior. (Tigerman 2007: 63)

For the corporate market in the second half of the twentieth century, a number of manufacturing firms began to specialize in working with architects and designers not only to produce comprehensive ranges, but also to supply expertise in office planning and design. Architectural practices also developed interior design departments. The use of new building techniques including curtain walls, suspended ceilings and large, open-plan spaces all offered new and exciting challenges to the interior designers. These new spaces also required specialists in such areas as space planning, lighting design, acoustics and sophisticated climate control systems. There is now a much clearer understanding of the roles of interior designers in relation to other specialisms and professions.

structure

The Interior Design Profession

A number of interrelated aspects define a profession. These include:

- The use of particular skills based on theoretical knowledge
- A structure for the development and supervision of education and training in these skills
- The competence of professionals being ensured by examinations
- The establishment and maintenance of a code of conduct to ensure professional integrity
- The performance of a service that is for the public good
- A professional association that organizes its members and controls the number, selection and training of new entrants

Professional Associations

The tradition of maintaining some exclusivity in a trade, craft or profession has a long history. In 1834, English architects had organized themselves into a professional body. In 1857, American architects founded the American Institute of Architects. Professional recognition of interior designers had to wait a while.

The Institute of British Decorators, founded in 1899, became the Incorporated Institute of British Decorators, with a clear intention 'to encourage and promote the profession of interior decoration in all its branches and to improve and raise the status, training and qualification of its members' (V&A). The Institute encouraged and influenced the development of courses in interior design within the UK, held international and national conferences and produced various publications, including a code of professional practice for interior designers. In 1953, it was renamed the Incorporated Institute of British Decorators and Interior Designers, and then in 1975 it again changed its name to the British Institute of Interior Design. In 1987/8, the Institute merged with the Chartered Society of Designers.

In the early part of the twentieth century in the United States, professional associations were being established (see Martin 2007). Nancy McClelland explained the need:

> Not so long ago architects were forced to organize in self-defense, to protect themselves against untrained men who claimed all the rights and privileges of trained men. Decorators today are in a similar position. They are demanding sound training and real knowledge from those who wish to enter the ranks of recognized workers. The day has gone by when a woman who has never done anything but make a lamp shade or

move her furniture around until somebody said, "the group is attractive," can call herself a decorator.

Real decoration is, in its fundamental principles, an architectural affair. It goes far deeper than the making of lamp shades, the hanging of draperies, or the devising of enticing colour schemes. The architect and the decorator together, in creating and furnishing a house, work out the psychology of taste and the principles of the fine art of living. (McClelland, in Fleischman: 245)

Although, in 1914, thirty-eight members established The Decorators' Club in New York, and ten years later Sherrill Whiton founded the New York School of Interior Design, it was not until 1931 that the American Institute of Interior Decorators was founded, in Grand Rapids, Michigan. In 1936, it changed its name to the American Institute of Decorators (AID). In 1955, the AID published a manual of professional practice, highlighting changes within the profession.

In 1957, the National Society for Interior Designers (NSID) was founded in the US and in 1961 the AID changed its name again to American Institute of Interior Designers (AIID). A little later, in 1963, the International Federation of Interior Architects was formed in Denmark, then in 1965 the Interior Decorators' & Designers' Association (IDDA) developed in Great Britain, and in 1969 the Institute of Business Designers was formed to advance the profession in the field of specific business-related design practices in the United States.

By 1975, a merger of the American AIID and NSID created the American Society of Interior Designers (ASID); whilst in 1979 the International Society of Interior Designers (ISID) was founded. In 1994, the merger of the US-founded Institute of Business Designers (IBD) and Council of Federal Interior Designers (CFID), plus the International Society of Interior Designers (ISID), created the International Interior Design Association (IIDA).

Internationally, there are other professional organizations that work alongside interior designers, such as the International Federation of Interior Architects/Designers (IFI), which was founded in 1963, and 1992 saw the founding of the European Council of Interior Architects (ECIA) as an umbrella representative body for European professional interior architects' associations.

In 2002, the British Interior Design Association was formed from the merger of the IDDA (Interior Decorators' & Designers' Association) and the British chapter of the IIDA.

Registration and Licensing

The idea of registration for interior designers as a step to ensure professional recognition began in the 1930s. In 1938, Quebec province in Canada passed the first registration law, limiting the use of the title Certified Interior Designer. It was some time later, in 1951, that the first attempts to license interior designers developed in the USA, but it was not until 1982 that Alabama passed the first Interior Design Title Act. This restricted use of the title Interior Designer to qualified individuals. Since then, a number of other jurisdictions have followed. Recently there has been considerable lobbying in the USA, in the name of free competition, to stop regulation of the profession by government intervention.

Education

In 1563, the Italian painter and architect Giorgio Vasari encouraged Cosimo de Medici to establish the first regulated academy of art. Following Vitruvius's ideal, students learned the academic subjects, whilst the masters, in their own workshops, undertook their practical training. This developed so that the academy offered both practical training and theoretical lectures in accepted artistic practice. This two-fold approach, separating theory and practice, has underpinned training for art and design ever since, for better or worse. Recent changes in curricula indicate that there are attempts to merge, or at least link, theoretical and historical studies with studio practice.

By the 1790s, there were well over one hundred art academies in Europe, but certainly the most influential by the mid-nineteenth century was the *Ecole des Beaux Arts* in Paris. This school created a further separation of theory and practice. The architects had separate offices where real commissions were undertaken and the atelier or studio in the academy was mainly used for education in theory, so students often had little comprehension of practice until they left the academy. By the end of the nineteenth century, the legacy of the Beaux Arts training was to encourage accurate copying of Renaissance styles, as opposed to eclecticism and this remained a strong influence in Europe and the USA up to World War I.

In the twentieth century, the Parsons School of Design in New York was the first educational institute in America to offer a programme in Interior Design. Founded in 1896, it was in 1904 that Frank Alvah Parsons joined and, in 1910, he became the School's president. In 1939, nine years after the death of Frank Alvah Parsons, the School officially adopted his name.

The Parsons School continued to develop its programme in design and was important in spearheading new thinking in design education during the late 1960s. Important curriculum changes that moved away from decorating the homes of the middle and upper classes, towards work on the design of urban and socially conscious projects, set the pattern for many later programmes in other institutions.

The University of Washington in Seattle established the first university interior design programme in the mid-1920s. In Canada, the University of Manitoba established the first Interior Decoration Diploma in 1938, and in 1945 changed it to a four-year degree. During the 1960s and 1970s, interior design programmes developed in universities throughout North America. Florida State University offered one of the earliest interior-design-focussed doctoral programmes in the mid-1960s. The University of Tennessee established its multi-disciplinary doctoral programme, with an emphasis on environmental factors, in the early 1970s (Spanbroek and Lommerse 1999).

In Britain, the Royal College of Art established a postgraduate Department of Interior Design in 1951, which changed its name to Environmental Design in 1972. The teaching of architecture was brought back into the curriculum in 1975. Interestingly, it was in 1993 that the amalgamation of the Architecture and Interiors programmes occurred. In 2005, the department was renamed as Architecture. A few polytechnics and private schools offered undergraduate courses in the 1960s, and these developed and grew over the next forty years. In 2010, British higher education institutions offered 43 courses in interior architecture and 114 in interior design.

In the USA, The Interior Design Educators' Council (IDEC), founded in 1963, began to publish the *Journal of Interior Design Education and Research* (later *Journal of Interior Design*) in 1975. The establishment in 1970 of the Foundation for Interior Design Education Research (FIDER), also in the US, was intended to review and accredit programmes in interior design. In 1973, the first six accredited programmes in American universities were run. In 2006, FIDER changed its name to the Council for Interior Design Accreditation (CIDA).

In 1972, The National Council for Interior Design Qualification (NCIDQ) established a common qualification examination for interior designers in North America. NCIDQ serves to identify to the public those interior designers who have met the minimum standards for professional practice by passing the NCIDQ examination.

The educational content of the curriculum of contemporary degree-level interior design courses should include the following indicative areas:

- The development of appropriate attitudes, traits and values towards professional responsibility, accountability and effectiveness.
- The understanding of the fundamentals of art and design; theories of design; sustainable design; human behaviour; and discipline-related history.
- The ability to understand and apply the knowledge, skills, processes and theories of interior design.
- The development of communication and personal skills.

- The use of appropriate materials and products, used within the context of building systems.
- The recognition of the need to understand and apply the laws, codes, regulations, standards and practices that protect the health, safety and welfare of the public.
- The essential role of business and professional practices.

Industry

The business of interior design is an important element of the economy. For example, in 2007 in the USA there were around 11,000 companies with revenue of seven billion dollars working in the field. A typical firm is based in one location with fewer than four employees and revenue of $620,000 per year. Approximately 30 per cent are self-employed, with the fifty largest firms only accounting for 10 per cent of the total revenue (First Research Inc. 2009).

The profession relies upon a huge infrastructure of makers and suppliers to create networks of connectivity between the profession and the industry. In addition to components suppliers, various craftspeople including builders, decorators, joiners, fitters and other tradespeople, the interior design industry also employs a range of other professionals including surveyors, architects, lawyers, lighting designers, etc. The following selected list (based on the domestic interior) hints at the extent of the range of suppliers: accessories, acoustics, antiques, art, bedding, cabinetry, display/storage, drapery, electrics, fabric and trim, flooring and carpets, furniture, glass, hardware, home automation, kitchen bathroom equipment, lighting, shutters and awnings, stone, ceramic and tile, and textiles and soft furnishings.

The extent of the services used by interior designers is also demonstrated by this partial list: CAD and computing, cleaning, delivery, electricians, florists, framers, painters and decorators, photographers, plumbers, restorers and conservators, and upholsterers, amongst many other more specialized services.

The issues that face the interior design profession in the twenty-first century are likely to be similar to others. As Christine McGuire has suggested:

Predictions for the future of individual professions strongly suggest that most, if not all, will continue to be faced by more external regulation, increased competition from outside the field, intrusion of newer occupations, louder public demands for more high-quality service at lower cost, and increasingly rapid and pervasive technological changes that drastically alter practice. (McGuire, in Curry and Wergin 1993: 15)

chapter 4

the processes of design

CHAPTER OVERVIEW

This chapter looks at some general issues that have a wide resonance with all design practice. For example, a major factor for design practitioners is the way in which their principles and values connect with the ethics of their discipline. This includes taking into account the values relating to aspects of practice such as aesthetic, social, environmental, gender-based and economic considerations. An introduction to a general model of addressing a design problem follows some discussion of the generic design process. This process includes the stages of discovery, defining, developing and delivery. The chapter then considers some of the methods and tools used by designers. These include processes such as cost-benefit analysis, critical path analysis, evidence-based planning and design, interaction matrix, morphological analysis and synectics.

introduction

The idea that design equals activity rather than outcomes is the approach to 'design' taken here. There have been many, many attempts at defining design, all of which have particular strengths and weaknesses. For example, Kevin McCullagh has pointed out that 'design is not a fixed process; each design discipline and designer within that discipline works differently, as do individual designers tackling each project differently. The design process is highly dialectic, iterative, complex and – above all – human activity' (McCullagh, in Dudley and Mealing 2000: 48). This statement would seem to rule out any possibility of a ge-

neric way to think about design in anything other than broad generalizations. However, McCullagh also says that 'any human activity which involves problem identification, reflection, experiments and proposals is a manifestation of the design process (48). Therefore, we can break down the design process objectively into some sequences of thinking, planning, acting and reacting.

design

Engineer and educator Bruce Archer, a staunch advocate of research as the basis of design, defined it as follows: 'Design is that area of human experience, skill and knowledge which is concerned with man's ability to mould his environment to suit his material and spiritual needs' (Archer 1973). Reference to sustainable design and the issues of environment, economics and human society must qualify this. More specifically, we could say that interior designers give shape and structure to interiors through sustainable methods, and satisfy the functional, psychological and aesthetic needs of users.

Design is also a methodical process, as it requires designers to carefully consider issues and problems in our physical environment, and then to suggest suitable solutions. Finally, design is also imaginative, as designers must turn concepts into realities, taking into account the constraints and drivers that affect individual projects. Put another way, successful designers need to be able to combine the skills of decision-making and advocacy with those of enquiry and analysis, all balanced by the designer's own experience base.

Designers are subject to a wide range of external influences. These include other disciplines, visual stimuli from their own and other cultures, historical references and, not least, the demands/wishes of the clients, indicating a need for a broad-minded and open approach. These stimuli offer the designer source material for ideas. They also raise questions and may inspire solutions for problems.

overview of process and practice

Design processes have been discussed and analysed widely over the last fifty or so years, but there is still little general agreement. This is not surprising since design is such an overarching term in itself, and covers so many sub-disciplines; indeed each project is individual, so there may seem little scope for an authoritative process. Designers also have to adapt to changeable market conditions, variable customer tastes and the dynamics of change. In addition, the various stages of a design commission often overlap. However, although there is clearly some form of generic design process, it must be borne in mind that, as the focus narrows on the details of the project, the process will become increasingly specific. More mechanistically, design is a response to the flexible and fixed limitations of a brief. Certain aspects of the brief, such as function, statutory demands and client requirements, will be specified whilst other aspects will offer a freer opportunity to the designer.

Almost all designers follow processes that have common elements. The initial starting point is the understanding and development of the client's needs and wishes, sometimes called programming. This stage might involve site visits and discussions with clients and other parties to evaluate the perceived needs. There will be an assessment of the nature of the space(s) and inventories taken of existing fixtures and fittings or new-build requirements outlined. After this initial assessment stage, the designer formulates a plan and makes estimates of the costs. Designers work in a variety of ways, using sketches, plans, blueprints and CAD combinations to prepare imagery. The use of computers in design has developed with advanced processes such as parametric design (Figure 4.1). These programmes can link dimensions and variables to

Figure 4.1 Frame Bar Athens, by Dimitrios Tsigos, showing thermo-formed surfaces in Staron using CAD parametric design processes, 2007.

geometry so that when the values change, the design changes as well. This allows the designer to create modifications very quickly and simply. The formal presentation to the client then follows this preparatory work.

Once the design has been approved, following any amendments based on the client's requirements, the designer will begin specifying all the required materials, finishes, equipment and furnishings; the designer will also contract other suppliers and service providers, as necessary. At this point, designers undertake any legal submissions for code compliance, etc. Most designs also require the hiring of contractors to undertake particular work, such as lighting, plumbing or electrical wiring.

Lastly, the designer plans the project delivery schedules, co-ordinates the work of others into the schedule and ensures a timely and on-budget completion. After final installation and snagging, the designer undertakes post-occupancy evaluations and organizes adjustments as necessary.

As an important counter to this simplistic approach to an outline of the design process, philosopher Donald Schon explains the reality of designing. Apart from the obvious conception, representation and production of things, Schon says that 'Designing in its broader sense involves complexity and synthesis. In contrast to analysts or critics, designers put things together and bring new things into being, dealing in the process with many variables and constraints, some initially known and some discovered through designing' (Schon 1987: 41–42). For Schon, the role of the designer is to 'juggle variables, reconcile conflicting values, and manoeuvre around constraints – a process in which, although some design

products may be superior to others, there are no unique right answers' (41–42). An important consideration that is worth remembering is that, in most cases, the decisions of designers will affect others.

The constraints that Schon and others mention include both internal and external. The internal are related to the project itself, e.g. budgets, existing services, issues of circulation, relationships between spaces, roles, etc. There are also constraints in relation to the practical technology, visual issues and symbolic or expressive constraints. Even more removed are the external constraints such as site, legislators and any other parties involved. There are also fundamental constraints such as human needs and practices, ecology, sustainability, etc. Schon's point about the impact of designers' decisions and their unintended consequences on others is important. In order to try to be prepared to deal with all these issues, designers need to work within a set of principles and values.

guiding principles

More than ever, designers have to be responsible and accountable for their actions in many ways, therefore it is imperative that they possess an understanding and consideration of the ethics, morality and values that relate to their business.

Ethics and Morality
Ethics is the science of morals. Sometimes people interchange the term ethics with 'morality'. We can divide ethics into three aspects: descriptive ethics, referring to beliefs about what people

consider to be right; prescriptive ethics, referring to how people ought to act; and applied ethics, relating to how we put moral knowledge into practice. Ethics are therefore of concern to interior designers in three ways. Initially, they relate to professional activities in conducting business.[1] Secondly, they shape the explicit professional proficiency needed in areas such as accessibility, usability, safety and environmental concerns. Thirdly, there are the wider issues relating to morality and the obligations of being a human and working with others. These include concepts of justice, value, natural and legal rights, duties, equality, freedom, trust and consent.

Put another way, the designer's first ethical position must be to act responsibly in and on the world. An ethical approach to this will encompass the process of envisioning possibilities that relate to a whole range of issues including, but not limited to, individuality v. conformity, consumption v. sustainability, space use, materials honesty, aesthetics and function, and universal design.

For the individual designer, the ethical aspect covers issues of professional behaviour, professional expertise and professional morals. The issues that this raises create a maze, confounded by acceptable standards of behaviour, responsibility, consciousness and identity through actions. The philosopher Roger Scruton explores the connections between values and ethics and explains how they are not straightforward. He says 'In every serious task there are factors which, while of the greatest importance, cannot be assigned a relative value – not because their value is absolute, but because a man may not be able to judge in advance just when he is prepared to tolerate their remaining unsatisfied' (Scruton 1980: 29).

Values

Values are not simply preferences; they are morally justified, by reason, by judgement or by a combination of these, and will vary depending on the particular approaches of the individual and the society within which they are working. Designers must not only express values in their thinking but also demonstrate these qualities in their outputs.

An individual's values, inculcated from early in life, consist of attitudes, beliefs, orientations and underlying assumptions. Closely linked to these are the broader ideas, opinions and culture to which an individual is exposed. The designers' personal preferences, aspirations, past experiences and projects will all affect the values they bring to projects. Values are often organized into value systems – the ordering and prioritization of different values on an individual, professional and societal level (Holm 2006).

Aesthetic Design Values   The aesthetic design values come from the range of influences that impact upon a practitioner. These influences will obviously include personal artistic and self-expressive values as well as attitudes to the more general issues of spaces, structures, functions and materials. Aesthetics derived from the classic, traditional, organic, minimalist, regionalist or vernacular inform these. In addition, the value of aesthetics as the basis of many types of human communication and self-expression through structures, shape and colour is self-evident. The appreciation of the inter-relationship between aesthetics and the workmanship that brings artefacts into the environment is also crucial.

Social Design Values   For many designers, part of their agenda is to try to effect social change for the better. At the basic level, an understanding of the interconnections between societies and their religious, social and economic values and philosophies is important. At another level, there are the needs of individuals and a consideration of how these needs will be met. Examples of how this might work include relations with stakeholders and the use of participatory design; crime prevention using defensible space and environmental design (CPTED); community engagement; and trying to find simple solutions for developing-world problems.

Stakeholder Values   The values associated with stakeholders relate to an understanding of the client, their needs, expectations, priorities and emotions. Designers can produce work that will reflect these values and reinforce their worth to the stakeholder. The example of an office renovation for the New Orleans branch of an international engineering company shows two ways of working closely with a client. The metal staircase was adapted from the client company's own industrial products to an office setting (Figure 4.2). The architects designed a polished stainless steel staircase that uses the standard stringers, stanchions and railings. However, the design enhancements make the monumental staircase more relevant to a design community than an industrial setting. This change of use benefited the company as it allowed them to take this new application and broaden their market range.

In the boardroom of the same New Orleans project, the goal was to create an energizing yet casual workplace for engineers and customer service personnel (Figure 4.3). The boardroom is equipped with the latest communication and visualization technologies, designed to reflect the client's state-of-art designs, and to stimulate the creativity of their employees.

Environmental Design Values   The Roman architect Vitruvius's comments on 'on-site resources such as proper orientation, thermal mass, shading, ventilation and local construction materials' (Holm 2006: 247) demonstrate an early interest in the issue of environmental design values. Since the mid-twentieth century, there has been a growing awareness of the need to engage with issues surrounding sustainability, reuse and modification and environmental health. The significance of assessing the effects of technology is also important here. Hence, the environmental values associated with design have taken centre-stage.

Design Values   These values use existing designs as a starting place for new solutions. They include an understanding of materials and their embedded values and ideals as well as knowledge of aspects of materials in relation to users and the signifying function of materials and objects. These values encourage the understanding of people holistically through such means as the four-pleasure framework, which includes physio-pleasure (pleasure derived from the senses), socio-pleasure (pleasure derived from relationships with others), psycho-pleasure (related to people's cognitive and emotional reactions) and ideo-pleasure (concerning people's values) (Jordan 2000).

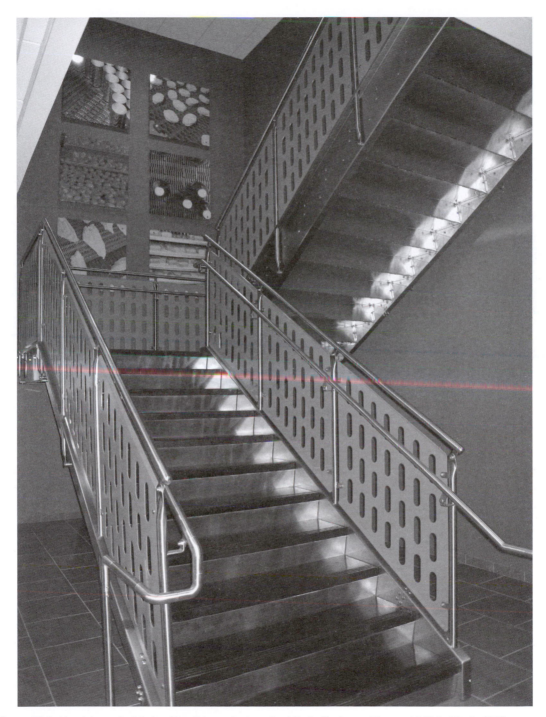

Figure 4.2 Lobby staircase for Intralox, New Orleans, in pierced red steel with chromed frames, HMS Architects, 2009.

Figure 4.3 Boardroom for Intralox, New Orleans, HMS Architects, 2009.

Gender-based Values   This set of values relates to a consideration of the history and practice of gender difference and representation, and the equality of opportunity. Leslie Weisman considers that 'the man-made environment is a form of social oppression, an expression of social power, a dimension of history and a part of women's struggle for equality' (1992: 3). The unpicking of issues surrounding women and their relation to housing and home-making has been part of this process.

Economic Values   These values reflect a designer's understanding of the economic constraints of the marketplace: knowing the cost of materials, processes and designers' time; the relationship between costs and other aspects of materials and processes; and an understanding of the distinction between value, price and cost.

Technical Values   Issues such as effectiveness, sturdiness, flexibility and the qualities of fitness to purpose define the justifications for the selection process of the technical aspects of a project. A knowledge and understanding of one's own values, and those of the fields in which we work, are important to professional designers as a way of enhancing their awareness, which in turn encourages more successful strategies in their work.

the design process

Having considered the 'problem of the process' in ethical and moral terms, we can now consider the general issues of design. As already suggested, many theorists and practitioners who have written about design have suggested that design is a process that follows a sequence. Although we cannot reduce it satisfactorily to a set of processes in the studio, the idea of a sequence does give a framework for analysis and, more importantly, for management of the process.

General Model for Addressing a Design Problem

In stressing at the outset that this linear image is for illustration and demonstration purposes only, it is clear that in reality the actual design process is complex, interwoven, reflexive and unpredictable. Design practice is often based on precedent, habit, typologies and conventions relying upon existing principles, as opposed to exploration, creation and the establishment of principles during the actual process of designing. In truth, much design work is probably a combination of both approaches. For example, in interior design terms, the production of spatial meaning and spatial problem-solving are equally important.

At this stage, the interesting distinction between charges and briefs defined by the art historian Michael Baxandall is worth noting (Baxandall 1985: 36).[2] He considers that charge refers to known solution types specified before any design work starts (i.e. to design a restaurant), whereas the brief includes additional aims brought about by designers during the process, which cannot be intimated before they begin to consider the job. Both these are implied in the following framework.

The Discovery Stage   This initial stage includes identification and elucidation of the problem and the consideration of a range of possible solutions. These have to be considered in line with values and the given constraints and limits. Memory, often as history (aesthetic values), informs the idea. Consideration of the functional and psycho-social needs of the users, including the practical, symbolic, psychological and narrative functions of the work (design values) will inform these initial stages. Market research and user research, for example, will assist in this part of the planning process. Indeed evidence-based design, using information discovered through a range of methods of research related to the real issues, is the way forward.

The Defining Stage   This second stage is the definition, interpretation and alignment of these discovered needs. Tough analysis of context, feasibility, connectivities and 'brand', etc., will inform the analysis. The need to consider other parties in the planning – including clients or sponsors, users and affected non-users, allied professionals, officials, and contractors and suppliers – is evident (social values), so early consultation in this defining stage will often avoid problems later.

The Development Stage   This stage marks the point in the project where designers develop potential solutions, through multi-disciplinary working and management-planning tools and methods. They express their ideas through a synthesis of visuals, layouts and plans to suggest a range of possible solutions. At this stage, the client makes final choices and selections.

The Delivery Stage   This final stage includes the implementation and delivery of the project, its testing and post-installation evaluation.

The abstraction in this generic linear model means that its actual use is limited in real situations beyond a simple starting point.

Another Model

Another way of looking at the design process is to consider it as a system of analysis, synthesis, appraisal and decision-making. In this method, the analysis involves the exploration of relationships, looking for patterns in the information available, and the classification of objectives. Analysis is therefore the structuring and organizing part of the problem-solving process. Synthesis is the stage in which designers begin the generation of solutions for the brief. Appraisal involves the evaluation of suggested solutions against the objectives in the analysis phase. Based on the state of the design brief/solution, the decision sequence is either advanced or rejected. Return loops can exist for some or all steps in the decision sequence to check progress and suitability (see Markus and Arch, in Hutton and Devonal 1973).

Designers can apply this process to outline proposals, scheme design and detail design, being aware that 'return loops' are in constant use between the parts of the process. However, even by allowing for return referencing between each stage, it is difficult to chart a real design process in such a way.

Bryan Lawson points out that the reality of designing is rather messier than a simple linear model! For example, he cites two architectural practitioners, Robert Venturi and Eva Jiricna, who often start a project by considering the details that will in turn inform the 'bigger picture' (Lawson 2005: 39). In an interior project, there may be a particular object, or issue, that can be the basis of design decisions. Whichever outline model we choose, it will have limitations when considered for specific briefs. We therefore need to apply a range of secondary tools and methods.

methods and tools[3]

Cost-Benefit Analysis

Simply put, this process adds the total value of the benefits of a course of action, and subtracts the costs associated with it to calculate any benefit. Life cycle assessment is important here, as designers often specify the payback period on a project as being over a particular period. Cost-benefit analysis may be limited in its usefulness as it usually considers financial data and financial benefits only. The inclusion of intangible elements in the analysis will be more useful, though more difficult to assess, since we have to estimate these, and therefore will encounter issues of subjectivity. An example of a specific would be a cost-benefit analysis of the employment of ergonomically designed office furniture, which would consider not only the financial costs but also the human costs, reductions in sickness, improved outputs etc.

Critical Path Analysis (CPA)

Critical Path Analysis is a planning tool for all the tasks that pertain to a project. The tool assists in the preparation of a schedule, and of resource planning. The value of CPA is that it allows monitoring of progress against goals, ultimately aiding completion on time – a key element for successful interior design. CPA requires three components to work successfully. First is a comprehensive list of the activities and processes required for project completion; secondly, details of the time (duration) that each activity will take to complete; and finally, a note about the relational dependency between the various activities.

Determining Components

A system of design planning that undertakes the understanding of the client and their needs, the policies and culture (values) of an institution, and any other components of a client's circumstances, in such a way as to allow future independent alteration. Developed by Christopher Alexander, it attempts to consider the full pattern of relationships that occur when, for example, designers introduce new objects into spaces. Whilst this is often intuitive, the idea of the system is to attempt to map it.

Evidence-based Planning/Design

Similar to the above, but here a designer, together with an informed client, would use qualitative and quantitative evidence from a range of dependable documents, resources and 'best-practice' guidelines to assist in the decision-making process. Using the evidence in conjunction with critical thinking is essential to develop an appropriate solution to the design problem. The results of the process should be able to improve demonstrably

the performance of the enterprise. This method is applicable to many types of commercial designing projects, but is particularly suited to healthcare environments, due to the nature of the industry and its critical clinical and safety issues (see Ulrich, Zimring et al 2004).

In a similar way, behavioural-based architectural planning uses literature searches and review, diagnostic interviewing, diagnostic observation, questionnaires and surveys, and work sessions to confirm or adapt findings (see Hershberger, in Bechtel and Churchman 2002: 292–305).[4]

Interaction Matrix

This process tool assists in visualizing and tabulating the interaction of components of a project with other selected factors. It could consist of a simple chart to show the components of the project and the particular aspects of the environment/space. It then plots the interactions to ensure that full acknowledgement is given and that they can work properly together.

Morphological Analysis

This approach studies the structure, shape, form or content of something and then considers how these interconnect to create a whole, or Gestalt. In this case, morphology considers the connections between interior designs, functional implications, cultural meanings and the designer, so can therefore be physical, social or mental. It examines the relationships between the design objectives and the qualitative and quantitative limitations. Finally, it is useful to consider the relationships between the work and its impact on culture and environment. For example, a morphological approach could link interior design with, for example, social changes, and then challenge assumptions (Hanson).

PRSM

An interesting development is the Personal Resource Systems Management Model (PRSM) devised by Barbara McFall. This is an analytical tool for investigating person–environment interactions. This systems analysis puts the user at the hub of six dimensions (i.e., intellectual, organizational, social, material, natural and financial). The user interacts with these in one or more of three ways (e.g., mental, emotional or physical), resulting in varying degrees of satisfaction (McFall and Beacham 2006: 21–34). The resulting analysis may well more accurately reflect the user's needs than simple observation, for example.

The PRSM is particularly useful for understanding person–environment interactions. By arranging the matrix in Figure 4.4, where each cell represents a separate interaction, the researcher will be able to identify trends and similarities in the qualitative data they have assembled.

Synectics

Synectics is another problem-solving technique that encourages the lateral thinking processes of a team to reveal thoughts that they were unaware of: 'Trust things that are alien, and alienate things that are trusted' is a key idea. Synectics is similar to brainstorming, but is more involved as it tries to make the psychological processes behind creative work accessible. The use of analogies is key

to the success of the method. The three basic ideas behind synectics are that the emotional aspects of creativity are more important than the rational, intellectual ones. This means that the irrational takes priority over the rational and is a valuable instrument in its own right. The key idea is that the designer makes connections between seemingly disparate elements in an attempt to provide new perceptions about problems.

The process begins with the design problem that is to be analysed and then comprehended. At this stage, designers employ various mechanisms to reverse 'normal thinking', i.e. to make the strange familiar and vice versa. This is where analogies come into the system. By considering how designers have solved other related problems, e.g. in nature (see bio-mimicry below), a solution might be revealed that had not previously been considered. Secondly, the designers can put themselves directly into the situation. In wayfinding terms, for example, if you wanted to get from A to B, how would you do it? Thirdly, consider the most outlandish solution and work back from that, establishing the practicalities on the way. By integrating psychological states such as immersion, detachment and speculation with the problem and with potential solutions, we may reach improved conclusions.

All the above methods are still fairly generalized and applicable to many branches of design. In the next chapter, we will consider the actual process of interior design.

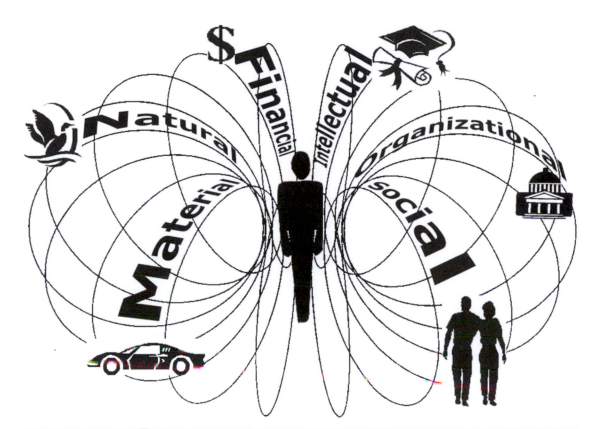

	Mental	Emotional	Physical	
Intellectual				Intellectual Satisfaction
Organizational				Organizational Satisfaction
Social		Emotional-Social Quality of Living		Social Satisfaction
Material				Material Satisfaction
Natural				Natural Satisfaction
Financial				Financial Satisfaction
	Mental Well-being	Emotional Well-being	Physical Well-being	**Total Quality of Life**

Figure 4.4 The PRSM Matrix, © B. McFall 2009; used with permission.

CASE STUDY 4.1 Nike's East London 1948 Space

Here we explore the process of design for a retail installation by the Wilson Brothers for Nike's East London 1948 space named Raise Your Game, completed in 2009 (Figure 4.5). Initially based on the concept of the pop-up retail store, it is now a fixture. The site was potentially awkward. Situated in two railway arches, it not only meets the retail needs but also acts as a gallery and social meeting place. As 1948 is the weekly meeting place for a local urban running club, this is the basis of the design ideas. One of the key visuals was the floor. The 'Running Man' floor graphic, which incorporates three maps used by the club, has red (5k), yellow (8k) and green (10k) lines that refer to local tube lines in the area passed on the respective runs. The line width is the same as traditional sports-pitch markings, and 'X' marks the 1948 space location on the map. The floor is also a focal point, made from 100 per cent recycled rubber using Nike's GRIND sports surface material, featuring recycled rubber sport shoes.

The displays are ultra-flexible, using a set of twelve modular units that are alterable at will. These steel and laminated plywood units refer to tiered stadium seating, another sporting allusion. Detachable (and multi-positional) hanging rails make a contextual reference to the mass of football goal posts seen at the nearby playing fields at Hackney Marshes. The centrepiece of the interior is a 6×8 metre dimmable neon football-pitch installation, hanging horizontally from the ceiling, which provides a visual focal point. The design process, following a path of evaluation, definition and development, focussed closely on the sport aspects, the local nature of the project and the demands of the company and the clients, and thus created a set of successful interior spaces.

Figure 4.5 Nike pop-up shop in East London showing the neon lighting based on a soccer field layout, Wilson Bros, 2009.

CASE STUDY 4.2 Dental Spa

This patient-centred design for a dental spa is located in Georgia, USA. Patients in dental surgeries are often anxious, so creating an interior design with a non-clinical ambiance is both sympathetic and sensible. In this example, the use of varied lighting using custom copper and bronze wall sconces, luminous pendants and accent lighting for artwork, as well as colour-balanced task/ambient lighting, all go a long way to achieving the desired environment. The 'Tuscan style' waiting room achieves a friendly and domestic atmosphere (Figure 4.6). The use of natural stone and wood in both clinical and waiting spaces, combined with a high-tech plasma screen in the reception area, headphones with satellite radio, Olympus movie goggles and a custom-designed 2.5-metre water wall for white noise, further demonstrate the approach to client satisfaction (see Figures 4.7 and 4.8).

Figure 4.6 Dunwoody Dental Spa view of corridor and surgery spaces, Georgia, USA, by LeVino Jones Medical Interiors Inc., 2005.

Figure 4.7 Dunwoody Dental Spa waiting room, Georgia, USA, by LeVino Jones Medical Interiors Inc., 2005.

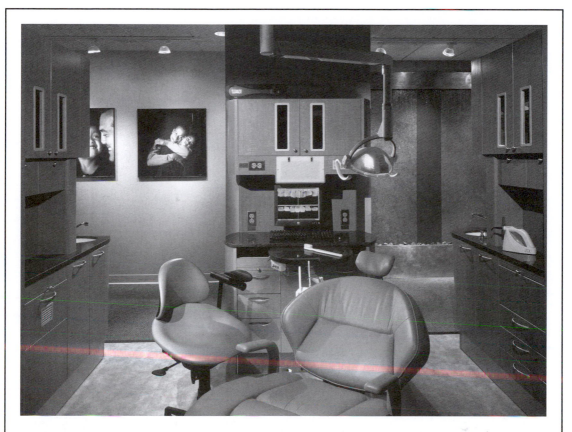

Figure 4.8 Dunwoody Dental Spa surgery, Georgia, USA, by LeVino Jones Medical Interiors Inc., 2005.

CASE STUDY 4.3 *Shiramatsu ga Monaka* (Japanese Sweet Shop)

Completed in Sendai in 2008, this project, featuring a long-established Japanese-style confectionery store, represents a design concept called 'Japanese modern' (*Wa*-modern), which combines the spirit of old Japan and its craft skills with a contemporary edge (Plate 8). The values of aesthetic design and social design are evident in this work. The site of the work was an existing property with a narrow storefront (16 metres) and long depth (20 metres), which is traditional for *Machiya*-style pieces of land in this region.

The space features a light wall to create the image of a light shining through a paper screen, which penetrates through the stairways, visually connecting the upper and lower floors. In order to create a dignified and harmonic space, the designer employed porcelain tiles for the floor, diatomite plaster for the wall and rusted iron for the exterior wall, and fixtures and fittings are finished in a white, lacquer-like style.

chapter 5

the process of interior design

CHAPTER OVERVIEW

The previous chapter introduced some generic design concepts. This chapter takes into account specific aspects of interior design planning and process. First, it addresses the 'language' or tools of interior design. The principles of interior design are fundamental positions that underlie the practice of interior design. They are well known, and can appear intuitive, but some understanding of issues such as proportion, scale, balance, rhythm, contrast and unity will not only enable the designer, but will also allow manipulation and adaptation to occur successfully.

Various elements make up the distinctive parts of an interior. In this chapter, we explore the role and nature of line, form, texture and pattern, and the context in which they are located. Following an understanding of the principles and elements of the discipline, we examine the actual interior design process. By adhering to the general linear procedure as a model, we can see the various aspects of the development of a scheme. The first phase is the formulating, inception and feasibility stage, which helps to create a client–designer relationship. The programming stage, influenced by research, follows this. The chapter then considers the nature of outline proposals and design work, including preparation of concepts, surveys and methods of representing designs to clients. Finally, we consider the delivery stages and project supervision and the important roles of evaluation, reflection and feedback provided by post-occupancy evaluation.

introduction

According to the NCIDQ (The National Council for Interior Design Qualification), 'The interior design process follows a systematic and coordinated methodology, including research, analysis and integration of knowledge into the creative process, whereby the needs and resources of the client are satisfied to produce an interior space that fulfils the project goals' (NCIDQ). This encompassing, though bland, definition mentions all the elements we would expect to find but in no way indicates anything of the excitement of the creative process and the wide knowledge base required.

The necessarily broad approach that interior designers have to take is indicated in architect

Hugh Casson's comments that, to succeed, they have to 'be something of an impresario, a mixture of architect and illusionist, scholar and artist, medicine man and psychologist, acutely sensitive to gradations of character, to atmosphere and to the *genius loci et temporis*' (1968: 17).

Henri Focillon put it another way when he wrote lyrically about the builder [aka the interior designer]: 'He is a geometrician in the drafting of the plan, a mechanic in the assembling of the structure, a painter in the distribution of visual effects, and a sculptor in the treatment of masses' (1948: 22).

These inspiring descriptions indicate the range of skills and knowledge a designer might acquire and use in the process of creating interiors. Like all creativity, there is an element of intuition and inspiration, but creativity can also be located on a scale ranging from the routine, to the interpretive, to the original. The development from project-based problem solutions to knowledge-based innovative and artistic creativity is the key skill. Part of the basic skill set is an understanding of the language of design; another part is to appreciate the principles and elements employed and their potential.

language of design

In 1856, The French architect and designer Viollet-Le-Duc considered: 'The first condition of design is to know what we have to do; to know what we have to do, is to have an idea; to

---

Henri Focillon (1881–1943)

Henri Focillon was an influential French art historian and theorist. His book *The Life of Forms in Art* (1934) explains his particular approach to understanding visual culture by emphasizing considerations of style and practice over any contextual explanation. According to Focillon, the dialectic relationship between the given forms and qualities of materials and the designer-maker's individual form-giving motivation is what creates style. His idea was that the 'life forms' were founded in the ability of designers or makers to produce new solutions based on their experience of dealing with space, materials and processes. Although his formalist ideas are not fashionable, his interest for designers is in his idea that 'art' is a constant exchange between objective materiality and the subjective designer's will.

Viollet le Duc (1814–1879)

Eugène Emmanuel Viollet-le-Duc was a French architect and theorist who promoted the Gothic Revival in France. He contended that Gothic architects considered issues of function along with the construction techniques of the time, which thus produced that particular style through the language of Gothic. For the nineteenth century, he advocated the use of new materials for both new and restoration work. For example, in his *Entretiens sur l'architecture* (Discourses on Architecture) he recommended iron for frames to facilitate the lightness achieved by Gothic work.

express this idea we must have principles and form; that is grammar and language' (1875: 350).

Also in 1856, Owen Jones published his famous *The Grammar of Ornament*, in which he expounded thirty-seven general principles in the arrangement of form and colour in architecture and the decorative arts. There have been many attempts and numerous publications ever since given over to defining a design language.

Writing in 1915, Frank Parsons explained in his *Interior Decoration*, *Its Principles and Practice*: 'Man expresses his ideas or conveys his thoughts to others by means of language, and language consists of a set of symbols which serve to establish a standard system of communication between all persons by whom these symbols are understood'. Parsons continued specifically in relation to interior design: 'Determine what you want your room to express when it is done, and then purchase only those letters that are required to make up the statement. All this must be given in the language of colour, form, line and texture, governed by the principles which are the very structure of language' (1920: 17, 246, 247, 274). Forty years later, Frank Lloyd Wright, in his *The Natural House*, reiterated the point: 'the grammar of the house is its manifest articulation of all its parts, this will be the "speech" it uses … The man who designs the house must speak a consistent thought-language in his design' (1954: 181–183).

These ideas of language encompass the principles and elements of interior design in such a way that they comprise an alphabet and lexicon of spatial elements and an inventory of materials; a grammar or syntax of how the above are combined into a satisfactory whole, and a style manual that recommends artistic, aesthetic

approaches to achieve particular effects. The language reflects the cultural, psychological, symbolic, ethnic and gendered aspects of the society that uses it. Put another way, the vocabulary would represent the basic elements of a designed space (see elements below). These principles inform the design. Derivations are the results of the process of applying a common set of conventions to a set of elements in a designed space, and the design languages are the families of products derived from a common set of 'rules' (Bruton 2007: 311).

This, of course, seems to indicate a mechanistic way of putting an interior together. However, if we return to the comparison of project-based and knowledge- based approaches to design and Schon's idea that designers 'engage in a conversation with the situation they are shaping' (1985: 103), it is likely that the language can be used simply (as in routine), fluently (as in interpretive) or eloquently (as in originality).

principles of interior design

Principles are general, but fundamental, positions that underlie many of the processes of interior design. They are not a straightjacket and should not stifle creativity if that means breaking the rules. Indeed, much of the history of interior design has been a series of breaks or adaptations of previous rules. For example, in the case of Deconstructivists, the need to have something to react against such as accepted principles means that they can distort and adapt them to create new imagery. However, an understanding of these essential ideas is important, in that they provide a set of keys to unlock the overarching considerations of interior designing. The old cliché – only when you know the rules can you break them – still has some validity about it.

Proportion

Proportion, although simply defined as the relationship of one part to another or to the whole, in terms of size, amount or degree, is not straightforward. An alternative definition says that proportion is a system of composition in relation to visual order, giving weight to compositional elements. Proportion is a key to creating ideal shapes, and specific proportions have become codified by particular cultures, in various times, to represent these ideals.

In terms of proportion, mathematics can create visual harmony in design but it can also create disorder. For example, Euclidian geometry (based on plane and solids) became the guiding principle for the twentieth century Modernists, and non-Euclidian (based on the hyperbolic and elliptic) for the more recent Deconstructivists. However, certain systems or proportions are so ingrained that we take them for granted, although they have had their critics. Artist, photographer and Bauhaus faculty member László Moholy-Nagy, writing in 1929, commented: 'Systems of proportions are for the past, today they are only used by eclectics. Formulae can never be the basis of creation. For creation it takes purpose and conscious analysis' (in von Meiss 1990: 64). Many would agree with this judgement but proportion is still an essential element in the interior.

Systems of proportion are varied and include the Arithmetic (1, 2, 3 …) the Geometric (1, 2, 4 …) and the Harmonic (6, 8, 12 …). When applied to interior spaces, proportion systems can simply be ratios. For example, sixteenth-century architect Andrea Palladio explained that:

There are seven types of room that are the most beautiful and well proportioned and turn out better: they can be made circular, though these are rare; or square; or their length will equal the diagonal of the square of the breadth; or a square and a third [4:3]; or a square and a half [3:2]; or a square and two-thirds [5:3]; or two squares [2:1]. (In Tavernor and Schofield, trans, 2002: 52 [57])

The most well-known proportion system is the so-called Golden Section (1:1.618), whereby the longer side of a rectangle relates to the shorter side, as the sum of both is to the longer. The Greek mathematician Euclid gave the first recorded definition of the golden ratio in his *Elements* and it has remained in the designer's armoury ever since.

The numerical sequence called the Fibonacci Series, devised by Leonardo of Pisa (1175–1230), has each number as the product (sum) of the previous two (i.e. 1, 1, 2, 3, 5, 8, 13 …). The connection with the Golden Section is interesting as the division of any number in a Fibonacci sequence by the next highest gives 1.61, which is very similar to the ratio of the Golden Section. Their location in natural examples such as flower petals and galaxy spirals makes them appear to have a built-in aesthetic, which, according to some, is intrinsically attractive. In man-made examples, the music of Mozart and Beethoven, Virgil's poetry and Le Corbusier's Modulor all appear to rely on the application of the Fibonacci series.

Le Corbusier described the geometry of the Fibonacci series as 'rhythms apparent to the eye and clear in their relations with one another. Moreover, these rhythms are at the very root of human activities. They resound in man by an organic inevitability, the same fine inevitability which causes the tracing out of the Golden Section by children, old men, savages and the learned' (1946 [1927]: 68). This idea of rhythm is perhaps useful in understanding why proportion has a hold on our psyches. Le Corbusier devised a system of proportion that he called Le Modulor. This linked to the Fibonacci in that: 'A man with upraised arms provides, at the determining points of his occupation of space – foot, solar plexus, head, tips of fingers on the upraised arm – three intervals which give rise to a series of golden sections, called the Fibonacci series' (1961: 55). The basis of this system was proportions and intuition, not literal body shapes.

Although not fashionable, proportional relationships have a deep-seated root in human nature, and there is often a clear perception of which schemes are visually satisfying proportionally, as opposed to those that are not. The Finnish architect Eliel Saarinen put the issue of proportion most elegantly when he said: 'Always design a thing by considering it in its next larger context – a chair in a room, a room in a house, a house in an environment, an environment in a city plan' (in Enquist 2002). There seems to be something human-centred here about the approach to proportion that removes it from mathematics and relates it to perception. It also refers to scale.

Scale

Scale is the relative dimensions of parts to a whole. Scale also has psychological aspects.

Scale incongruence and inconsistencies create disharmony for humans, so, dependent upon the space in question, some order, symmetry and contextual understanding is often required to enable people to relate to the space. If the opposite effect is required, changing the scale may create a disorientating effect. We use pre-determined standard sizes or scales for components for ergonomic reasons, cost reasons and, sometimes, to ensure psychological satisfaction through familiarity.

When working with scale, many designers advise being bold. Society decorator Nancy Lancaster said: 'Scale is of prime importance and I think that oversized scale is better than undersized scale' (in Wood 2005: 127). However, like much else in designing, the use of scale relates to the answers to the particular questions posed. What is important in a space? Is its relation to humans important? How far can general acceptability or common ground influence our sense of place? To what do we want to call attention or what do we wish to hide?

Balance

According to Edith Wharton, 'the desire for symmetry, for balance, for rhythm in form as well as in sound, is one of the most inveterate of human instincts' (Wharton and Codman 1978 [1897]: 33). Balance is the visual weight of interior components and furnishings that creates a sense of equilibrium in an interior. Visual weight and textures, surfaces, shapes and colour can all influence the perception of balance. The axis or fulcrum of a design is therefore often critical, as this is the basis for perceptual and conceptual factors, although balance does not equate to symmetry. Distinct parts can act with similar strength in a composition but need not be symmetrical. The example of the eighteenth-century Rococo interior, where asymmetry is fully developed, is based on a more intuitive arrangement or composition that 'looks right' and in balance, through using unlike elements that act with similar weights or strengths.

Symmetry

This term generally has two major meanings. The first is a perceived sense of proportionality and balance that, for many people, represents a pleasing arrangement. For Vitruvius, symmetry was an agreement between the various elements of a building and the total work and he referenced the symmetry of the human body as a guide. Symmetry relies on equilibrium, so, as in balance, the role of the axis is important. The staircase of the Amsterdam Scheepvaarthuis demonstrates this well (Figure 2.3). The second meaning is a precise and clear concept of balance or repetition of like shapes etc. The rules of geometry often demonstrate these. Art historian Dagobert Frey puts symmetry another way. He explains that: 'Symmetry signifies rest and binding, asymmetry motion and loosening; the one order and law, the other arbitrariness and accident, the one formal rigidity and constraint, the other life, play and freedom' (in Weyl 1983: 16). Symmetry can be used as a platform for further development, for example by using a lattice of lesser components derived from the original pattern or the creation of new symmetrical patterns from two simpler ones. The geometric transformations such as rotation, scaling or reflection and repetition are all examples of this.

Reflection symmetry uses mirror-line symmetry so that anything that directly reflects as a mirror image is in balance. It can be orientated in any direction, whereas rotation symmetry is based upon like components that revolve round a common centre. This can occur at any angle or frequency. Translation symmetry refers to the same elements located in different parts of a space.

Edith Wharton considered symmetry as a mark of civilization. More pragmatically she declared that 'It is, therefore, not superfluous to point out that, in interior decoration as well as in architecture, a regard for symmetry, besides satisfying a legitimate artistic requirement, tends to make the average room not only easier to furnish, but more comfortable to live in' (Wharton and Codman 1978 [1897]: 34).

More recently, Rudolf Arnheim saw a fundamental role for symmetry in design. 'Architectural [and interior] design has in all cultures so insistently relied on symmetry because buildings serve as an element of stability and order in the midst of human experience, which is pervaded by struggle, accident, discords, change and irrationality' (1974: 152). A powerful reason for its adoption when appropriate.

Axis and Alignment

An axis is a path type that is often the primary organizing element of a set of spaces or layouts. The basis of the axis is direction and the concept has a number of variants including the major and minor axes of a space or plan, the point or origin, and combinations and shapes that vary according to design intentions. Doors, for example, may act as starting points for axes. Paths trace axes, so are often not necessarily obvious. For example, equal axes may feature around a central point; linear axes will direct towards a goal; and bent,

Rudolph Arnheim (1904–2007)

Rudolf Arnheim was a German theorist and perceptual psychologist. His pioneering notion of 'visual thinking', based on the idea that vision itself is the primary tendency for thought, is the driving force behind his works. His idea that knowledge of the world is an objective sensory experience helped to develop his theories of the importance of perception in understanding one's surroundings. For interior designers his *Dynamics of Architectural Form* is useful in the analysis of order and disorder in design, his discussion of the importance of the visual, and his consideration of the relations between practical functions and perceptual expressions in spaces.

curved or random axes will create directional flow. In one London tearoom from the 1950s, the use of horizontal alignment in the light fittings and cornices with the vertical wall panelling and furniture is clear (Figure 5.1).

Alignment to an axis refers to the state of edges or centres of components that have a relationship with the axis. In interiors, this often relates to the building skeleton, although purposeful non-alignment may be a feature of the design.

Rhythm and Repetition

Repetition or rhythm is a simple composition technique that offers a sense of coherence to an interior through the addition or division of elements, or by the use of a simple series of motifs. To control space and create harmonious effects, the use of rhythm and repetition may contribute

to interior design planning and offer elements of visual coherence. Various ways of achieving rhythm are through (a) progression, where the rhythm is based on succession in size or colour; (b) alternation through changes in line and flow or radiation of line from a focal point; and (c) repetition of colour, shape or material, even if differing in size.

The use of repetitive or rhythmic hierarchies, progressions (visual and physical) and durations (experience) can create a sense of coherence. This can occur even with heterogeneous items; if parts of them all have common characteristics, they will maintain the effect. Achieving this through material, scale or texture, as well as shape, is part of the designer's skill. The use of a zigzag theme in the interior of the London Peppermint Park bar, from 1979, shows the theme repeated in the bar surface and the sub-ceiling and the mirrored walls reflect the repetition (Plate 9).

Architect Thomas Beeby believes that 'ornament is based on a unit and the finite number of different geometric manipulations that can be enacted upon it to produce the various types of symmetry and rhythm which lie at the heart of ornament. In ornament, symmetry results from a proportional relation of part to whole and rhythm is produced by the dynamic repetition of proportional parts to a uniform beat' (in Kiernan 1977: 12). Manipulation through translation, rotation, reflection and inversion can extend the repertoire. Translation is the simple repeating of the 'unit' with no alteration in size or direction. Rotation is the process of directing the 'unit' to the four major orientations. Reflection allows the 'unit' to refer to its likeness along a vertical axis, while inversion allows reflection over its horizontal axis.

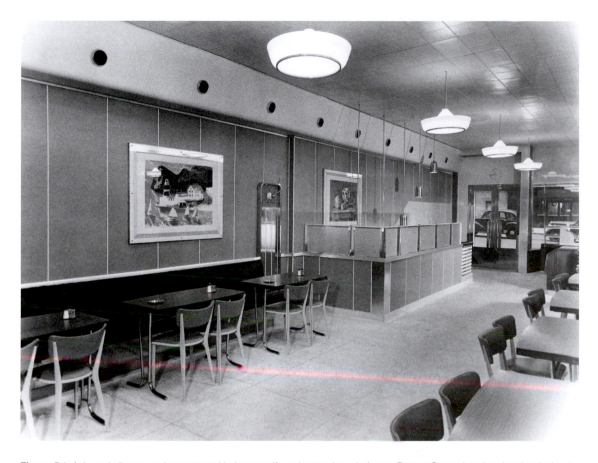

Figure 5.1 Axis and alignment demonstrated in Lyons self-service teashop, in Lower Regent Street, London. Interior design by Richard Lonsdale-Hands Associates in dove-grey, scarlet and royal blue, 1951.

Combinations of these systems can develop further unit structures.

Contrast and Opposition

This element uses the idea of mutual reinforcement of difference with no particular hierarchy implied. This can take many forms including positive/negative; light/dark, solid/void, large/small, natural/artificial, etc. Contrast can help establish differences and distinctions through dialogue and spatial separation and between symmetry and asymmetry. Specially, we define opposition as contrast that uses equal values of colour, weight, shape, etc.

Unity

The relationship between the separate parts and the whole of a design or scheme relates to unity. Unity gives a sense of completeness to a composition, even if the viewer has to complete it. The impact of the Gestalt theories of visual perception and psychology has a bearing on the understanding of this process (see below). Visual unity arising out of a mix of elements is *one* possible aim of interior design. The value and degree of unity will depend on the project brief and the design concept. Having a central theme, however, is often sensible as it offers consistency. We may achieve unity by using repetition, congruent materials choice, colour palette or repetition of elements. Interiors for retail 'brands', such as coffee shops or fast food outlets, often demonstrate a unity that becomes recognizable worldwide.

Harmony

Harmony is the accord created between different elements of a design or composition to produce a unity of effect and thus create a connected whole. This may not be the particular goal of any project but there is usually a good reason for attaining harmony in an interior, as it relates so much to human needs. The Eastern traditions of creating harmonic spaces, which include Feng Shui and Vaastu Shastra, do have followers. Feng Shui, an ancient Chinese system of space planning and use, uses astronomy and geography to help one improve life, by harmonizing energy flows through spaces. The Indian Vaastu Shastra considers various aspects of creating living environments that are in harmony with physical and metaphysical forces. The Vaastu is conceptually similar to Feng Shui although it differs in detail. For most interiors harmony is desirable and the avoidance of dissonance a useful goal.

Having established the main principles relating to interior design, we can now consider the elements associated with them.

elements of design

The elements are the distinctive parts that make a complete whole. Charles Eames said of design that it is a 'plan for arranging elements in such a way as to best accomplish a particular process' (in Laurel 2003: 10). This simple statement belies the complexity of the elements of design outlined below.

Line

An extension of a point into space, a line is identified as an edge, although it has no width itself, only length. Thus, line can describe a shape by being the edge of an area or surface, colour, tone or pattern. In these cases, the line creates a combination. Lines may be straight or curved, heavy or light, soft or hard, or a mixture of them all. The vertical line emphasizes gravity and is the basis of frameworks and supports. In contrast, the horizontal line reflects grounded support and stability. In one example, of aluminium kitchen units (Figure 5.2), the units have a defining horizontal emphasis. The diagonal reflects activity and movement as it is between the vertical and the horizontal. The opportunity to create angles with diagonals in conjunction with the other line dimensions makes them highly useful. Curved lines may be geometric (i.e. circles, parabolas, ellipses, etc.) or free forms such as the *cyma recta*. Lines, through their particular delineations, can show movement, suggest rhythm or even signify emotions. The psychological effects of line create apparent changes in proportion, and have an impact on the perception of space so that horizontal lines appear to flatten, while vertical lines tend to heighten spaces.

Figure 5.2 Detail of horizontal emphasis in drawers of aluminium kitchen units designed by Vico Magistretti for Schiffini, 2010.

Shape or Form

Although often used interdependently, a distinction between the idea of 'form as shape' (Gestalt or as perceived by the senses) and 'form as idea or abstraction for a particular' (perceived in the mind) is useful. Form can describe the defining shape of the whole idea, both internally and externally, and may be natural or fabricated. Form identifies space as the prescribed idea of what we know to be a particular shape or interior. Form is partly responsible for identity creation. Le Corbusier saw form as 'an active, volatile, living force which animated the systems of a structure, lending tension and complexity to all the parts, which were none the less held together in a tight unity' (in Curtis 1986: 12).

Where do ideas of form come from? By relating architectural historian Mark Gelernter's five suggested theories of architectural form (1995) to interiors, we can gain some idea. He has noted five variations, outlined below, that attempt to describe the origins of form. He also points out their weaknesses.

First Variation   Functions (physical, social, psychological and symbolic) determine form, but clearly this does not occur through functions alone. Many spaces with similar functions are often quite different in concept and detail. 'Form follows function' has a certain attraction, but the variables are often so great as to diminish the idea to being an unworkable concept.

Second Variation   The designer's creative imagination conceives form. Certain designs have consistency as themes that reoccur in works, making them identifiable as those of one person. However, this idea does not allow for commonly shared notions and recurring themes found in many designs of a particular place or time.

Third Variation   Contemporary visual culture influences form through the designer's interaction with their surroundings and contemporary ideas. Even if one were able to define 'a spirit of the times', it does not account for changes or differences that occur simultaneously.

Fourth Variation   Socio-economic conditions influence form. Again, this is not sustainable since the forces of a social system only influence a designer indirectly. In any social system there are many competing forms, and design is often a leader rather than a follower in socio-economic change.

Fifth Variation   The fifth idea is that timeless principles form a theory of universal types and values. Although forms may be universal, there are myriad ways to interpret them.

These concepts of form-creation, expanded in the work of psychologist David Canter and Stephen Tagg, refer to form as a kind of spacio-sensory calculation (Malnar and Vodvarka 2004: 58). The forms of buildings and their interior spaces not only relate to the physical shapes, but also to the impact they have on the user. Shapes suggest semiotic messages and will therefore influence emotional responses and suggest particular activities. For example, a traditional courtroom interior has a stepped hierarchy of spaces, which reflects its authoritarian layout. The manipulation of these forms to be user-friendlier has resulted in many courtrooms reducing their hierarchical shapes and layouts.

Texture

The tactile nature of materials and their textures is increasingly significant in interior design, because not only has texture always had an important relation to colour, light and the sense of touch, but also because of the greater understanding of how it affects the human experiences of the space. If not fully considered, surfaces may often simply reflect the material's texture through fact rather than through deliberate and considered choices that can offer sensory experiences. The physical impressions created by materials through texture will create psychological responses dependent upon hardness, softness, tension and the semiotics of the material. For example, contrasting textures are useful for visual interest and for indicating changes in the layout of spaces. Textures can also increase illusions of changes to height, space, etc. The amount of light reflected by a material will also influence its apparent texture.

Pattern

We can describe any decorative arrangement as a pattern, although the repetition of motifs often represents pattern. Pattern may be intrinsic in the building design or applied to provide surface enhancement and can assist in unifying a design. However, a degree of control is important, although the 'pattern on pattern' arrangement can work well if carefully managed. In his autobiography, American decorator Billy Baldwin gives an example: 'It's a rule that pattern should not be played against pattern, that figured curtains need a plain wall. But nothing is more enchanting than the indoor garden that grows from flowering chintz, flowered walls, flowery needlework rugs' (1972: 26). Pattern can disguise shapes or act in a unifying role by visually linking components of a scheme.

Context

The importance of visual and cultural influences on interiors means that designers have to be continually aware of the history and contemporary use of all aspects of visual culture. An awareness of other features and stimuli that influence an understanding of interiors, such as the social sciences, psychology, behavioural sciences and anthropology, is also relevant.

An understanding of historical and contemporary visual culture is crucial to designers, as they are an integral part of it. The visual content of everyday life appears in multiple forms, such as printed images and graphic design, television, film and video, computer interfaces and software design, the Internet, advertising, fine art, photography, fashion, architecture, product design and the urban scene. The process of contextualizing this information is crucial to the interior designer at any particular time. Seeing the broader context of interiors as part of a system that combines texts and graphic design, logos, the design of functional objects, buildings and the urban landscape, will also enable interior designers to locate themselves in a cultural milieu.

the interior design process

The generic processes associated with the practice of interior design follow the general pattern established in Chapter 4, but in this section, we undertake a closer evaluation and analysis of the procedure as it works specifically in interior design.

To consider the interior design process in more detail, a number of aspects that connect and interlink with each other can be considered together in the following eight-point model (see also Chapter 13: The Business of Interior Design).

1. Formulating: Inception and Feasibility
2. Programming: Research and Scoping
3. Outline Proposals – Scheme Design – Detail Design – Product Information
4. Representing
5. Presenting
6. Moving and Implementing
7. Project Supervision – Site Operation – Completion
8. Evaluation – Reflection – Feedback – POE [Post-Occupancy Evaluation]

Although these aspects of the design process appear linear or cyclical, the actual practice will of course be a continuous movement between the elements.

1. Formulating: Inception and Feasibility

This initial stage refers to establishing, considering and exploring the outline design brief or project. Key issues include the identification of the various elements and ways of understanding them and then restating the issues and their sub-issues. To achieve this, the framing process allows for viewing the challenges from a number of different though structured aspects. Do not underestimate the importance of these critical perspectives. Stephen Cairns and Jane Jacobs's explanation of the network demonstrates something of the complications. They point out that there are 'complex and often contradictory relationships between decorative and consumption practices and ideals, orders and grammars that resided both in the site of the home and elsewhere – on design drawing tables, in bureaucracies, in magazines, in commercial premises, in a resident's imaginative and practical world, in the very colour of paint, texture

of walls, and pieces of furniture, be they newly acquired or handed down' (2006). In attempting to deal with this complexity, the role of programming is essential. Before that next step though, we need to establish the relationship between client and designer.

Client/Designer Relationships   Like many other professional categories, interior designers have developed roles as consultants rather than proscribers, so a professional relationship indicates a degree of confidentiality. Interior designers need to understand their clients' values, requirements, brand or style and the context of the works. Depending on the nature of the project, the designer may be working with a single customer, a couple, a procurement team or a board of governors, as well as, in most cases, other professionals. In any event, the client will often have ideas of what they want and it is the designers' responsibility to temper these ideas with careful interpretations and guidance.

2. Programming: Research and Scoping

Programming is the systematic research that explores the context of the design project and informs the decision-making process, which in turn defines the requirements to complete the project successfully (see Kriebel, Birdsong and Sherman 1991: 29–36). Programming or scoping has a number of benefits. Firstly, it involves all interested parties in defining the nature of the problems and identifying the positive attributes residing in current spaces, facilities and furnishings. Secondly, it is clear that the process of gathering and analysing data early on will benefit design decisions and will minimize the need for subsequent redesigns.

Programming strategies include the methods designed and used for collecting, organizing, synthesizing and assessing the information needed to design the interiors of any type of building. The information needed would include such aspects as the initial concepts; the goals and objectives of the client; any projections as to change; actual and future space requirements; furniture, furnishing and equipment needs; costings; and appropriate codes and regulatory concerns. Much of the research of a project will involve 'measuring' in its broadest sense. This part of the process must be relevant to the client's strategies; it must be a reliable method, with a high degree of validity and efficiency, which does not discriminate. The value of 'evidence-based' design is clear here.

Research Designers of interiors need to study and research at least four considerations. The first is the physical control. What controls, including mechanical systems, will the interior need? Secondly, what is the functional frame that prescribes the size and quality of interior space and access; thirdly, the social milieu that will use the spaces, noting the wide range of social interactions within and without a structure; and fourthly what is the cultural symbolization embodying common values and symbol systems to be used? Evidence to support these analyses will be very helpful in the following steps.

Balancing the research between qualitative, quantitative, direct (e.g. cost benefit analysis) and indirect measures (e.g. levels of absenteeism in a work situation) is important. It may be necessary to instigate a control group to act as a base. The research methods will inevitably be both subjec-

tive and objective and will include, for example, interviews and focus groups that might discuss tasks undertaken, explain the use of technology and consider issues around space use, facilities, etc. Other research techniques might include analysis of physical spaces, such as the actual use of space evidenced by wear patterns, personalization of space and analysis of use through behavioural observation.

In terms of cultural or geographic analysis, the example of the Hotel Associa, in Shizuoka, Japan, demonstrates an attempt at making connections to the locality. As a local, city-based hotel, the theme of the design portrays the rich surrounding environment and the historical background to both the local people and the hotel guests. Shizuoka is located at the foot of Mount Fuji, with splendid natural surroundings (Figure 5.3).

The image shows part of the lobby of the hotel. The surrounding environment and its history are simply expressed with stone masonry work reflecting the castle town. Particular planting expresses the temperate climate of this region and the rich natural environment.

Part of the methodology of research is participation. Although this can be fraught with difficulties and worries over blandness or an inability to please everyone, and even acknowledging the definition of a camel as 'a horse designed by committee', the process does have benefits. It is important to ensure that when consultation occurs, the designer bears in mind the following. To integrate appropriate suggestions at an initial stage, involve the users/clients early on. We gain

Figure 5.3 Associa hotel lobby, Shizuoka, Japan, showing masonry wall and feature planting to reflect the particular location, ILYA Corp. 2009.

little by consulting after the event. Secondly, offer concrete alternatives/options for people to react to, and present possible scenarios in a format that is comprehensible to the audience. This is especially the case for spatial issues where the use of three-dimensional models may be very helpful.

Techniques to develop programming include brainstorming, as a way of generating ideas and concepts that will help us consider outline solutions. The concept of reframing is also of value in the programming scheme. This method allows for a selection of paths for thinking through multiple approaches to a design question. These include transforming the known; using alternative metaphors; finding analogies; employing various theoretical perspectives; eliciting various stakeholders' conceptual frameworks; and translating a problem or design into different media for conceptualization (see Krippendorf 2006: 216 and also Chapter 4/Methods and Tools).

3. Outline Proposals – Concepts Surveys

As touched on above, exploring different concepts will help us to draw up some outline proposals, while no complete outline is possible without actually undertaking a survey of the space in question.

Concepts   Concepts are abstract mental suggestions or thoughts based on inclusive considerations of needs/desires that define what we want to achieve. Joy Malnar and Frank Vodvarka suggest that concepts 'should [first] be viewed in terms of cause not effect [addressing the problem]; second there should be some prior basis for a concept's assumptions [research]; and third a concept ought to be inclusive in its breadth of concerns' (1992: 75).

Discussing the work of the architect and interior designer Adolf Loos, Benedetto Gravagnuolo considers a contrasting approach to how a concept is developed: 'The artist, or rather the architect [designer], thinks first of the effect he is aiming at, then he constructs the image of the space he will create in his mind's eye. This effect is the sensation that the space produces in the spectator: which may be fear or fright … respect … pity … the feeling of warmth, as in his own house … forgetfulness, as in taverns' (1995: 23). This is a poetic description of conceptualization but it does demonstrate an alternative approach that starts with a possible solution.

The initial stages of any conceptual process should be as value- and criticism-free as possible to allow for the largest number of ideas to develop. In these ways, making unusual or 'off-the-wall' suggestions become confident processes. At the conceptual stage, all ideas should be welcome and a process of association should be encouraged to develop ideas further or move them in another direction. This synectics approach functions well in team-working situations.

Survey The basic measuring of space is an important part of creating outline proposals with plans drawn up to scale. At this stage, the designer lists all the services needed as well as details of items that will affect the layout, such as windows, fixtures, etc. Undertaking a flow analysis of traffic at this stage, along with various other considerations, will assist in defining the nature of the possible work, i.e. renovation, re-siting of activities in spaces, or simply redecoration and accessorization. Assessment of the non-measurable aspects – including the state of fabric repair, electrics, joinery, HVAC (Heating, Ventilation and Air Conditioning), the orientation of spaces, the nature of existing textures and finishes, the actual versus potential use, and the possible reuse of existing furnishings – are all part of this aspect.

Only when the research, concepts and survey are complete can the designer move to the next stage.

4. Representing

The process of representing, through drawing, models, mood boards and computer models, defines and explores the problem and prepares potential solutions for the client's consideration. The appropriateness of the type of representation is important. In fact, a range of presentations is useful for the 'conversation' with the client and other members of the design team. The representations may be outline proposals, scheme plans and designs, layouts, etc. From these representations, the designer draws up the materials selection, the purchase lists and estimates for presentation and client approval. Particular institutions may have particular requirements relating to the submission of design works. For example, the US Army Corps of Engineers has a code for their requirements for the submission of interior design documents, which includes:

- Drawings
- Specifications
- Design Analysis
- Cost Estimates
- Color Boards
- Structural Interior Design
- Comprehensive Interior Design
- Construction Schedule
- Architectural Sketches/Renderings
- Architect-Engineer Design Quality Control Plan
- Miscellaneous

(USACE 2003)

In the UK, the RIBA/BIDA (Royal Institute of British Architects/British Institute of Interior Design) Form of Appointment for Interior Design Services (ID/05) covers a comprehensive range of related services in interior design; in the USA the AIA (American Institute of Architects) has similar documents.

Now we can consider the representation methods in a little more detail.

Figure 5.4 Presentation sketch of spa reception area, Neil Pearson.

Sketching The most basic and effective method of quickly defining an idea is by using pencil and paper (Plates 12 and 13). The immediacy and portability of a sketch is valuable but so also is the ability, whilst with a client, to demonstrate a number of variations and build up an idea quickly so as to create a dialogue. The skills of sketching and drawing are also demonstrations of professionalism. Designers use sketches as the basis for later drawings, which are more specific. They can define spatial relationships and placement of furniture and, by various colouring and shading techniques, can give an image of the space in

use (Figure 5.4 and Plate 10). The development of visuals, using isometric, axonometric and perspective models, either with hand-drawn images or with two- and three-dimensional computer modelling, is crucial to the concept development (Figure 5.5). In some cases, clients receive, as part of the concept package, computer-aided drawings, rendered with images and textures to create a 'virtual reality' image of the spaces.

Orthographics Orthographics refer to drawings with no perspective, such as 'working drawings' or plans and elevations. Drawn to scale (often

Figure 5.5 Presentation concept sketch for luxury office interior, Mark Humphrey.

1:50 for interiors), they may be more detailed, often up to full size. Sections are either vertical or horizontal 'snapshots' of the proposed or existing space. Commonly, a section defines the vertical and plans the horizontal.

The isometric projection is a method of visually representing three-dimensional objects in two dimensions, in which the three co-ordinate axes appear equally foreshortened and the angles between any two of them are 120 degrees. The axonometric or planometric projections work by drawing a plan view at a 45-degree angle, with the depth added vertically. These are essentially scaleable drawings, which can offer a visual representation of a space or objects within spaces. The example of a design for the interior decoration of the RMS *Queen Elizabeth*, for the Cunard White Star Line, shows an isometric projection by the architect Grey Wornum. It shows a typical

Art Deco patterned flooring scheme for a deck entrance (Plate 11).

Plans Plans are the key working tools of the designer and contractors. They show important information about the organization of spaces and how this in turn affects access, privacy, circulation and location of equipment and HVAC systems. However, they can be much more than simply operational tools. The architect Louis Kahn said: 'I think that a plan is a society of rooms. A real plan is one in which rooms have spoken to each other. When you see a plan, you can say that it is the structure of the spaces in their light' (in Hing 2006: 11). Therefore, a plan can be lyrical as well as functional.

There exist a number of types of plans used by interior designers and there is no universal standard for their use or order. The project will dictate the requirements, although there are some that are always essential.

Site plans identify the location of a property in its local context. It is a 'bird's-eye' view of the site to show boundaries and contiguous spaces. They should indicate the location of utilities, roads, driveways and paths, and other features that refer to the nature of the terrain. The site plan is separate from any new landscaping requirements.

Floor plans are a crucial part of the plan set, usually starting with the lowest floor and ending with the roof plan. The floor plan should illustrate the position of walls, partitions, doors, stairs, equipment, furniture and all relevant dimensions, etc. (Figures 5.15 and 6.9). Architects and designers

use various plans to avoid confusion, especially if there is a need for demolition, partition erection or the repositioning of fixtures and fittings. Floor plans are often close to the beginning of the full plan set.

Reflected Ceiling Plans (RCPs), showing ceiling layouts, appear in the plan set after the floor plans. The RCP is an overhead view of the ceiling drawn to scale (often the same as the floor plan). It shows the position of light fittings, t-bar ceiling patterns and any suspended items. Interior designers should supply the mechanical and electrical engineers with an RCP so they can add information regarding items such as circuitry, ducting, etc. (Figure 5.17).

Interior elevations illustrate the internal walls of a space. Exterior elevations show the external walls of a structure. Starting with the main or front elevation, all the building elevations appear after the plans in the set. The elevations show detail that is not evident from the plan including mouldings, signage, window size and shape.

Sections include cross-sections of the entire building, as well as various wall sections and detail sections (Figures 5.16 and 6.10).

Detail drawings, often drawn as sections, give graphic and textual information. Individual projects will vary, so the quantity of detail drawing will vary considerably, but all should identify building works required and specific contractor's details, as well as schedules, structural plans for larger projects, mechanical drawings for HVAC systems, and lighting and electrical layouts.

5. Presenting

This is the final part of the preparatory process before final agreement and contracting. Presentations are vital to the process of gaining business and vary in content, depending on the project (McLain-Kark, Dhuru, Parrott and Lovingood 1998: 1–11). They may simply be portfolio presentations of drawings and plans, mood boards and concept boards (Figure 5.6), or computer modelling (Figure 5.5) and animations; they may be PowerPoint presentations, showroom displays or a combination, including the use of scale models – for example in large-scale work. Clients easily comprehend scale models but need to avoid details and colour scheming as models work best when they reference spatial relations and material use. An interesting development is the use of 'rapid prototyped' rooms, which employ the actual equipment, furniture and fittings planned for a room or space with the walls, dividers, etc., made up from heavy-duty cardboard materials. This mock-up approach allows for the testing of various layouts before they are committed to, and is particularly associated with healthcare and hospitality design.

6. Moving and Implementing

Once there is acceptance of the scheme, the 'moving' – getting on with the job – and implementation phase follows. At this stage, it is wise to check that all items are in place for the work to begin and for satisfactory completion for all parties. Bearing in mind that this is a contractual relationship, the designer needs to consider the following:

- Is it clear what work we are, and are not, undertaking?

- Is there any more research required before starting?
- Are completion dates viable and agreed?
- Are responsibilities and limits clearly established?
- Are pricing and payment terms agreed?
- Are terms and conditions fully understood and agreed?
- Does the client understand that changes to an agreed design will incur extra costs?
- Has a formal and binding contract been signed off?
- Has everything been confirmed in writing?
- Are there any loose ends that need tying up?

When the client has approved in principle, the next task is to begin the developmental process. Revisiting the primary generators is helpful in refreshing minds so that the processes of detail design, project planning and budgeting can go ahead smoothly.

Upon signature of contracts that define the project, the final specifications, working drawings, schedules for construction and installation, and final cost estimates are drawn up so that contractors are selected and purchase orders raised.

Team Composition Charretes are planning teams composed of designers, users and other decision-makers, who gather information on project requirements and reach consensus so that all parties have a full understanding of the scope, conceptual design ideas and budgets for the project. Charretes should complete within a short time period and should include meetings between users and professionals for the benefit of

Figure 5.6 Layout board for a scheme based around nautical imagery, Lena Anderson.

both parties. In order to achieve the best from the process, everyone involved needs clear outlines of the development of the project and its outcomes.

It is important that the members of the team have the technical and policy awareness required, as well as the authority to make firm resolutions.

Although it is at the proposal stage that teams are often established, it is at the moving stage that the project teams are briefed with the proposal, research outcomes and timetables. Continuity of staff engagement (and any substitute arrangements made) is essential, as are the channels of responsibility and the location of tasks. Businesses must identify these on a master schedule. An explanation to clients of the level of involvement of the principals or partners of a business or client is important, and, equally, to agree what plans are in place to deal with any changes in the client team.

7. Project Supervision – Site Operation – Completion

Project supervision in interior designing is both mechanical and creative. Analysis of work and judgements are developed, based on experience or established principles, and should be both objective and subjective. Supervision of site operations, including construction, deliveries, installation and snagging, is an important role and becomes the front face of any interior design business.

8. Evaluation – Reflection – Feedback – POE

The whole process of evaluation is ongoing and part of the reflective designing process. Indeed, evaluation will often mean 'going back to the drawing board' during the development of a project. This is part of the process of monitoring design decisions as they progress, to ensure the satisfactory relationship between the core ideas, principles and concepts and the design process and outcomes.

One particular aspect of appraisal, once a project is complete, is Post-Occupancy Evaluation (POE). Craig Zimring defines POE as 'the systematic assessment of the process of delivering buildings or other designed settings or the performance of those settings as they are actually used, or both, as compared to a set of implicit or explicit standards, with the intention of improving the process or settings' (in Bechtel and Churchman 2002: 307).

The importance of POE is clearly in the feedback that it can obtain to allow assessment of the facility. The assessment will assist in fine-tuning the project, diagnosing trouble spots, analysing any innovations introduced, evaluating changes to the strategy of clients and maintaining quality levels. However, it is also important that any lessons learned be acted upon, not only for the project under review but also to inform future project planning in order to avoid repeating errors and to ensure successful future outcomes.

CASE STUDY 5.1 Kitchen Remodelling Example, 2008

Here the designer explains her approach to this project (Figures 5.7–5.11):

The project was a 1911 duplex townhouse located in historic, downtown Frederick, Maryland. As the house was a historic building, the designer had no flexibility with the footprint.

The client, who was born in Peru to an American missionary family, wanted a comfortable, welcoming environment, mildly informed by Peruvian colours and art. Although her children had grown and left home, they often come back to spend time as a family together. For the kitchen, the client's goal was a family-friendly space, conducive to cooking together, where she could entertain family and friends in a semi-formal manner.

BEFORE

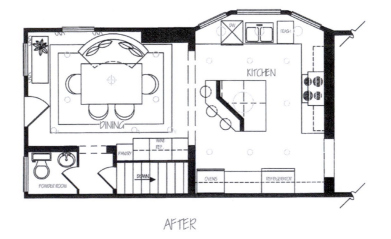

AFTER

Figure 5.7 Plan of domestic space for renovation, Frederick, Maryland, before project, Jenny Boylan, 2008.

Figure 5.8 Domestic space before project, Frederick, Maryland, Jenny Boylan, 2008.

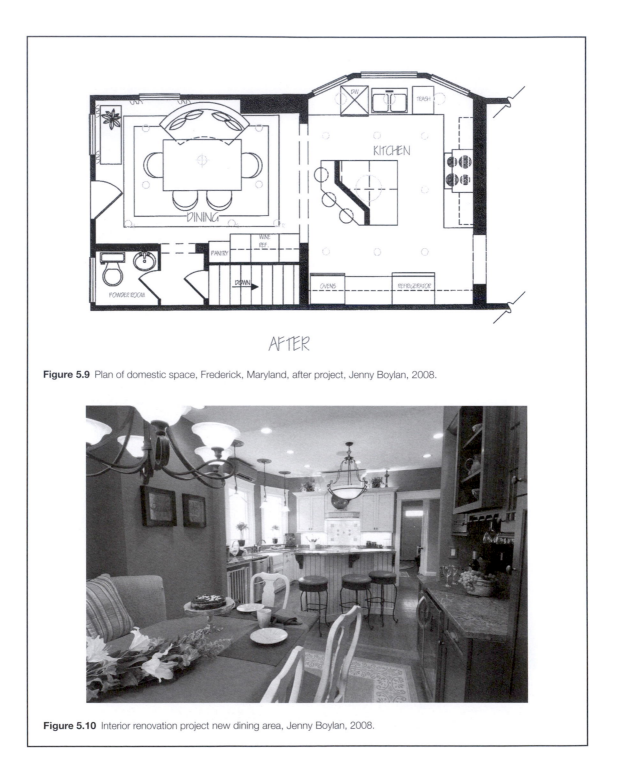

AFTER

Figure 5.9 Plan of domestic space, Frederick, Maryland, after project, Jenny Boylan, 2008.

Figure 5.10 Interior renovation project new dining area, Jenny Boylan, 2008.

Figure 5.11 Interior renovation project new kitchen area, Jenny Boylan, 2008.

The transformed space was originally two separate rooms. The kitchen is positioned at the back of the house while the dining room is in the larger, adjacent space. After some study, we made the decision to switch these functions, so the new workspace would occupy the larger, adjacent, light-filled space. We achieved a relaxed, open flow by removing the wall between the two spaces. Traffic moving through the rooms now glides outside the work area, by the optimally angled, granite-topped island.

A bowed set of three double-hung windows in what was the old dining room faced the uninspiring brick wall of the neighbouring house, just five feet away. The solution: shorten the windows, frame them with exuberantly painted mouldings, and camouflage the view – now, etched glass windows splash a muted radiance into the space by day, and luminous texture by night. A curved banquette provides the lingering guest with a comfortable seat, and rests perfectly within what was an inconvenient jog in the wall.

We specified custom mouldings to match the originals, out of respect for the original architecture. Reminiscent of that earlier time, she chose to punctuate the cabinetry in places with glass-fronted cupboards (JB Interiors, Inc.).

CASE STUDY 5.2 Sage Art Gallery Project

This project is for a proposed art gallery for the Sage College, Albany, New York State (Figures 5.12–5.14). The proposed Sage Gallery is designed to support the display of both three-dimensional and hanging works in its 223-square-metre exhibition space.

The Gallery is intended to host exhibitions across all artistic media, attracting entries by award-winning artists from across the country and abroad. Several exhibitions are planned for installation each year, including an exhibition of student work at the end of spring term. The space must therefore be flexible, and easily adapted to a variety of exhibition types.

The central open space is intended to serve as a passage between the lower gallery space and the spiral stair gallery. The main lobby is a multi-functional space used for large events, meetings and receptions but can also be used as a private space for small meetings. The main entry way is designed as a curvy space that slows down visitors in order to prepare them for the experience waiting to happen inside. The spectacular spiral glass stair gallery space intends not only to celebrate the creativity of contemporary artists featured but also to act as a focal point and specific image or icon for the gallery.

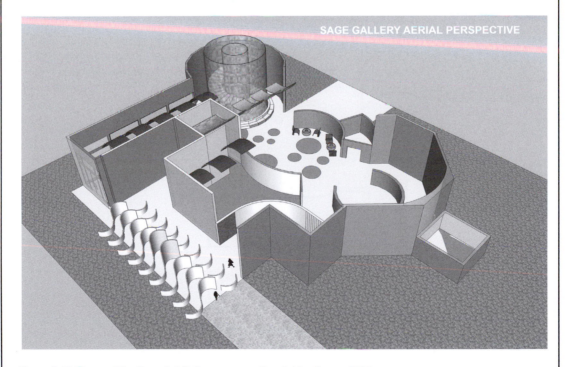

SAGE GALLERY AERIAL PERSPECTIVE

Figure 5.12 Proposal for Sage Art Gallery, perspective, Adrian Avram, 2009.

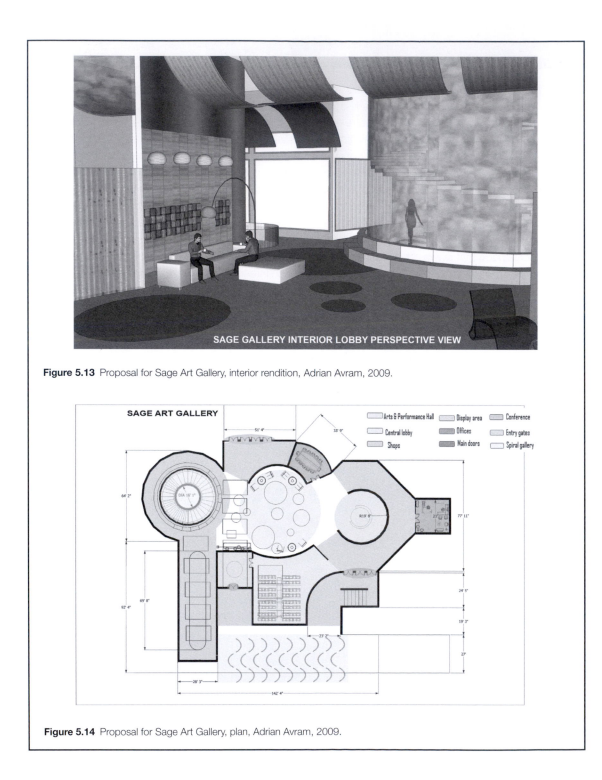

Figure 5.13 Proposal for Sage Art Gallery, interior rendition, Adrian Avram, 2009.

Figure 5.14 Proposal for Sage Art Gallery, plan, Adrian Avram, 2009.

CASE STUDY 5.3 Octium Jewellery Store, Kuwait, 2009

Octium is a luxury jewellery shop that features the work of a very exclusive selection of artists and designers. Spanish designer Jaime Hayon has harmoniously merged tradition, modernity, materials and technology into a fantastical space (Figures 5.15–5.18 and Plates 12–14).. One of the most important and innovative characteristics of this project is the division of areas and the ways of displaying the jewellery.

After passing through an imposing façade in St Laurent dark marble and an impressive brass door, the visitor enters a surprisingly contrasting interior that is completely organic and very soft. Inspired by traditional Mediterranean constructions where lime was used for finishes to give an organic feel to interiors, there are no corners inside the shop.

Innovation and detail are key aspects to the project's conception. Almost every single element was custom-designed and made for the project. These vary from a large, very theatrical furniture piece where ceramic lamps fall inside the display elements, which present a selection of work from a particular designer, to a seven-metre centipede-like display element made in natural walnut with brass crutch-like legs that honour Dali's influence.

There is a striking central area with a very complex, multi-legged rounded table with rising cylinders that exhibit jewellery, and a light installation on top of this element where cylinders of different diameters hang from the ceiling like stalactites. There are also two desk environments that allow the visitor to experience a more traditional jewellery exploration experience in comfort.

Everything from furniture and chair finishes to lamps and handles was custom-designed and made especially for Octium. The use of contrasting finishes like glossy lacquered woods, natural walnut, shiny ceramics and luxurious fabrics give a general feel of tradition and technology joined in a balanced proportion.

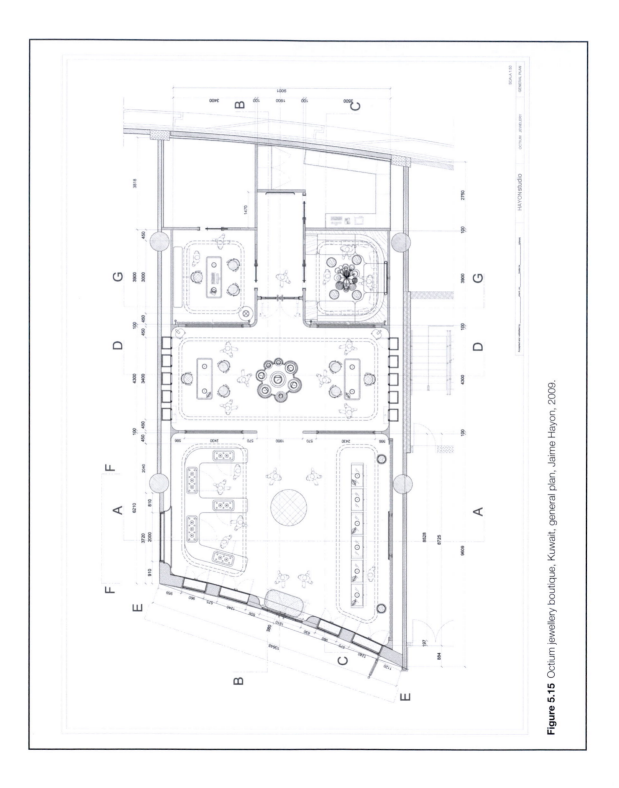

Figure 5.15 Octium jewellery boutique, Kuwait, general plan, Jaime Hayon, 2009.

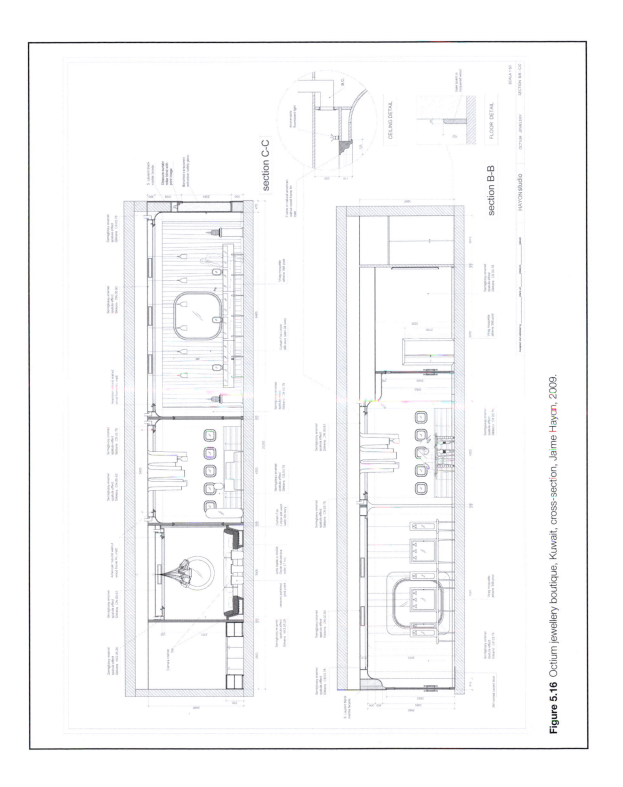

Figure 5.16 Octium jewellery boutique, Kuwait, cross-section, Jaime Hayon, 2009.

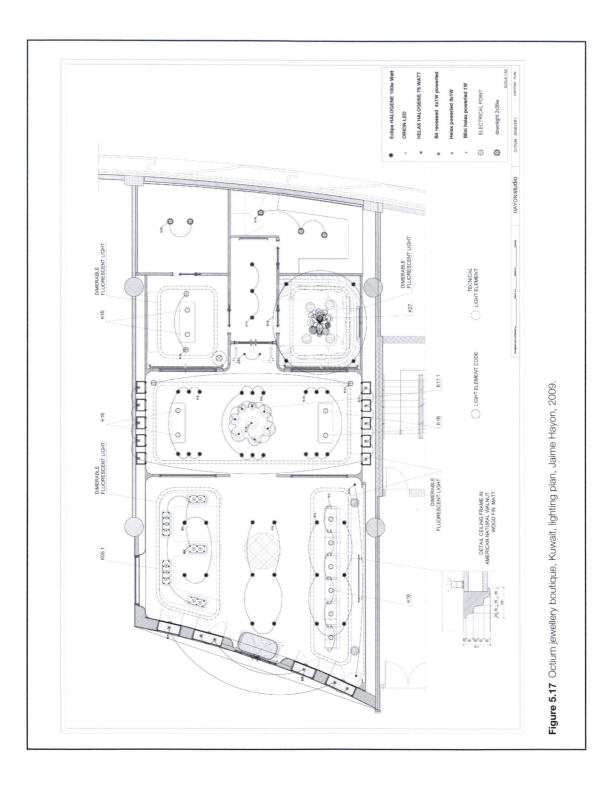

Figure 5.17 Octium jewellery boutique, Kuwait, lighting plan, Jaime Hayon, 2009.

Figure 5.18 Detail of Octium jewellery boutique, Kuwait, interior showing custom-made display cases, Jaime Hayon, 2009.

chapter 6

space

CHAPTER OVERVIEW

This chapter addresses one of the key aspects of interior design, namely space. It begins by defining the nature of space and considering some of the philosophers who have considered the issue of space. Discussions centring on representations of space and the spaces of representation consider the reality of spatial practice. Some analysis of the concept of place follows. We then explore the sense of place, which then leads to a discussion of place attachment theory.

Following on from this, the chapter then considers various aspects of space in use, including aspects of the psychology of space and our perceptions of it. More specifically, the chapter examines considerations of boundaries, thresholds and spatial movement including circulation, path configuration and spatial sequence. The consideration of human space needs through issues such as personal space, privacy and crowding follows. This leads to the important issue of the organization of space through planning, layout and space syntax. Finally, the chapter introduces some consideration of the nature of wayfinding.

introduction

Space is arguably the key aspect of interiors and is perhaps the most complex aspect of their design. Indeed, as Patricia Pringle says: 'the emerging discipline of interior design is differentiated from interior decoration or architecture by its being a discipline of spatial performance and experience rather than one of composition or style' (in Attiwill 2004: 6). At one time, people considered space as relatively neutral but now the impact of technologies, consumption, surveillance and other transformative aspects, such as the recognition of sexuality, gender and race, act upon it. We now conceive of space in a number of ways, including the philosophical, psychological, physical, social, political, active and imagined.

defining space

We can consider space from a number of viewpoints. Space is clearly a permeable volume bounded and formed by the physical nature of a building. Therefore, architectural interior space is a volume enclosed by the arrangement of a building. René Descartes developed the mathematical idea of [Cartesian] space as a series of co-ordinates or points that made up a volume, which was inherently neutral. The basic Cartesian view is one in which the placement of objects in relation to each other, by the use of the co-ordinates of height, width and depth, relates to traditional concepts of symmetry and axes. This static approach was the basis of the nineteenth-century Beaux Arts ideal of interior layouts of space based on axes and hierarchical orderings.

However, spaces may house objects and equipment that define the space and may accommodate people and allow events to occur. Therefore, we can visualize space as the distance between objects, which is variable and relational and thus dynamic and not static, as in the Cartesian view. Space is also temporal, since we negotiate spaces through time. Finally, if surfaces are considered as components of space production, then, as Mark Wigley suggests, '… the interior is not defined by a continuous enclosure of walls but by folds, twists, and turns in an often discontinuous ornamental surface' (2001: 11). In addition to this, the active participation of human beings gives shape and purpose to interior spaces. Therefore, spaces become the stages upon which we act out our lives (see proxemics, below). One example of the change from fixed box spaces to 'open-plan' living space is in a maisonette in a London public housing project – the first instance of open-plan living design in a British public housing maisonette. Built in 1957, in Golden Lane, it took Modern Movement ideas about effective use of space in a one-bedroom apartment and enlarged and adapted them for a maisonette. Although not universally accepted at the time, the gradual move away from single-use rooms to multiple-use spaces reflect the ideas of space efficiency circulating by the 1950s (Figure 6.1).

We can generalize the nature of spaces into (a) the cellular, where boundaries meet at corners, thus creating individual rooms; (b) the free or undivided space with simple boundaries; and (c) the open, where irregular shapes fit within a continuous boundary that defines several areas. Whichever of these is under discussion, acknowledgement of the permeability of spaces and the issue of movement between separated spaces are critical to the conception of successful layouts.

The conceptual understanding of space in relation to this experience of movement, construction and representation is important for interior designers. According to John Peponis and Jean Wineman:

Built space is a field of structured co presence, co awareness, and encounter. The potential of these three factors arises as a by-product of movement. Secondly, we frame these factors according to the manner in which the space labels are distributed over a particular layout. The space labels carry cultural assumptions about rules of behaviour, roles and meanings of spaces, so space configuration is socially encoded. Thirdly the framing of exploration and search is another function of the social production and occupation of space. (In Bechtel and Churchman 2002: 286)

Figure 6.1 Open-plan maisonette living room, Golden Lane estate, London, 1957.

The notions of presence, awareness and encounter remind us that space means little until humans engage with it. It is clear that space is complex in its definition, let alone in its usage.

philosophy of space

The nature of space has fascinated people since ancient times. Both Plato and Aristotle addressed the issue in metaphysical terms. The Chinese philosopher Lao Tzu (sixth century BC) wrote succinctly:

> We fire clay to make a cup,
> But we use the empty space in the centre
> We build walls to make a room,
> But we use the empty space they surround.
> (Tao Te Ching)

Twentieth-century philosophers have challenged the Cartesian neutrality of space. For example, Henri Lefebvre has noted that 'space is never empty: it always embodies a meaning' (1991: 154). As a society always produces space, we can understand its meaning. He says: 'Space has been shaped and moulded from historical and natural elements, but this has been a political process. Space is political and ideological. It is a product literally filled with ideologies. There is an ideology of space … The production of space can be likened to the production of any given particular type of merchandise' (1976: 31). Lefebvre goes on to say that spaces are 'at once a precondition and a result of social superstructures' and 'any space implies, contains and dissimulates social relationships' (1991: 85 and 82–83).

Henri Lefebvre (1901–1991)

Henri Lefebvre was a French sociologist, philosopher and theorist who argued in *The Production of Space* that space is a social product, or a complex social construction, built on social meanings, that affects people's spatial practice and awareness. In particular, the idea of lived-in space has a range of important attributes that go far beyond its physical construction. However, he decried the obsession with the visual that he thought tended to limit an understanding of space, as he considered that all the senses should be experiencing space.

In a different vein, Martin Heidegger sees the key social relationship as a link between space and dwelling. He says that to dwell 'refers to a manner in which we humans are on earth', there-fore to be human means to dwell (in Heidegger 1971: 147). He goes on: 'Man's relation to locations, and through locations to spaces, inheres in his dwelling. The relationship between man and space is none other than dwelling' (157). He goes on further to suggest that place is more important than space, and suggests that it is the concept of boundary that allows the defining of space in order that the boundary is not a stop but a starting place from which spaces are created (154).

Heidegger sees a place as a fixed and set entity, and we can criticize this as ignoring the role that place has in social processes as well as its potential for change, as suggested by Lefebvre. In Lefebvre's view, space is crucial to humankind because it is in space that people interact with each other and their environments (see human space needs below). In his view, these social spaces replace the commodified absolute

---

Martin Heidegger (1889–1976)

Martin Heidegger was a philosopher who considered that the way people exist is through the notion of dwelling. For Heidegger, the important issue was the distinction between the perceived and the real. We see and experience things through the senses, which explains how things appear; Heidegger wanted to locate what things actually are. Space relates to being in the world and for him it was architecture that made the world visible. Space is a result of clearing away to allow for dwelling to occur. The situations of buildings relates to their 'being' where they are particularly located.

spaces. Lefebvre breaks down the production of social space into three aspects: spatial practices, representations of space and spaces of representation, which are useful to consider further as they co-exist and interact.

spatial practice

This refers to the production of the built environment that we live in or use; it 'embraces production and reproduction, and the particular locations and spatial sets characteristic of each social formation. Spatial practice ensures continuity and some degree of cohesion' (Lefebvre 1976: 33). These are experienced spaces, the 'where' that things occur. The space labels given by particular groups will indicate the 'what' that occurs.

Jean Baudrillard (1929–2007)

Jean Baudrillard was a French sociologist, thinker and theorist. For Baudrillard, it was consumption, rather than production, that was the main drive in capitalist society. He argued, in his *System of Objects* (1968), that needs are created, rather than inherent. Baudrillard thought that all purchases, because they always signify something socially, reflect the nature of the purchaser/user. He saw goods having a range of values, including a functional value or basic purpose; an economic value; a symbolic value that is relative to other objects; and finally a sign value that may imply particular social values, such as style or position.

Jean Baudrillard considers changes in spatial practice from a sociological viewpoint:

> Whereas the old-fashioned dining room was heavily freighted with moral conventions, "modern interiors" in their ingeniousness, often give the impression of being mere functional expedients. Their "absence of style" is in the first place, an absence of room, and maximum functionality is a solution of last resort whose outcome is that the dwelling place, though remaining closed to the outside, loses its internal organization. Such a restructuring of space and the objects in it, unaccompanied by any reconversion, must in the first instance be considered an impoverishment. (1996 [1968]: 17)

The way forward, in Baudrillard's view, is to consider the gap between 'integrated psychological space' and 'fragmented functional space' (1996 [1968]: 19).

Changing the closed function of fragmented space was a challenge for architect and designer Alvar Aalto. Writing in 1930, he put forward the idea that if the actual functional requirements of space are analysed and used as starting points, rather than the given forms of standard practice such as designated rooms, then space will be used much more efficiently (in Greenhalgh 1993: 139). This sounds more like the integrated social space that Baudrillard discusses. Plate 15 shows a mock-up of a space intended for a pied-à-terre for a single man as part of an exhibition on one-room living.

Cultural customs and attitudes also inform spatial practice, and practitioners must understand

and incorporate them into spaces where appropriate. For example, gates and transitional spaces define both physical and psychological boundaries in Islamic design (Serageldin 1995: 193–206).

representations of space

Representations of space are mental images that help to make sense of spaces and surroundings, organize our knowledge and understanding of them and through them, and legitimize particular approaches to the manipulation of space. Lefebvre refers to the idea of conceptualized space and representational space. He considers 'conceptualized space, [to be] the space of … planners, technocratic sub dividers and social engineers, all of whom identify what is lived and what is perceived, with what is conceived (arcane speculation about numbers, with its talk of the golden number, moduli and "canons", tends to perpetuate this view of matters)' (1991: 38). For Lefebvre, 'conceptions of space tend … towards a system of verbal (and therefore intellectually worked out) signs' (39). These become archetypes in the collective unconscious. Contemporary attitudes to design tend to try to consider the reality of space-use expressed as 'spaces of representation' by Lefebvre, rather than preconceived concepts of how spaces should be.

spaces of representation

In this scenario, conceptualized spaces become lived space. These spaces are the occupied, transformed and felt experiences of particular spaces, so are both conceptual and lived-in. These spaces '[embody] complex symbolisms … linked to the clandestine or underground side of social life' (Lefebvre 1991: 33). Here this is 'space as directly lived through its associated images and symbols, hence the space of "inhabitants" and "users" … it overlays physical space, making symbolic use of its objects'. It 'may be said … to tend towards more or less coherent systems of non-verbal symbols and signs' (39). For Lefebvre, 'representational space is alive: it speaks. It has an affective kernel or centre: Ego, bed, bedroom, dwelling house; or square, church, graveyard. It embraces the loci of passion, of action, and of lived situations, and thus immediately implies time' (42). It is space as used space, not directly relating to construction but connecting to symbolic and artistic productions to counter the rational and logical aspects of representations of space.

Lefebvre further points to the crucial importance of space: 'To underestimate, ignore and diminish space amounts to the overestimation of texts, written matter and writing systems along with the readable and the visible, to the point of assigning to these a monopoly on intelligibility' (62). He continues: 'It is clear, therefore, that a spatial code is not simply a means of reading or interpreting space: rather it is a means of living in that space, of understanding it, and of producing it. As such it brings together verbal signs … and non-verbal signs (music, sounds, evocations, architectural constructions)' (47). In other words, space and its planning and understanding go well beyond blueprints and plans to encompass all the senses, the emotions and the imagination.

Michel de Certeau (1925–1986)

Michel de Certeau was a French Jesuit and scholar. In his important work, *The Practice of Everyday Life*, he built up a theory of the processes of everyday life through the activities of producing and consuming. De Certeau suggested that daily existence is repetitive and unconscious, so he tried to show how people instinctively navigate through everything they do. His distinction between monolithic 'strategies' and the individual's opposing 'tactics' is the basic concept. These navigations are particularly relevant to issues of space and place.

Michel De Certeau comes to the theorizing of space from a different angle. He suggests that what activates space are movements seen through time, speed and directions. He sums it up neatly by saying that 'In short space is a practiced place' (in Ballantyne 2002: 74).

The connections between space and human activity, whether described as dwelling, self-representation or practice, are evident. However, the discussion of space (as well as many other concepts) is linked at some level to issues surrounding function that are themselves often rooted historically and culturally. How particular spaces are used is part of an ingrained social understanding. Frank Lloyd Wright expanded upon the theme of humanity in space planning in 1931, when he gave a lecture entitled 'The Cardboard House'. He exhorted designers (architects) to make all the parts of a house 'come together as enclosed space – so divided that light, air and vista permeated the whole with a sense of unity'. In particular he stressed the need to 'eliminate the room as a box and the house as another by making all walls enclosing screens – the ceilings and floors and enclosing screens to flow into each other as one large enclosure of space, with minor sub-divisions only'. The relation to humanity and space use was developed in the same lecture: 'Make all house proportions more liberally human, with less wasted space in structure, and structure more appropriate to material, and so the whole more liveable' (in Benton, Benton and Sharp 1975: 64).

The apparent trend towards denial of the liveable in recent 'post-functional' interiors seems to extend this. Discussing a dining room by architect Peter Eisenman, Roger Kimball suggests that Eisenman developed a design that was as free as possible from functional planning. Importantly, 'these dislocations … have, according to the occupants of the house, changed the dining experience in a real and, more importantly, unpredictable fashion' (in Mitchell 1993: 22). Although these dislocations might appear problematic for interior designers, who should put the needs of the client first, in this example it does appear that the users of this non-traditional space have had the benefit of a new set of experiences.

place

The idea of place in relation to space is important for interior designers to grasp. Place is less abstract than space, but each defines the other. Space suggests movement, whereas place indicates pause. The geographer Yi-Fu Tuan explains the moving process from space to place as learning to move around a maze: 'At first, only the point of entry is clearly recognized; beyond lies space. In time, more and more landmarks are identified and the subject gains confidence in movement. Finally, space consists of familiar landmarks and paths – in other words, place' (1977: 71).

Sense of Place

We define a sense of place, or *genius loci*, as a social experience of belonging that exists independently of any one individual's perceptions or experiences, yet is reliant on human engagement for its existence. One may derive a sense of place from natural environments, e.g. gardens, but this is often in a combination of natural and cultural features in the landscape, and includes the people who occupy the place through their individual history.

Fifty years after building the Unity Temple (1906–1908), Frank Lloyd Wright eloquently described the total effect of its design and the nature of its space:

I think that was about the first time when the interior space began to come through as the reality of the building, when you sat in the Temple, you were sitting under a big concrete slab that let your eyes go out into the clouds on four sides. Then there were no walls with holes in them. You will notice that features were arranged against that interior space allowing a sense of it to come to the beholder wherever he happened to be. And I have been working on that thesis for a long time because it was dawning on me that when I built that building the reality

of the building did not consist in the walls and in the roof, but in this space within to be lived in. (Caedmon Records 1955)

Although Wright does not say it directly, he is surely referring to the 'sense of place' that his building created. The internal space, the use of geometry and symmetry in the Unity temple, reflect not only Wright's ideas about design but link well with the congregation's religious needs (Plate 16).

Michel de Certeau also makes important distinctions between space and place. 'A place (lieu) is the order (of whatever kind) in accord with which elements are distributed in relationships of co-existence. … A place is thus an instantaneous configuration of positions. It implies an indication of stability' (in Taylor and Preston 2006: 79). Eugene Walter suggests that the place is an extraordinary mix of emotions: 'a place is a location of experience. It evokes and organizes memories, images, feelings, sentiments, meanings, and the work of imagination. The feelings of a place are indeed the mental projections of individuals, but they come from collective experience and they do not happen anywhere else. They belong to the place' (in Malnar and Vodvarka 2004: xi).

In any event, the role of designers in assisting with the creation of a sense of place is clear: 'Place is special, a space of particular qualities and impact informed by some perceivable difference from another place, hence a "sense of place", [which implicates] design as either somehow sharing in place or as the instrument for achieving it' (Johnson 1994: 392).

Gaston Bachelard again relates sense of place to experience when he considers that place is

Gaston Bachelard (1884–1962)

Gaston Bachelard was a French philosopher who based his study of architecture not on its histories but rather on the actual experiences of users in buildings and spaces. His *Poetics of Space* reflects on particular spaces including lesser-known ones, such as the cellar and the attic. The message for designers is to base their work in the experience of the users rather than use loose or general concepts that might or might not engage with the viewers and users of spaces.

subjective, whilst space is objective: 'Space that has been seized upon by the imagination cannot remain indifferent space subject to the measure and estimates of the surveyor' (1995 [1959]: xxxii). In other words, 'inhabited space transcends geometrical space' (47).

A sense of place is not just personal. It is important to business in that it is more than simply a location; it is an identity. People/customers will make connections to the 'place of business' or the brand identity through a sense of place as much as other attributes. A good example of this is the Starbucks coffee shop chain, which has become a 'third place' where their interior spaces are neither home nor work. The attraction of European coffee houses, where it is traditional to relax and take time over your coffee and socialize with friends in sophisticated atmospheres, combined with the high American standards of service, has created a very successful space that has became 'a place' (see Waxman 2006: 35–53).

An interesting example of space use that integrates four differing space types is the Blue Frog acoustic lounge in Mumbai, India. Built in 2007 in a converted warehouse, it collapses a theatre, restaurant, bar and club into one space but maintains the performative characteristics of each particular space type. It is a series of intimate spaces in one that offer a range of visual, flavourful and audio experiences for the users and creates its own particular environment (Figure 6.8 and Case Study 6.3).

Environmental psychologist Lynne Manzo's work on place meaning also has resonance for interior designers. Her researches have revealed how the socio-political foundations of our emotional relationships to places, particularly the impact of gender, race, class and sexuality, require the full extent of the human experience to be considered by designers when researching and working on people–place relationships. A number of points are of interest. For example, researchers found that non-residential settings and areas may provide a greater feeling of 'at home-ness' than residential settings for many users. They also found that experience in a place might be more important than the features of the physical environment in establishing the meaning of a place. Thirdly, they found that users may most frequently feel ambivalence toward significant places and that, not surprisingly, a person's race, gender and sexual orientation may well influence the feelings and meaning they experience in a place (Manzo 2005: 67–86). These points indicate that an understanding of place is not straightforward. However, successful spatial arrangements can often lead to place attachment.

Place Attachment Theory

A place is a 'space that has been given meaning through personal, group or cultural processes' (Altman and Low 1992: 5). Place attachment revolves around individuals' personal characteristics, behaviours and self-image, the availability of facilities and resources, and a 'sense

disruption; they create navigation issues and a sense of place. Geographer Daniel Montello notes these triggers as follows:

- *Sensory access* – what can be seen, heard, etc.
- *Attention* – what is looked at, listened to, etc.
- *orability* – what is remembered, what is *tten*, etc.
- *avioural affordance* – where one can *eat*, etc.
- *ct* – mood, comfort, stress, fear, aes-*cs*, etc.
- *ality* – pedestrian flows, noise, eye con-*, social distance, etc.

(Montello 2007: iv–2)

ciation of these features is valuable when *ing* aspects of human–space relation-*xamples* abound that demonstrate how *fy* spaces and places to compensate for *d* omissions, and how, if left unmodified, *action* results.

dividuals, there appears to be a hierarchy *relations* with space that begins with a *other* people in the space. This is fol-*by* the recognition of and connection to *rticular* movements within the space. The *f* brightness and their distribution will cre-*al* points, as will high contrast, vivid colour *fferentiation* within spaces. In addition, *patterns* and the play of the Gestalt idea of *ty* and proximity will influence the process *ssing*. Finally, the issues of common mean-*d* personal identity will have an effect on the *es* to space.

perceptions of space

We do not measure our perceptions of space in terms of order or disorder, nor are they in-built, but they are our individual responses to particular configurations of forms informed by social consensus, often mediated by critics and writers. The Dutch architect and designer Gerrit Rietveld said in 1957: 'If, for a particular purpose, we separate, limit, and bring into a human scale a part of unlimited space, it is (if all goes well) a piece of space brought into life as a reality. In this way, a special segment of space has been absorbed into our human system' (in Greenhalgh 1993: 227).

Elements such as scale, vertical/horizontal alignment, colour, number and repetition enliven this metaphysical approach. Expression of activities through the selection of geometries, circulation patterns, roles of structure and systems, use of solid/void, light/shade, and colour/texture will all affect the perception of space. Nevertheless, we must remember Bachelard's words on the need to experience spaces not simply as abstract ideals:

> To sleep well we do not need to sleep in a large room, and to work well we do not have to work in a den. But to dream of a poem, then write it, we need both ... Thus the dream house must possess every virtue. However spacious, it must also be a cottage, a dovecote, a nest, a chrysalis. Intimacy needs the heart of a nest. (1995 [1959]: 65)

The idea of human body-centred space reminds us that we base our perceptions on haptic as well as visual experiences. These haptic events include hearing where the auditory and acoustic experiences are more than just in relation to entertainment and conversation. Secondly, there is the sense of smell, which tends to identify places and times forever in the mind. Thirdly, there is the sense of touch that occurs when we encounter surfaces that are tangible and memorable. Finally, there is the often-underrated kinaesthetic sensation of bodily movement in and through the environment. It is clear that by linking considerations of these senses with the physical aspects of space, designers are likely to influence behaviour (see also Tversky 2003: 66–80).

space use

Baudrillard suggests that: 'Space is at his [the interior designer's] disposal like a kind of distributed system, and by controlling this space he holds sway over all possible reciprocal relations between the objects therein, and hence over all the roles they are capable of assuming' (1996 [1968]: 26). However, as we have seen, people are involved. Indeed, by usurping control, the user may adapt space in direct opposition to the designer's intentions.

How space is used can be analysed in many ways. There are five general aspects: boundaries and thresholds; spatial movement; circulation; path configuration; and sequence and focus.

Boundaries and Thresholds
We have already seen Heidegger's idea of the boundary as enclosure. Robert Venturi expressed the importance of the entrance as a boundary or

meeting point of interior and exterior forces when he suggested that the wall is an event that distinguishes two types of space – interior and exterior (1966: 86). The transitional elements that enable spaces to operate on boundaries, e.g. doors, are themselves visual experiences, and of course, the entrance itself is a haptic experience. However, the boundary directly relates to human behaviour in that it is a spatial form, created by society.

Le Corbusier succinctly defined the importance of the threshold and its role as 'the little vestibule that frees your mind from the street' (1946 [1927]: 183). More recently, Norberg-Schultz explored the links between inside and outside: 'the basic property of man-made places is therefore concentration and enclosure. They are "insides" in a full sense, which means they "gather" what is known. To fulfil this function they have openings which relate to the outside' (1980: 10). All these notions link boundaries and thresholds to issues of interaction.

Thresholds do not need to be at the interior/exterior junction. Hotel architect Morris Lapidus used the idea of internal thresholds and related the idea of entrance to the theatre or stage set. Here he is creating an artificial threshold:

> To get into the dining room you walk up three steps, open a pair of doors and walk out on a platform, and then walk down three steps. Now the dining room is at exactly the same level as my lobby, but as they walk up, they reach the platform. I've got soft light lighting this thing up, and before they're seated, they are on stage as if they had been cast for the part. Everybody's looking at them; they are looking at everybody else. (In Caplan 2005: 183)

Interior Spatial Movement

To improve the experience of an interior, circulation spaces ought to have equal value in relation to other spaces, so that they do not become simply transitory. Animating these spaces by providing distractions such as seating, object displays or other visual stimuli will be helpful. One particular aspect of spatial movement is circulation.

Circulation

Space planning is involved with the planning and arrangement of all routes: primary, secondary and tertiary, as well as escape and service routes and waiting areas. The aim of circulation planning, working in conjunction with wayfinding, should be to produce rational and clear pathways and routes. It should avoid making paths through reception areas, for example, although the reception areas might well be the starting point of an axial progression. This planning process should also avoid incompatible uses, say between customers and service engineers, and should try to minimize movement by linking related areas. Examples of the well-known kitchen triangle or the hospital sequences of preparation room, operation theatre and recovery room demonstrate this.

Diagrams overlaid on plans help to develop circulation planning and could include routes such as the straight line, the line with branches, or the radiating ring circulation. Furniture and equipment layout will affect circulation in particular spaces so designers need to consider this when planning. Furniture layout is therefore part of the methodical review of requirements including seating, work surfaces, storage, equipment and any special needs as appropriate to the space, e.g. beds, bathroom fittings, kitchen equipment, etc. (see, for example, Plate 32 and Figures 5.15 and 6.9).

The locations of differing spaces will affect the efficiency of circulation. Therefore, the relationship of space to entrance and exit points, the journey importance and the traffic type is an important consideration. We also need to consider the conflict between vertical and horizontal circulations (see, for example, Hölscher, Meilinger, Vrachliotis, Brösamle and Knauff 2006: 284–299).

Path Configuration

The configuration of paths influenced by factors such as distance, direction, orientation and the origin/destination planned is another planning tool. Cognitive mapping informs the understanding of pathways and routes. The urban planner Kevin Lynch explained that: 'In a successful cognitive map people need to identify (*Identity*) objects; e.g. a door as an entity; secondly they recognize a relationship (*Structure*) i.e. where it is, and then thirdly it must register some meaning (*Meaning*) for them, in the case of a door – a hole for getting out' (1960: 8). A well-known example of linear path configuring that suggests movement to a goal is in Daniel Libeskind's Jewish Museum in Berlin; a more banal example is the circulation path model used in IKEA home furnishing stores to control customer traffic flow through the building.

Sequence and Focus

A pathway sequence is a set of space relationships in and through an interior, often along an axis. A perfect example of this would be the traditional *enfilade*, whereby the alignment of the doors of the first room with the doors of connecting rooms, via a single axis, provides a view through the whole group of rooms.

Swiss-born architect Bernard Tschumi suggests three aspects of a sequence: the transformational, based on the device, procedure or methodology of design such as rotation, insertion, fusion etc.; the second is the spatial or structural construct, for example an axially-based sequence; and thirdly, the programmatic or socially symbolic aspects (1996: 154). The spatial sequences are structural and independent of meaning, but the operational processes derive from the appearance and shape of the spaces creating a tension between spaces and their use, which is often problematic. In commercial interiors, modes of spatial arrangement have considered such issues as flow of work, intersection meeting points for informal contact, and layouts that encourage 'social networking', to assist frequent connectivity and interactions.

Prospect Theory

The combination of being able to see without being seen is the basis of the idea of prospect theory. In other words, from a place we can survey space. It manifests itself in people's preference for sides rather than centres, covered spaces within reason, and open spaces with views, all of which promote the feeling of security and screening. The use of multiple vantage points within an area, and the screening of large spaces with refuges that have good sight lines, are possible approaches in large, undifferentiated spaces. A balance of elements works best.

The other aspect of prospect planning is in the relationship that prospects have to refuge spaces (where refuge means enclosure). For example, Frank Lloyd Wright's interiors were more refuge-dominant, whereas Le Corbusier's were prospect-dominant in that the interiors were exposed.

human space needs

There is a conflict in the issue of space, which Lefebvre has already defined. He suggests that 'the user's space is lived – not represented (or conceived). When compared with the abstract space of the experts (architects, urbanists, and planners), the space of the everyday activities of users is a concrete one, which is to say subjective' (1991: 362). His argument suggests that as architects and designers do not live in other people's spaces, they have little control over their use.

People animate, occupy and define space. People require spaces to provide sensory interest and stimulation. Since spaces reflect social organization, they need to provide security, identity, stability and a chance to interpret the unwritten rules of space usage in society. All these will vary depending on the age, personality, health and actual spatial needs of the individual. However, we base cultures partly on their formal integration of spaces, using classification of interiors as a guide to behavioural contexts. These socially constructed spaces identify people along with them so that social organization often means relating to sets of unwritten rules, which underpin interpersonal contact in spaces.

These relations make connections between place, performativity and the notion of the self. Erving Goffman developed this idea in his *Pres-*

Erving Goffman (1922–1982)
Erving Goffman was a Canadian sociologist and writer. He considered that individuals would try to control or direct the impression that they make with others by altering their location, look and conduct. Similarly, others will be attempting to read this individual. Goffman created a 'dramaturgical analysis', which made a connection between the performance of everyday life and a theatrical performance. He explains this by thinking of a front or stage where the individual is in an arena with an audience, so they have to present a public face. Conversely, there is a back position, which may often be a private place, where the person can remove the public persona and express their identity.

---

entation of Self, where he claimed that the 'self is a product of performance in social interaction' (1959: 252). The example of Lapidus's threshold, above, demonstrates this. Goffman argues that 'self-presentation is a crucial determinant of one's very sense of self' (170). This presentation process shaped the self. 'The individual is able to present an image of self that is accepted by others in social situations that is mainly determined by social categories, status and resources' (171). People undertake all this in selected social spaces.

Goffman also gives an analysis of interactions within spaces that are useful here (240). He investigates individual identity, group relations, the impact of environment, and the movement and interactive meanings of information. He sees people as actors, presenting themselves in a specific spatial context. Their 'performance' creates impressions conveyed to the 'audience' on a 'stage setting', (space) that itself is part of the performance. The interior therefore acts as a setting for the social roles assumed by the actor.

The defining of space by people shows that the individual's physical identity as a human being, distinct in the world, is as important as their social/cultural identity as a member of a group with shared values. Sociologist Andy Crabtree points out that for most people: 'Spaces and spatial arrangements are known in common and essentially tied to situated activities through observable practices for their production and accomplishment' (2000).

Designers can respond to these needs by interpretation and understanding of behaviour through observation, evaluation and user participation in planning. The strategy that links designing with occupants' ability to individualize their space (e.g. offices) or control their local environment also allows for an address to some of these issues. This aspect refers to the possession and 'defence' of physical space as well as to the marking and identity of the user of the space. Territoriality uses organizing mechanisms to defend boundaries, etc., and marking that will often reflect the nature of an individual's personality. The example of the display of collections or of family photographs is well known.

personal space

Personal space is the area surrounding an individual, or the area that they consider their own territory. Any undesired intrusion into that space produces uncomfortable feelings and may provoke a reaction. The basis of these psychological phenomena is in the perceived surrounding space of an individual. For example, people in densely populated areas usually require smaller spaces for themselves, whilst larger personal spaces often reflect affluence, exclusivity and privacy.

Privacy

Privacy is an important aspect of personal space. As with personal space, privacy requirements are dependent upon the individual's needs, which usually go beyond simple space issues. Privacy is 'the selective control of access to the self or one's group' (Altman 1975: 18). Privacy expert Alan Westin has given four aspects to the concept of privacy (Westin 1967). These are: (a) solitude or being alone; (b) anonymity or avoidance of interaction; (c) reserve or 'keeping oneself to one's self'; and (d) the intimacy that relates to group privacy and emotional bonds. This unpicking of privacy shows that interior designers need to consider carefully an apparently simple concept. When clients convey that they need privacy, what do they really mean? Privacy has two further aspects: the withdrawal from society and the personalization of space. Privacy adjustment is therefore not just spatial; it is visual, auditory and tactile.

The anthropologist Edward Hall devised a system of 'distance zones' to express the behavioural aspects of space and territoriality. In his work *The Hidden Dimension* he suggests that personal space is both a form of non-verbal communication and a dynamic, and he introduces the concept of proxemics, where the understanding of space is 'a specialized elaboration of culture' (1966: 1).

The theory of proxemics in relation to space is important in considering space usage. Hall suggests three approaches. Firstly, there is fixed-feature space, which refers to buildings and their functions as rooms, compartments, etc. Secondly, there is semi-fixed-feature space, which varies culturally but is affected by adjustable arrangements such as furniture. Here the layout in space can be 'sociopetal' (bringing people together) and 'sociofugal' (keeping people apart). Then, thirdly, there is the informal space that surrounds individuals and controls access to one's territory. These spaces have been calculated as distance 'rings' around the body that move from the intimate (0–18in) for close friends and family; personal (18–48in), including casual friends, co-workers etc; social (4–12ft), maintained by those who know of one another but only come together for common purposes; and the general public (12ft +), which refers to strangers.

Density and/or Crowding

In space planning, density is a term that formulates the possible total occupancy of a building in order to arrive at an objective measure of persons per unit of area. This will inform such planning issues as circulation and exits required in an emergency. In the case of crowding, this is an individual psychological condition that relates to a sense of overload; therefore, individual sensitivities can often be quite different in the same situation. Clearly, these are also culturally defined. The perception of space in relation to issues of density and apparent or real crowding is an important issue for space planners and interior designers.

Environmental psychologists have suggested that density and crowding can have an adverse effect on mood and even cause stress-related illness. Therefore, interior designers should try to minimize the unpleasant effects caused when crowding occurs. Efforts to decrease the perception of confinement or increase the apparent size of a space often prove useful. Features that reduce feelings of crowding and density within buildings include:

- Fenestration, especially windows that can be opened and, additionally, provide views.
- Other visual escapes such as doors, and artwork on walls.
- Well-defined corners, as opposed to curved walls.
- Higher ceilings or roof spaces.
- Doors to partition or enlarge spaces, thus providing control.
- Room shape: square rooms feel less crowded than rectangular ones.
- Using partitions to create smaller, personalized spaces within an open-plan office or larger workspace.
- Providing increases in cognitive control over aspects of the internal environment, such as ventilation, light, privacy, etc.
- Positioning furniture at the sides of a space.

In any event, it is worth remembering that the perceived level of density may well be more than the reality (see Bell, Greene, Fisher and Baum 2001).

organization of space

The planning, layout and use of spaces are key parts of any successful interior design. The simple but dramatic example in Figures 6.2 and 6.3 demonstrates how altering a room about two metres square created an illusion of space. Although rather idiosyncratic, the adaptation of space, using mirrors, lighting, accessories and scale, demonstrates the process well.

For architect and designer Marcel Breuer, space organization was fundamental: 'In an ideal (or more properly stated, the correct) situation, the interior is no longer an independent unit set into the house, but is constructively tied to the building itself – properly speaking; it begins with the floor plan, rather than after the completion of the building as was earlier the case' (in Wilk 1981: 184). Whether this ideal situation is possible or not, planning remains a crucial aspect of space organization.

Planning

The planning of spaces ranges from simple, intuitive layouts through to complex, computer-generated schemes to maximize the space usage. There are a number of basic conceptual styles that space planners consider, although they will of course vary with the building's shape and intended use. These 'styles' include:

- A main area with secondary attached spaces
- Linear rows of spaces with parallel corridor access
- Single- and double-sided corridors
- Inner and outer units with internal access
- Clusters in a space
- Grids in a space
- Modular development of any of the above
- Open, landscape or free plan

Layout

A number of issues arise regarding space planning and layout that will vary in impact, depending upon the nature of the building and its use. These issues include security, the technical systems required, human factors and universal design matters, and appropriate codes and standards. In addition, the internal spaces of a building need arranging in a sequence compatible with the degree of privacy associated with the spaces; otherwise, some awkwardness may befall friends, guests, clients, or even family.

One particular aspect of layouts is that the designer should be aware of any fixed, semi-fixed or dynamic features. Another is the evaluation of the activities in the planned or given spaces derived from the programming stage. Designers should usually place related activities in proximity and, conversely, unrelated activities are usually set apart. For both individual and group space needs, the layout planning needs to consider territorial issues such as boundaries, the nature of any workspaces, the appropriate size and density, and the need for environmental stimulation. A more sophisticated approach to spatial layout planning is the concept of space syntax.

Space Syntax

On the basis that spaces are an underpinning of social organization, space syntax explores these relations (see Space Syntax and Bafna 2003: 17–29). Space syntax therefore covers a set of theories and techniques for the assessment and analysis of spatial configurations. Spaces are broken down, analysed as networks of choices and then mapped to identify or create the appropriate connectivities between the sub-divided areas.

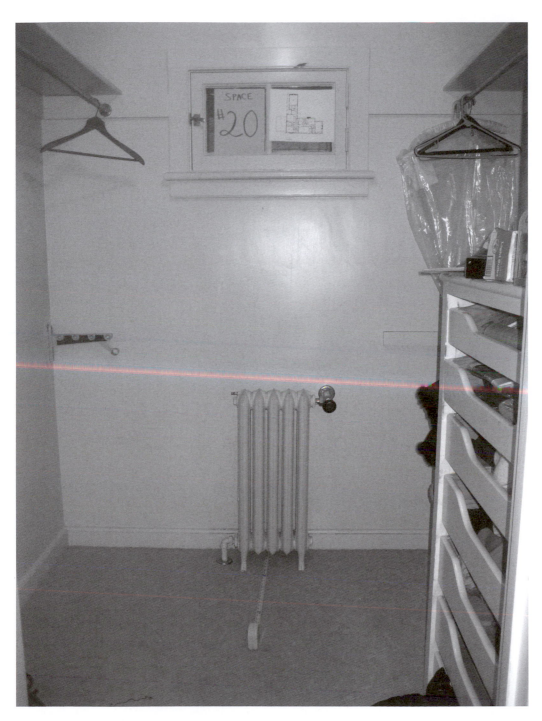

Figure 6.2 Small space conversion Before, Jodie O'Connor.

Figure 6.3 Small space conversion After, Jodie O'Connor.

The use of plans is the basis of this approach since from this point it is possible that they can assist in the analysis of a space's potential usage, privacy requirements, routing, etc. This approach is particularly valuable in interior spaces where wayfinding is an important element. Galleries and museums, transport hubs and healthcare buildings will particularly benefit from this type of analysis. Designers use space syntax to predict the correlation between spatial layouts and social effects such as crime, traffic flow and sales per unit area in, for example, commercial interiors.

The use of axial lines (one-dimensional) and 'convex maps' (two-dimensional) as elements in the programming of an interior is particularly valuable in complex spaces. Axial line-mapping charts all the lines that cross more than one space to reach another. This approach, based on the 'longest line of sight and access' through open space, is valuable, for example, for planning wayfinding uses. The convex mapping approach uses the plan to divide spaces into the fewest number of the largest spaces available and to define the points of access between them.

wayfinding

Wayfinding planning is a crucial aspect in the success of interior spaces and their circulation and negotiation. Whilst it has its own specialist consultants, an overview of issues is a useful contribution to the interior designer's knowledge. Wayfinding is an aspect of environmental psychology, so 'successful wayfinding involves knowing where you are, knowing your destination, knowing and following the best route to your destination, being able to recognize your destination on arrival, and reversing the process to find your way back out' (Carpman and Grant, in Bechtel and Churchman 2002: 427).

Wayfinding is a concept of orientation and routing that includes: signage and other graphic communication; other clues built in to the building's spatial planning; logical space arrangement; audible communication; tactile elements; and provision for special-needs users. For individuals, the issue of being lost in a labyrinth is real and may be confounded by the individual's narrowness of vision and inability to conceptualize spaces on 'the other side' of divides, for example. Therefore, the following tools will greatly assist the wayfinding capabilities of the space users:

- Visual access or visibility via clear lines of sight.
- Architectural definitions of space by separation of areas with particular elements.
- Features that act as landmarks and points of reference.
- Signage and numbering systems with signs particularly at decision points
- Considered building layout and spatial sequencing

To ensure maximum efficiency in wayfinding, the specific design elements of signage are important. These include coding to simplify decision-making, zoning to divide space into areas, and signage for information. In addition to the planning, the operational elements need sustaining through staff training, along with wayfinding maintenance and upkeep.

The Wayfinding Process

Behavioural elements, i.e. seeing the target destination, following a prepared path, using identifying signs and landmarks, and forming a 'cognitive map' of the route, are the basis of wayfinding. Initially, there is an orientation process based on a sense of direction. This series of active sensory perceptions creates a network of references through which the space can be understood. The second stage is the wayfinding route decision, whereby the individual creates cognitive maps that code proximity, distance sequence and pathways. Thirdly, there is the process of actually navigating and route monitoring. Finally, through the culmination of the above actions, the individual reaches the destination.

ANALYSIS Office Spaces

Offices, like rooms, have a simple definition that belies their complexity. They are, in essence, places of business; therefore, they have a different basis for space use and organization from 'domestic' space. There is always an imperative of efficiency in office space layout and design, but this needs tempering with working conditions, image and optimum performances.

Workplace designer Francis Duffy defines four categories of office model:

- Hive: Here workers operate under precise instructions, having little leeway and little interaction or autonomy. This space requires simple, open-ganged cubicles, for example. The image of the 'typing pool' in the 1960s Nestlé office building in Vevey, Switzerland (Figure 6.4), shows a concern for efficiency, but there are also some considerations of employee comfort.
- Cell: Here individual spaces such as offices or high-partitioned areas allow for autonomy without much interaction. Highly talented skilled workers might use these spaces.
- Den: This works for a highly interactive group of people working together with differing skills. Ideally, it is a mixed space with continuous meeting areas and local, individual workspaces.
- Club: For high-level work that requires talented workers to be both collaborative and solitary in their working methods. Here, a wide range of changing tasks are undertaken, thus the space needs to be complex, easily manipulated and able to accommodate a variety of tasks.

(Duffy 1997 and also specif. 60–61)

Whilst these may offer simple and easily visualized labels for workspaces, practice indicates that there are a number of typical layouts used for space planning. In any event, planners need to consider the concept of 'your office is where you are', which takes into account the development in personal computing and flexibility in locations of work.

A simple but typical space is the cell/corridor combination that organizes some offices. This is based on variable-sized spaces running along a corridor and placed so that each office has a window and corridor connections. This layout might reflect the independence of the occupants and single-use amenities.

Figure 6.4 Office workers in Nestlé building in Vevey, Switzerland, designed by architect Jean Tschumi, 1961.

The shared room or office space is often team-based, with an arrangement of open or screened workspaces. Open plan offers flexibility, through freely arranged workstations, with and without screening. A small open-plan layout would accommodate 4–9 persons; a medium open-plan would suit 10–24 persons; and a large open-plan 25+ persons. Recent research on open-plan offices has shown that closeness to a window and the height of partitions significantly influenced employees' awareness and satisfaction of these spaces. Being near a window apparently reduced distractions and interruptions whilst offering better levels of acoustical and visual privacy. Participants rated higher partitions (140cm) more positively than lower partitions (120cm), indicating the value of the privacy factors (Yildirim, Baskaya, Celebi 2007: 154–165 and see also Figure 6.5).

The Flex office offers individual workstations, planned in relation to actual time spent in the spaces, and therefore has room for less than 70 per cent of the workforce to be in the space at any one time. This type of space has shared amenities.

The Combi office has shared space with back-up spaces for team-working but it allows for both individual and teamwork, as workers using common facilities can move between tasks. Here an

Figure 6.5 Open-plan office with screens, HMS Architects, 2008.

assumption is that less than 75 per cent of work will occur in these spaces. Most interesting is the development that architect and workplace designer Francis Duffy points to as being what he calls 'short-life interiors of offices' (Duffy 1990: 7). He suggests that the office building is much less important than its interior, as it is in the interior where the real interest and activity occurs.

ANALYSIS Casino Interiors

Analysis of the interior design of casinos demonstrates how spaces can engage the users in the world of play. The proprietors of casinos know that the interior has a great impact on the behaviour of players, inasmuch as the gambling environment will influence gaming behaviour. There are two contrasting approaches to these types of spaces. David Kranes (1995: 91–102) sees casino spaces as playgrounds with features that generate positive emotions. Recent research has demonstrated that highly arousing environments increase gambling behaviour (Finlay, Marmurek, Kanetkar and Londerville 2007: 166–175). These emotions connect to the hierarchy of needs and offer features such as lofty ceilings and uncluttered layouts, but all with a feeling of stimulation, awareness and discovery:

What happens with The Mirage [hotel/casino] is the most delicious sort of player 'engagement'. Before one is even aware of the hotel casino, one hears water and sees greenspace. The signature palms are everywhere, planted in very appealing clusters and of varying heights. The carried spray from the falling water takes the edge off the day's reflected heat. Thus the potential player's senses are opened and relax immediately. And from that point, the entry is all enticement and adventure. (Kranes 1995: 99)

Krane's commentary on the moment of accessing the threshold is itself exhilarating: 'Crossing *into* any power-filled space will feel magical, vital, mysterious. The pulse quickens. The lungs fill. One feels a particular charge in the "crossing over." The adrenalin surges; yet it is a focused surge, not the surge of fear or anxiety' (1995: 9).

Bill Friedman, who has made a particular study of marketing these establishments, posits an alternative approach. He suggests that, rather than being barn-like, the interior design of these spaces be segmented; there should not be any long lines of sight or long aisles or passages. Low ceilings and a compact feel are preferable to spaciousness, and the gambling equipment itself should be the focus, not any distracting decorative themes, although there should be some variety in the overall ambience (2000).

Whichever approach the client takes, the impact of interior design on the ultimate success or failure of a casino business is evident.

CASE STUDY 6.1 ANA Intercontinental Hotel, Tokyo, Interior With Screens, 2007

This room was part of a renovation for the club-floor guest rooms on the upper floors of a high-rise hotel that has a commanding view of Tokyo city (Figure 6.6). A Japanese-style suite room was part of this renovation. This room, targeted towards the increasing number of guests from foreign countries as well as family guests, has its interior designed in a modern style with an international touch, whilst still incorporating many authentic Japanese elements. An essential ingredient of a Japanese-style room, the fusuma (sliding door) is located as a partition to divide the room into two. In addition, a glass partition, which sandwiches a hand-made Japanese paper and a pleated screen by the window, is used to bring light into the room softly, as though the light penetrates a paper screen. Other elements, such as tatami, white wood floor, black lacquer furniture and textiles, all express the Japanese taste. In contrast to the hustle and bustle of the city that spreads outside the window, the designer has created a most tranquil Japanese space.

Figure 6.6 ANA InterContinental hotel, Tokyo, ILYA Corporation, 2007.

CASE STUDY 6.2 Angry Monkey Offices, San Francisco, California, *c*.2002

The development of offices by Jensen Architects for this web services company introduces a use of space to allow for great flexibility. The large, open space has playful, custom-built mobile workstations that plug into the overhead power-data-telephone raceway at any point in the office space, allowing employees to relocate easily as job requirements necessitate. Each desk has a formed polycarbonate privacy screen. Other elements in the office include a two-storey-tall plant wall that screens the glare from eastern windows (Plate 17), a tunnel-shaped room that takes its form from the vertical bicycle storage, and a horseshoe-shaped dining counter for lunch and meetings (Figure 6.7). Built-in upholstered banquettes provide extra seating and give the space a relaxed, lounge-like atmosphere in the conference rooms.

Figure 6.7 Angry Monkey office interior with eating bench, San Francisco, c.2002.

CASE STUDY 6.3 Blue Frog Acoustic Lounge, Mumbai, India, 2008

The conversion of a north-lit industrial warehouse into an exciting space that is able to merge theatre, restaurant, bar and club is an interesting development. The performative characteristics of each space type have been integrated through a cellular organization built up from circles of varying sizes in a horseshoe plan. The centre of the plan focuses on a circular dance floor, with a stage at one side and tiered, cylindrical seating on the three other sides. These booths, which seat between four and ten people, are staggered to offer uninterrupted views of the stage but are linked by a glowing acrylic resin surface, which unifies the various sizes of booth. The project also employed acoustic consultants to provide a scheme that would deliver great music experience without disruption from other ambient noises (Figures 6.8–6.12).

Figure 6.8 Blue Frog acoustic lounge, Mumbai, overview of tiered circular seating layout, Serie Architects, 2008.

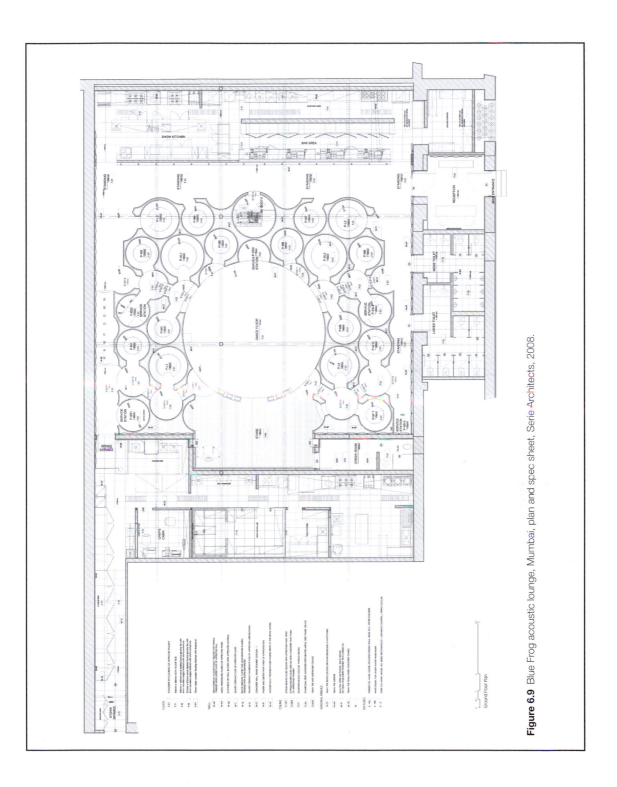

Figure 6.9 Blue Frog acoustic lounge, Mumbai, plan and spec sheet, Serie Architects, 2008.

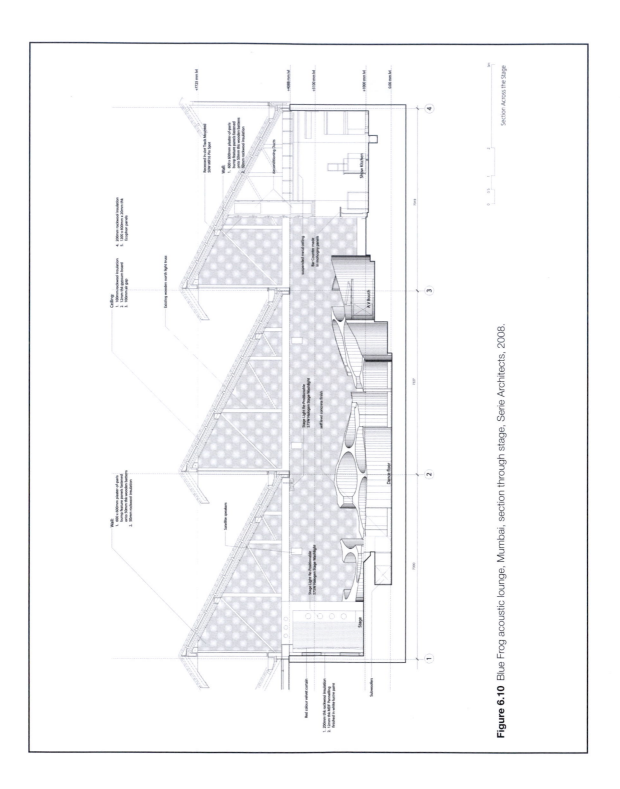

Figure 6.10 Blue Frog acoustic lounge, Mumbai, section through stage, Serie Architects, 2008.

Section Across the Stage

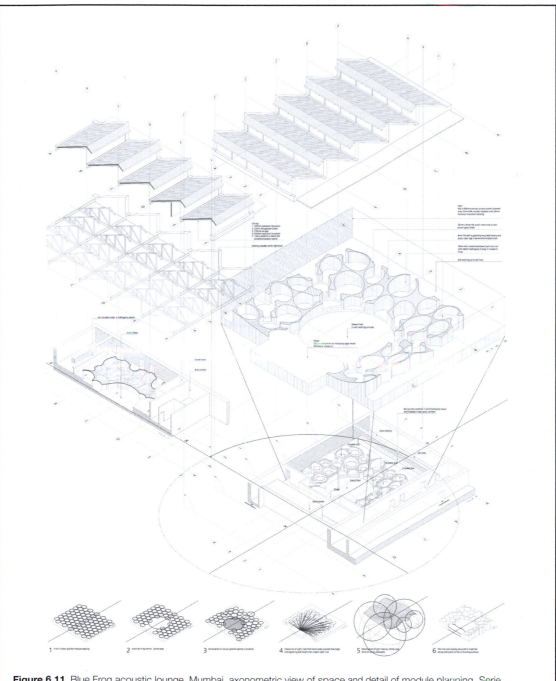

Figure 6.11 Blue Frog acoustic lounge, Mumbai, axonometric view of space and detail of module planning, Serie Architects, 2008.

Figure 6.12 Blue Frog acoustic lounge, Mumbai, detail of seating areas, showing flowing acrylic panels, Serie Architects, 2008.

chapter 7

colour and colour systems

CHAPTER OVERVIEW

This chapter on colour is not particularly involved with the mechanics of colour scheming: rather it considers colour from a variety of points of view, especially the psychological and symbolic aspects. Starting with a discussion about the nature of colour as a phenomenon, the chapter then considers particular colour theories. Colour theories are the backbone of our understanding of how colours work together, as well as providing notating mechanisms. An understanding of the basics of the psychology of colour is essential for designers. Furthermore, an understanding of the ways in which people perceive colour, and how designers can manipulate colour, is also discussed. The chapter then considers some of the myths that have arisen around colour and its use in interiors. The issues of colour perception and cultural symbolism demonstrate that there are no universal colour rules. This indicates that careful consideration of the clients' needs and the contexts of use are more important than colour clichés in an interior. However, mechanisms for colour description are essential to convey meanings, so the chapter moves on to look at colour systems, including the CIE (Commission Internationale de L'Eclairage), the Munsell System and the NCS (Natural Colour System). Finally, there is a brief consideration of the process of colour planning.

what is colour?

Trying to understand colour is not straightforward. The philosopher J.J. Gibson has suggested that: 'the meaning of the term colour is one of the worst muddles in the history of science' (Gibson 1968). It is not just limited to science. A definition to start with, which touches on the multiplicity of colour issues, is that: '... Colour is a sensation, produced in the brain, by the light which enters the eye, and that while a sensation of a particular colour is usually triggered off by the eye receiving light of a particular composition, many other physiological and psychological factors also contribute' (Rossotti 1983: 16).

By unpicking the definition, we can say that light is the key factor in humans' ability to sense colour. There are four fundamental aspects. The first is the nature, quality and quantity of light that will allow us to see colours. Simply, it is the effect produced on the eye and its associated nerves by light waves of different wavelength or frequency. Light transmitted from an object to the eye stimulates the different colour cones of the retina, thus making possible perception of various colours in the object. Second is the nature of the object and particularly its surface in relation to the quantity of light it absorbs, reflects and transmits. Surfaces absorb some wavelengths of light and reflect others. We see the reflected light as the colour of an object. Thirdly, there is the sensitivity of the individual's eye and its ability to register light and interpret it to the brain. Fourthly, there are individual (and cultural) psychological factors that will affect colour perception. Hence, individual perceptions do not necessarily relate to prescribed palettes or definitions.

talking about colour

Jacob von Falke's *Art in the House* (1871) text seems remarkably familiar today, as he discusses colour:

> Ordinarily, and one may say absolutely, colour is of more importance in the decorative appointments of a house than form … It is colour which chiefly gives character to a house, and by its help we may produce any desirable effect. A room may be made to look narrower or broader, lower or higher, by means of colour. If we desire to make it grave or cheerful, bare or rich, simple or splendid; if we would impart to it a cosy and attractive or a poetic aspect, make it look warm or cool; if we would fashion for

ourselves a place to dream in, or one fitted for serious and solitary meditation, or one suited to social enjoyment, our first and last medium is colour. (von Falke 1878: 172)

There is a particular vocabulary of terms associated with colour studies. Colour terms are usually learnt by association, so that objects such as a red sunset, a green field or a yellow sun will identify colour names such as 'red', 'green' and 'yellow'. This does not always follow, as culturally defined objects such as post boxes, for example, differ in colour around the world. Because of this difficulty in definitions, there have been many attempts to systemize colour data.

The first term generally associated with colour is hue, which expresses the basic quality of the colour. In the Munsell notation system, for example, there are five basic hues: red (R), yellow (Y), green (G), blue (B) and purple (P); and five intermediate hues: yellow red (YR), green yellow (GY), blue green (BG), purple blue (PB) and red purple (RP).[1]

Chroma, saturation, intensity and value are also important colour terms. The chroma is the difference from grey at a given hue and lightness in the Munsell system. Saturation refers to the degree of purity of a hue. Intensity is the relative brightness or dullness of a hue. Value refers to a hue's relative brightness, the increments from white to black, with white being the highest value. Those hues with a high content of white have a higher luminance or value.

The Munsell system is one of a number of various schemes considered further below. Firstly, an understanding of the development of colour theory is of value to contextualize the issues.

Plate 1 French bed and wardrobe by George Smith, from his *Collection of Designs for Household Furniture and Interior Decoration*. Engraving, London, England, *c*.1808.

Plate 2 Decorative details of the Moorish villa Wilhelma, Stuttgart, by Karl Zanth, 1851.

A CRAFTSMAN LIVING ROOM, SHOWING RECESSED WINDOW SEAT

Plate 3 Interior of a 'craftsman house' showing recessed window seat, by Gustav Stickley, *c*.1910.

Plate 4 Design for the interior decoration of a stairwell for 44 Belgrave Square, London, by George Aitchison, 1869.

Plate 5 Design for the dining room in the 'House For an Art Lover' by C.R. Mackintosh, 1901.

Plate 6 Breakout area in office interior, with typical Swedish furnishings, 2002, Lena Anderson.

Plate 7 View of the dressing area with built-in combined storage/vanity unit made from single plastic moulding in the 'House of the Future' at the *Daily Mail* Ideal Home Exhibition in 1956, designed by Alison and Peter Smithson.

Plate 8 Japanese Sweet Shop ground floor, 2008.

Plate 9 Interior view of the 'Peppermint Park' bar and restaurant, Upper Saint Martin's Lane, London, 1979.

Plate 10 Drawing of an open reception area, Neil Pearson, 2008.

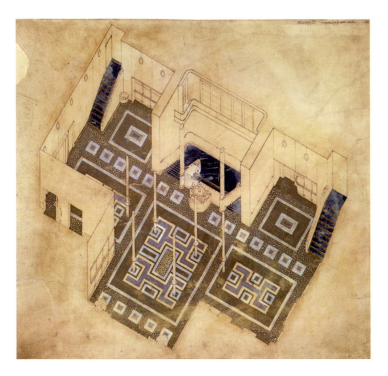

Plate 11 Isometric drawing by Grey Wornum of a design for design for the deck entrance and decorative floor for RMS Queen Elizabeth, 1946.

Plate 12 Octium jewellery boutique preliminary sketch, Jaime Hayon, 2009.

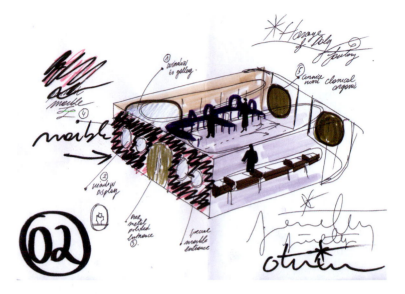

Plate 13 Octium jewellery boutique preliminary sketch, Jaime Hayon, 2009.

Plate 14 Octium jewellery boutique interior overview, Jaime Hayon, 2009.

Plate 15 Room setting of a pied-à-terre for a businessman in the exhibition 'One Room Living' at the Design Centre, London, 1972.

Plate 16 Frank Lloyd Wright, Unity Temple, Oak Park, Chicago, 1906.

Plate 17 Angry Monkey offices San Francisco showing interior plant wall, Jensen Architects, *c*.2002.

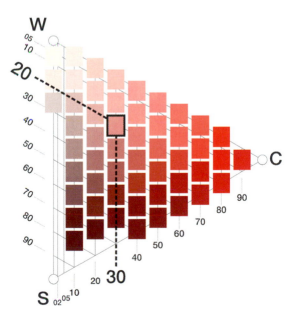

Plate 18 Natural Colour System example.

Plate 19 Example of Swedish interior scheme using the Natural Colour System by Lena Anderson, 2003.

Plate 20 ANA Manza Resort Hotel lobby, by Ilya Corporation 2009.

Plate 21 Jalouse club, London, showing the dynamic moving crystal glass ceiling with over 2,900 glass diamonds, designed by Mark Humphrey, 2009.

Plate 22 Part of dining area in a kitchen-diner; lighting example, by Lighting Design International.

Plate 23 'Wok' lighting dishes in baggage reclaim area, Barajas airport, Madrid, 2006.

Plate 24 Alessi Flagship store, New York, by Hani Rashid, 2006.

Plate 25 Spartanburg Health Center coffee shop.

Plate 26 Barsegh traditional house in Isfahan, 1971.

Plate 27 Baccarat showrooms, Moscow, by Philippe Starck, 2008.

Plate 28 Eames's house, Los Angeles, by Charles and Ray Eames, 1950.

Plate 29 Interior view of open-plan flat on ground floor of Spencer House, Greenwich, London, created in a semi-detached residence dating from 1670, converted by Geoffrey and June Holroyd in 1966. Shows living/dining area with overhanging sleeping area built at higher level at one end of room.

Plate 30 Santa Marta church, Venice, showing reuse as an exhibition and conference venue by Vittorio De Feo, 2004.

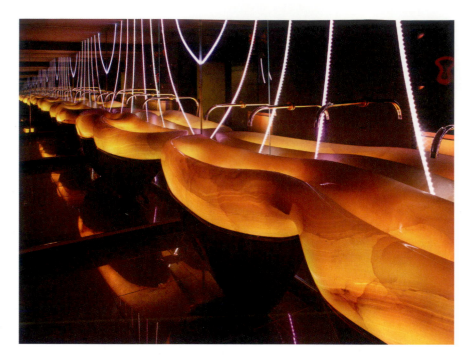

`Plate 31` Solid illuminated onyx vanity basins in Jalouse private members club, London, designed by Mark Humphrey, 2009.

Plate 32 Angry Monkey furniture layout plan, Jensen Architects, *c*.2002.

colour theories

Although artists such as Alberti and Leonardo had long interested themselves in the nature of colour, significant theoretical positions developed in the eighteenth century. The earlier work of Isaac Newton (1643–1727), whose experiments with light demonstrated that a prism could break down white light into a spectrum of colours, influenced these developments. He observed that the coloured light did not change its properties when it illuminated an object, so realized that the colour of a surface is the result of its interaction with already-coloured light rather than being inherent in the object.

Building upon Newton's theories, others were particularly interested in considerations of the effects of colour. One of the main issues was contrast, especially the contrast between opposing hues (complementaries) that created after-images and the contrasting shadows in coloured light. One of the first to investigate these phenomena was the German poet Goethe in his *Theory of Colours* (1810), and a little later, the Frenchman Michel-Eugène Chevreul developed his Law of Simultaneous Colour Contrast (1839).

The law of simultaneous contrast identified by Michel-Eugène Chevreul refers to the manner in which the adjacent colours of different objects affect each other. The influence of the background upon a foregrounded colour is a classic example and has been widely used for a range of visual effects.

The importance of Goethe's work for art and design was that, while Newton saw colour in a scientific way, Goethe saw it from an artistic viewpoint. Unlike Newton, Goethe's concern was

> **Johann Wolfgang von Goethe (1749–1832)**
> Although best known as a writer and all-rounder, his work on colour is still of interest today. In his book *Theory of Colours* (1810), Goethe provides a broad explanation of how we perceive colour in various conditions, and regards Newton's scientific explanations to be very particular. Goethe was not so much interested in the measurement of colour, as he was with colour and its qualities. There is now an accepted difference between Newton's scientific approach to the optical spectrum and Goethe's considerations of the actual perceiving of colours through the human eye.

less with the systematic measurement of colour: rather he was interested in how people really saw colour phenomena. In his *Theory of Colours*, Goethe wrote a general analysis of how people perceived colour in a range of situations. Importantly, the difference that Goethe saw was that the spectrum was not simply light fractured into seven colours, but that there were boundaries that overlap and make other colours.

During the nineteenth century, colour theory developed considerably, particularly through the efforts of Owen Jones, whose mantra was, 'Form without colour is like a body without a soul.' His interior schemes for the 1851 Crystal Palace Exhibition in London used a pale blue for the vertical metalwork of the interior, which probably enlivened the sense of open space. The girders had their undersides finished in a strong red; and he used the same colour for many of the background screens for the exhibits. Finally, any moulded details and the flutes on columns were finished in a yellow. Jones had based his scheme on his understanding of primary colour polychromy derived from his studies of architectural works from Ancient Egypt, Ancient Greece and the Alhambra (see Flores 2006).

During the twentieth century, experimenters highlighted the links between colour and experience even more, as an interest in the psychology of colour developed. The Swiss artist, designer and theorist Johannes Itten stressed in his *Elements of Colour* the importance of broad colour knowledge for the designer: 'The artist (or designer), finally, is interested in colour effects from their aesthetic aspect, and needs both physiological and psychological information' (1970: 12).

In a later work, titled *The Art of Color*, Itten takes the discussion of the emotion and symbolism of colour to extremes: 'Colors are forces, radiant energies that affect us positively or negatively, whether we are aware of it or not … The effects of color should be experienced and understood, not only visually, but also psychologically and symbolically' (1974: 16).

Other artists associated with the Bauhaus in the early twentieth century, including Wassily Kandinsky, Faber Birren and Josef Albers, made advances in colour theory and they emphasized the visual and emotional over the scientific. For example, Josef Albers, in his *Interaction of Color*, stated that his book 'reverses the [previously established] order and places practice before theory, which is after all the conclusion of practice' (1963: 1). In other words, he saw the visual sense as over-riding in practice.

Jean Baudrillard's writing on the use of unexciting 'functional colours', as opposed to bright,

> ### Johannes Itten (1888–1967)
> Johannes Itten was a Swiss expressionist painter, designer, teacher, writer and theorist particularly associated with the preliminary course at the Bauhaus school. In relation to interiors, his publications on colour are most relevant. Itten's approach to colour theory was radical because he considered colour not just through the physics of light but also through how particular colour relationships work when they are adjacent. Itten was also interested in how colour influences individuals both psychologically and spiritually. He argued for the idea that certain colours had innate qualities that would directly influence the viewer and their feelings.

sensual and 'vulgar' natural colours, demonstrates this. By functional colours, he means those that are 'reduced to an abstract conceptual instrument of calculation' (1996 [1968]: 37). In his *System of Objects* he suggests that: 'Colours are now contrasting ranges of shades, their value has less and less to do with their sensory qualities, they are often dissociated from their form, and it is their tonal difference that gives a room its "rhythm" … colours lose their unique value, and become relative to each other and to the whole' (1996 [1968]: 35). An illustration of this approach is in the recent thinking that the sales value of properties that conform to a 'neutral décor' scheme, which thus acts as a blank canvas for potential property buyers, will be beneficial (see Young 2004: 6–10).

psychology of colour

The Perception of Colours

In general terms, perception refers to how people become aware of and understand any sensory information that they receive. People base perceptions on the association between one's past events, one's culture and one's interpretation of the perceptions. If the observation or perception does not make any connections to these bases, it is likely to remain unperceived and therefore unrecognized. In terms of colour, the bases of past events, cultures and perception-processing are clearly crucial. Hazel Rossotti notes that 'since our experience of color is affected by our memory, by our knowledge of what color some object really is, we could claim that our color sensations are, in a sense, influenced by a lifetime of visual experiences' (Rossotti 1983: 17).

Light is the origin of the initial perception of colour. When light falls on an object, some of it is absorbed and some is reflected. The apparent colour of an opaque object depends on the wavelength of the light that it reflects. For example, a red object observed in daylight appears red because it reflects only the waves producing red light. The wavelength of the light transmitted by a transparent object creates the colour seen. An opaque object that reflects all wavelengths appears white; one that absorbs all wavelengths appears black. In addition to the light (and its own variables in terms of level, quality, colour and intensity), the size and shape, the distance from the eye and the other colours in the visual field will all influence its perception.

One of the key background ideas in colour and perception is the concept of its relation to the senses, or, to put it another way – the 'sensuous'. This relates to the idea of perceptions having qualitative sensations. Colours have apparent characteristics – the well-known distinction between warm and cold colours being one – but they can also have associations with weight, smell, sound and taste.

Manipulation of the Senses

Designers can achieve some manipulation of colour perceptions, to a degree, by using the principles of harmony, balance and contrast, for example. Colours can influence perceptions of space, distance and size, and will manipulate these perceptions depending on whether they are associated with, for example, surfaces, volumes, light, texture or shape. The physical reactions influence the perception of colour.

Recent research suggests that the brain does not passively receive the light messages. Rather, through the process of 'colour constancy', the brain decides what colour is perceived in order to ensure that the colour of objects remains reasonably stable under changing lighting conditions. This balance does not mean that we do not perceive differences; we just accommodate them.

Secondly, the phenomenon of simultaneous contrast that involves seeing the same colour as different, depending on its surroundings, has a bearing on both perception and planning. This effect works with every pair of bordering colours. For example, in a scheme with red and blue juxtaposed, the red may make the blue appear 'greeny' because it brings out its complementary colour green in the blue. Conversely, the blue makes the red seem 'orangey' because it stimulates its complementary colour yellow.

Complementary colours[2] of the same intensity placed adjacent to each other produce after-images that heighten our impressions. For example, red or yellow on a black ground appear bright and intense, whereas the same hues on a white ground appear to be darker.

Thirdly, there is the optical mixture that is the opposite of simultaneous contrast. In this process of assimilation, a background colour is, for example, lightened by white and darkened by black. This phenomenon is important in interior design as it affects placement of pattern and lettering, particularly with regard to scale and location. Fourthly, designers can manipulate the sense of spatial dimension, as we perceive distances differently in relation to the colours seen. We often see warm colours (i.e. those with longer wavelengths) as closer than cool colours, for example.

Apart from these physical reactions, colours affect the senses in other ways. They serve as the visual signifiers for the identification and re-identification of physical objects, e.g. red sun, and as conventions, e.g. the red fire engine. Deborah Sharpe suggests that 'man responds to form with his intellect and to colour with his emotions; he can be said to survive by form and to live by colour' (Sharpe 1974: 123). Robert Plutchik has devised a circumplex model that portrays the relations between emotional concepts that are comparable to the colours on a colour wheel. He assigns a colour to each emotion. Other emotional factors then relate to them.[3] These emotional responses are very real for many people so we must regard them seriously. As Baudrillard said above, colours are much more than function alone.

There have been many colour myths that generalize about people's reactions to colours.

For example, it is commonly said that red is exciting or increases hostile behaviour; that blue and green calm and soothe. A number of studies have evaluated the emotional aspects of colour, but overall the results seem to demonstrate ambivalence. However, this does not diminish the potential for colour to affect the emotions, as advertisers well know.

Designers often consider the importance of colour for its apparent ability to affect how we see shapes and size, and how it affects mood. Actual evidence of the influence of colour, however, is notoriously difficult to ascertain. In one experiment from the late 1970s, researchers used pink colours for their apparent 'tranquillizing effect' in a prison cell to try to reduce aggression. By repeating the experiment a couple of years later, it found no reduction in aggression – it was simply the novelty of the colour change that made the difference. However, the idea remained that pink would reduce aggression and many clinics, prisons and other facilities were re-coloured, despite the evidence to the contrary (see Kwallek).

Geoffrey Hayward, writing in 1974, pointed out that: 'colour schemes that have been found to exist with some frequency are assumed to be the ones that *should be* recommended; or architects [and designers] are used as judges and their conclusions are accepted as statements of fact' (in Lang 1974: 125). These colour choices are clearly located in our history, so the significances are not straightforward. In Baudrillard's *System of Objects*, there is a more structured argument against attaching simplistic meanings to colours:

In the traditional system, colours have psychological and moral overtones. Colour may be dictated by an event, a ceremony or a social role ... Tradition confines colours to its own parochial meanings and draws the strictest of boundary-lines about them. ... At the most impoverished level, the symbolism of colours gets lost in mere psychological resonance; red is passionate and aggressive, blue a sign of calm, yellow optimistic and so on; and by this point the language of colours is little different from the language of flowers, dreams or signs of the Zodiac. (1996 [1968]: 31)

Findings from other studies indicate that we associate a space painted in light colours with an open feeling and one painted in dark colours with a closed feeling, that we equate higher social status with darker colours, and that we feel that an environment increases in complexity with higher chromas (deeply saturated colours) and multiple hues (many colours). These generalizations seep into the psyche of the public and become 'facts'. Indeed, some have suggested that colour consultants have 'for the most part included myth, purloined scientific works ... and speculation' in their work (Sharpe 1974: 55).

However, researchers have found that chroma (the degree of saturation of a colour) does have a greater effect upon many of us than does hue. Therefore, it could be argued that stronger colours are arousing and weaker ones calming, irrespective of their particular hues. Taking this further, Frank and Rudolf Mahnke explain that 'Colour variety is psychologically most beneficial. It is not just that one colour is better than another for a specific purpose, that one may be considered psychologically exciting or another calming,

but a variety of visual stimulation and change in atmosphere is required in establishing a sound milieu' (1987: 6). In addition, the evidence from care home environments, for example, suggests that contrast range is more important than colour per se. The contrast perception deficit that is associated with Alzheimer's disease creates a need for careful consideration in the location, signage and colour choices of toilets, for example.

Colour consultant Carlton Wagner identified colours as either classifying or declassifying (1988). In one example, the failure of a store to sell an up-market black and white kitchen in a blue-collar suburb was 'consistent with the socio-economic preference predictions of Wagner, who noted that black/white kitchen interiors were preferred by the top 3% of income levels, while avocado and gold were the preferred hues of lower-middle income families' (Vodvarka 'Aspects of Color').

Wagner suggests that the classifying colours (e.g. those such as dark green, burgundy or dove grey) only have appeal to a relatively small number of people, whereas declassifying colours, such as yellow and orange, appeal to a relatively large segment of the population. This relates to Baudrillard's concept of 'black (or grey) [that] retains the meaning of distinctions of culture, as opposed to the whole range of vulgar colours'. Indeed Baudrillard goes on to comment on the psychology of these 'colours': 'black, white, grey – whatever registers zero on the colour scale – is correspondingly paradigmatic of dignity, repression and moral standing' (1996 [1968]: 31 and 33). For the architect and designer Marcel Breuer, white was 'a very versatile and beautiful colour: at the same time, it is the brightest colour. Living things appear more intense in a bright mono-chrome room' (in Wilk 1981: 184). This Modernist emphasis on the value of white is well known, but it is clear that in certain environments all white spaces can limit visual stimulation. Interestingly, the decorator Syrie Maugham's famous all-white room was given some relief by actually using 'shades' of 'whites' and multiple and varied textures.

colour and cultural symbolism

Colour conveys meanings in two primary ways, either through association of a particular colour with a natural phenomenon, or with culturally defined images. The communication of meaning as culturally determined associations comes from a multi-faceted range of sources.

Anthropologist Marshall Sahlins said: 'a semiotic theory of colour universals must take for "significance" exactly what colours do mean in human societies. They do not mean Munsell chips' (in Gage 1999: 20). Psychologist Mihayli Csikszentmihalyi takes this idea further and points out that the science of colour and the perception of colour are often quite different: 'However, it does not follow that people perceive color according to the analytical rules developed by physical scientists' (1991: 30).

This is a problem for contrived colour schemes with titles such as dyadic, triadic and split-complementary, for example, where the mechanistic function of the colour relationships is all that matters. The artist-educator Josef Albers advocated in 1971 that: 'we may forget for a while those rules of thumb of complementaries whether complete

or "split" and of triads and tetrads as well. They are worn out. Second, no mechanical colour system is flexible enough to precalculate the manifold changing factors … in a single prescribed recipe' (1963: 41–42). Csikszentmihalyi goes on to say 'in western culture, colors are seen in terms of a rational analysis of the physical properties of light. Having learned these properties one can't help but perceive colors in these terms' (1991: 30). However, we ought to temper this rational analysis with both the positive and negative cultural symbolism associated with colours.

These include cultural associations such as the image of green as the colour of eternal life in Japan, while in Ireland and the USA it represents luck. In the case of political or historical associations, the colour of flags and political parties are important sources of identity through colour symbolism. Symbolic religious associations of colour might include reds for the fire of the Sun and the fire of Hell. Any number of listings will identify colours with meanings, most of which are unproven, yet remain highly emotive.

Colour theorists frequently contradict each other, so it seems clear that no overall theories are completely satisfactory. Nevertheless, for all those who work with colour, a form of colour notation is necessary to ensure some consistency of specifications and common understanding, and various systems have been developed.

colour systems

CIE

The CIE system (Commission Internationale de L'Eclairage) is a spectrophotometric measurement of colour in light, which avoids the use of samples or tabs. The CIE's standard chromaticity diagram, based on perceptual-physiological measurements, represents an internationally approved technique of colour identification based on the additive mixing of light. The flat, tongue-shaped structure of the scheme contains colours ('chromaticities') occurring at mean brightness under a 'standard light source'. Used mainly in scientific applications, it deals with light sources and the colour qualities of the materials investigated. However, even as one of the most functional systems, it does not allow for the nature of reflected colour or how it is perceived, for example, and is therefore less valuable for interior applications.

Munsell Colour System

In this well-known system, three attributes describe particular colours: hue, chroma and value, with each colour attribute set out in ordered visual steps. The principle of 'perceived equidistance' is the basis of the system. Munsell introduced one hundred stages for hue, starting with five main colours and five additional colours, and adopts an ordering system with ten units of colour value (degree of lightness) from white (10) to black (1) and an open scale called 'chroma' (similar to saturation). Hue refers to the colour in the spectrum, is the basic name given to the colour, and is identified by a letter code based on the three primary (red R, yellow Y and blue B),[4] and the three secondary, colours (orange O, green G and violet V). The system progresses with tertiary colours that have two letters (i.e. BV for blue-violet) etc. The system designates the lighter colours towards white (i.e. above the middle of

the scale) as tints; below the middle towards black, they are shades. Examples might be BV/9, which would be a very pale lilac colour. Finally, the system divides chroma or degree of saturation or intensity of the colour into up to fourteen stages, from minimum to maximum. Thus, our example would read BV9/3.

Natural Colour System

The Scandinavian Colour Institute has designed a colour system based on how we see colours (NCS website). The NCS system starts with the four chromatic elementary colours, Yellow (Y), Red (R), Blue (B) and Green (G), and the two non-chromatic elementary colours, White (W) and Black (S). They describe colours in terms of their degree of visual resemblance to the elementary colours. These six elementary colours correspond with the perception of colour in our brain. These resemblances are the elementary attributes of yellowness, redness, blueness, greenness, whiteness and blackness. The basis of the NCS colour is how much a given colour seems to resemble two or more of these elementary colours.

All the colours in the NCS System have a percentage of whiteness or blackness, and this is best illustrated using the NCS colour triangle (Plate 18). The NCS colour triangle is a vertical slice through the NCS colour solid. C stands for maximum colour intensity or chromaticness, W stands for white and S for black. The scales for chromaticness, whiteness and blackness are divided into one hundred parts, which are read as percentages. So, in the example of notation '2030-Y90R', the 20 refers to the degree of blackness and the 30 to the intensity, and the amount of white is the balance of 50 (the total must be 100 per cent). The Y90R refers to the colour in reference to the elementary colours defined. Here Y90R means (Y) Yellow with 90 per cent (R) Redness.

Despite an understanding of the science of colour and light, the various colour theories, and the psychology and symbolism of colour, the planning process is at the heart of interior design practice.

colour planning

This process can be understood within a framework that includes four main aspects, the first of which is the role of colour in helping to express the nature of the overall design, e.g. hospital, retail or domestic planning, or of a particular space. Following from this is the use of colour to create the idea of 'place'. Thirdly, its function in understanding particular aspects of the built environment through communication, and lastly is the issue of style, fashion and contemporary concerns about colour in the environment. Johannes Itten sees colour planning as a form of expression:

> To compose in color means to juxtapose two or more colors in such a way that they jointly produce a distinct and distinctive expression. The selection of hues, their relative situation, their locations and orientations within the composition, their configurations or simultaneous patterns, their extensions and their contrast relationships, are decisive factors of expression. (1970: 91)

To begin to encompass these considerations, let us suggest an outline colour-planning process. Initially, a site audit should be undertaken to establish issues such as building orientation, proximity of other properties and whether there are any existing or new architectural or installed features that might influence planning. Secondly, there is the consideration of issues of accessibility and zoning. Thirdly, there needs to be an assessment of the quality and levels of light and how they will influence the scheme. Alongside these functional stages, we could consider the key colours as part of a consistent scheme. Finally, the issues of styling, appropriateness, psychological impacts and preferences will influence the colour choice.

Colour planning is fraught with any number of guides and truisms about how colours work together, their particular psychological effect, and so on. Many of these are grounded in some evidence derived from practice, though they can be limiting and misleading. The needs of the particular project and the client are paramount: and these range from the functional needs that pertain to most situations, such as the requirement of visibility, acuity, stimulation and freedom from ocular fatigue, to the emotional/psychological needs of particular clients or groups of users.

ANALYSIS Colour in Contemporary Hospital Design, 2004–2008

As long ago as 1869, Florence Nightingale was writing about the effects of colour in hospitals. In her *Notes on Nursing* she wrote:

> People say the effect is only on the mind. It is no such thing. The effect is on the body, too. Little as we know about the way in which we are affected by form, by colour, and light, we do know this, that they have an actual physical effect. Variety of form and brilliancy of colour in the objects presented to patients, are actual means of recovery. (1860: 84)

Jean Young made a summary of a recent research report and critical review of the research literature, *Color in Healthcare Environments* for the American Center for Health Design (2004), which showed that 'clearly, the research of color in health care environments is an important endeavour. Yet, the subject matter is complex and multi-faceted. Furthermore, mastering this knowledge for the application of research findings in healthcare settings requires caution, and sensitive creativity is paramount'. Young goes on to say: 'The authors of the color study would advise against the creation of universal guidelines for appropriated colors in healthcare settings. The complexity of user groups and the multiple uses of the environment make efforts to prescribe universal guidelines a waste of energy' (Young 2007).

Finally, therefore, considerations of geography, user characteristics and cultural matters have as great an effect as scientific analysis. Indeed, using an evidence-based approach would mean dismissing many 'pseudo-scientific assertions' and popular beliefs about the nature and impact of colour in these situations (Tofle, Schwartz, Yoon and Max-Royale 2007). This approach could encompass issues around the architecture and wayfinding with colour-defining hierarchies of spaces, landmarks and differentiations. Additionally, the integration of colour and any lighting arrangements will help to avoid problems of light adaptation. Clinical requirements often demand particular colours, for example the use of green for operating theatres to neutralize the after-image from red wounds, and the use of orange to stimulate energy in maternity wards. Textiles and furnishings will also be part of this consideration of colour in hospitals. Each part of the 'patient journey' needs specific consideration (Dalke et al 2006: 343–365).

CASE STUDY 7.1 Pharmacia Offices, Stockholm, 2003

The Swedish interior architect Lena Anderson designed the interiors for Pharmacia's two office buildings in Stockholm and started by having inspiration meetings with the people who work there (Plate 19). This resulted in a collage and the theme, based on 'Time and Space'. Time and Space led to 'Life and Man', which was presented as a poster in red nuances, followed by 'Countryside and Green' in green nuances and then finally to 'Sea and Sky', a poster in blue nuances. One building used blue colours with a little redness, whilst the other had blue colours with some greenness. The colours also changed slightly for each floor. The colour solution, based on warmth through textiles, wood and natural colours and a scheme based on red for life and people, blue for sky and sea, and green for land and flora, related to the environment. In addition, Anderson furnished each of the workplaces with a sit/stand desk with ash top, a personal pedestal in red and birch finish and two low cupboards with oak tops and birch sides. The use of the Swedish-based Natural Colour System helped in creating these schemes.

CASE STUDY 7.2 ANA InterContinental Manza Beach Hotel & Resort, 2009

This hotel is situated on Manzamo, a cape on the East China Sea near Okinawa. The renovation work was part of the re-brand of the hotel. While keeping the company brand reputation, the incorporation of the images of the ocean, using colours that reflected the emerald green waters, blue skies and white sand beaches found in the Manza location, were introduced into the design. The reception area, created by use of blue glass mosaic tiles for the counter, and lighting with blue LEDs, gives the resulting impression of images of waves and the floating ocean outside (Plate 20). The choice of blue as a perceived stable, calming and confidence-inspiring colour complements the connection with sky and water. Blue also appears to have associations with order and salubriousness and a soothing effect. These attributes appear ideal for a hotel reception area. The round waiting benches reflect the symmetry of the reception service desks.

chapter 8

light

CHAPTER OVERVIEW

This chapter considers lighting as a key element in bringing alive an interior design. Commencing with a consideration of the aesthetics of light in relation to space and shadow, it moves to consider the key issue of human needs and the role of lighting in meeting these. Although we divide lighting conveniently into functional, task and accent requirements, there is so much more to what seem simple terms. Planning a lighting project requires an understanding of the needs of the client, the specificity of the space and the users. By consideration of light sources and the role of daylight and artificial light, students can begin to see how to establish the lighting concept and particular criteria for a commission. The chapter also discusses the issues of sustainability and economics.

introduction

Light is electromagnetic radiation with a wavelength of 400–750 nm, derived from the sun or other high heat sources, which makes vision possible. Like other factors in interior design, this simple fact belies a whole range of other issues. These factors include health and safety, sustainable solutions, colour and the type and use of the space, as well as design choices relating to layouts and controls, equipment and luminaire selection, and other light sources and their treatments. However, for our purposes, lighting has three major aspects: the aesthetic/ design aspect, the human needs aspect and the economic aspect.

aesthetics and design

The significance of light as both a concept and a tool is clear. Light is the major enabler in assisting perceptions of interiors; however, it is far more than that. Light enables knowledge of surroundings and it defines various spaces, zones and boundaries within spaces. For Henri Focillon, light is defining. He said of an interior space: 'light not only illuminates the internal mass, but also collaborates with the architecture to give it its needed form. Light itself is form' (1948: 22). This significant role that light plays in creating places out of spaces was taken up by Chris Alexander, who explored the relationship between light and space usage: 'In a building with uniform light level there are few "places" which function as affective settings for human events. This happens because, to a large extent, the places which make effective settings are defined by light' (1977: 645).

These thoughts demonstrate how light, through its defining role, can create aesthetic moods and effects, identify 'place', accentuate form or create shadows in chosen parts of the interior. More than this, light affects our emotions and our physical and mental well-being. Jun'ichiro Tanizaki, writing 'In praise of shadows', considered that:

> The beauty of a Japanese room depends on a variation of shadows, heavy shadows against light shadows – it has nothing else. … This was the genius of our ancestors, that by cutting off the light from this empty space, they imparted to the world of shadows that formed there a quality of mystery and depth superior to that of any wall painting or ornament. (In Taylor and Preston 2006: 335)

The effects of shadows are therefore important in the planning of lighting schemes.

Shadow

Shadow is not only important for creating atmosphere and defining spaces, it also gives information about three-dimensional forms, contours, edges, distances and depth. Cast shadow, for example, is reliant on light, in that an object has its shadow attached (on the opposite side of the light source) and the object casts it. The dramatic photograph of architect Erno Goldfinger's staircase in his 1939 London house demonstrates the startling effect of shadows (Figure 8.1). The value of shadow, based on the comparison of light and dark, was not lost on earlier writers. Alberti, writing on light and shade in the fifteenth century, made an important point: 'Ivory and silver are white; placed next to the swan or the snow they would seem pallid. For this reason things appear most splendid in painting where there is good proportion of white and black similar to that which is in the objects – from the lighted to the shadowed. Thus all things are known by comparison' (1970 [1435–6]: Book One). The same applies to interior design.

Modern science explains that we base our visual perception on the quantity of contrast, not on the quantity of light, as our sight senses are contrast-sensitive. Thus, the direction and distribution of light will affect: the forming of functional zones; the defining of space; the emphasizing of features; the defining of layouts and patterns; and the creation of atmosphere through brightness contrast.

human needs and lighting

Light plays a crucial part in life, so it is little wonder that it is revered and its impact highly valued. Humans react to what they see; therefore, lighting is very important in people's responses to situations and spaces. Lighting can influence people's reaction to spaces in terms of perceiving a sense of pleasantness, relaxation, intimacy, apprehension, clarity and so on. Walter Gropius noted the awe-inspiring, even sacred, image of light: 'Imagine the surprise and animation experienced when a sunbeam shining through the stained

Figure 8.1 (Facing page) Staircase, 2 Willow Road, Hampstead, private house of architect Erno Goldfinger, 1939.

glass window wanders slowly through the twilight of a nave and suddenly hits the altarpiece. What a stimulus for the spectators!' (1962: 41). Indeed, the exploitation of the play of light has been a feature of religious spaces for many centuries. The twentieth-century designer Ettore Sottass, who goes further with the connection between the mystery of light and existence, also considered this sense of drama expressed by light: 'Light does not illuminate, it tells a story. Light gives meanings, draws metaphors and sets the stage for the comedy of life' (in Malnar and Vodvarka 2004: 207). Jean Baudrillard takes this idea further still. Discussing the importance of light and its role in human life, he puts it thus:

> Everything suggests that the source of light continues to be evocative of the origin of all things: even though it no longer illuminates the family circle from the ceiling, even though it has been dispersed and made manifold, it is apparently still the sign of privileged intimacy, still able to invest things with unique value, to create shadows and invent presences. (1996 [1968]: 22)

Whilst acknowledging the fundamental importance of light, we can now consider how to manage it. The pioneer lighting designer Richard Kelly based his ideas on lighting on his concept of 'light energy impacts'. He identified three fundamental types of light: focal glow or highlight, ambient luminescence or graded washes, and the play of brilliants or sharp detail. These relate to the more mundane descriptions of task lighting (focal glow), general lighting (ambient) and accent lighting (play of brilliants).

For Kelly, each of these aspects of lighting defines a particular psychological need as much as an aesthetic/design need (1955). In his example of focal glow, he considers the idea of focus, which is widely recognized and used in numerous examples, ranging from museums to dinner parties. It satisfies the need for visibility, but also creates a mood and an impression of being the centre of attention. The perceived contrast between things and their surroundings is often more important than light levels generally. As dominant colours and brightness attract the eye, so do contrasts in light levels. Therefore, it is sensible to make spatial information relate to colour and light patterns.

Kelly's second example, ambient luminescence, allows for general activity and safe movement. Viewed as a background, it has limited aesthetic input but is likely to reflect codes of practice and relate to energy conservation requirements. People see the brightness of vertical surfaces

---

Richard Kelly 1910–1977

Richard Kelly trained as an architect and lighting designer. He worked with many illustrious architects at the height of Modernism. His particular contribution was to recognize that modern materials needed a new approach to lighting to effect interesting results. His threefold approach worked by giving prominence to objects, lighting whole surfaces and forming sharp details. He used the terms 'focal glow', 'ambient luminescence', and 'play of brilliants' to illustrate his method. He was also a pioneer of recognizing the value of day lighting, long before it was fashionable again.

Figure 8.2 Detail of Cumberland Grill lighting, Cumberland Hotel, London, 1933.

more quickly than the horizontal, so wall-washers create visual boundaries, for example. However, diffused or shadowless lighting will reduce the level of visual cues that help to distinguish spaces.

Thirdly, Kelly describes the play of brilliants, where sparkling light encourages interaction and excitement. Mark Humphrey's crystal ball ceiling for the Jalouse club in London expresses this idea wonderfully (Plate 21). Accent lighting intends to be dramatic, to create a centre of attraction and focus the eye. The impact of well-planned accent lighting in displays such as those found in museums and high-status retail stores are well known. Kelly declares that: 'these three kinds of light make it easier to see (focal glow), make surroundings safe and reassuring (ambient luminescence), and stimulate the spirit (play of brilliants)' (1955). What more could we ask of light? The example of the Art Deco use of light to emphasize shapes, create accents and supply illuminations is clear in the lighting detail of the London Cumberland Grill, completed in 1933 (Figure 8.2).

economic aspects

As regards the economic aspect, issues centre around initial cost, the installation process and matters of maintenance and operation, all of which equate to the total cost of ownership. The energy use and the environmental impact of any lighting scheme need particular attention. The main aim of a scheme is to achieve energy-efficient lighting systems that meet the needs of the users in the most cost-effective manner, whilst meeting energy codes of practice. More specifically, lighting systems need evaluation through effective audits, which will result in recommended changes or specifications. To assist in this, the undertaking of lighting calculations to determine the correct light levels for particular tasks is invaluable. The strategies for determining efficient lighting management relate to this stage. The use of dedicated software to determine the life cycle costs is also a most useful tool, when appropriate.

planning a lighting project

It is clear from Kelly's descriptions that light is both an aesthetic medium and a provider or enhancer of visibility. These in turn relate to the general concerns of lighting as meeting the needs of ambient, task or accent roles. Reference to the three terms as layers is common, as they build up a lighting composition through specific choices to meet the range of needs within a plan. Since light is both a biological and psychological need (impacting on moods and energy levels, for example, particularly in areas with variable light levels and changeable weather patterns), design decisions also need to account for all human needs, not simply be task-based.

General lighting supplies a space with overall illumination. Sometimes called ambient lighting, it is essential for navigating spaces and is the basis of a lighting plan. This is often a single layer of lighting for a whole space, especially in buildings such as schools and offices. The relationship between the ambient light level and any task lighting will determine the visual impact of the space. If the general lighting levels are lower than the task lighting, for example, a more delineated sense of drama will occur.

Task lighting provides light to assist in the undertaking of particular and focussed tasks, usually close to the point of use. Recessed or track lighting, downlighters, pendants and portable lamps all function in this way. Task lighting is important for the health of eyes so should be shadow- and glare-free and be of sufficient power to prevent eyestrain.

Accent lighting produces visual interest in specific parts of a space. Used to highlight art works or other focal points, it draws attention to any features of a space that requires it. To be effective, accent lighting needs to be at least three times the level of the general lighting surrounding it (Plate 22).

Although every project will have different requirements, designers may use lighting to emphasize particular areas, to separate or divide one part of a space from another, to improve orientation or to direct the gaze. The creation of space and shape perceptions with light is normal practice. For example, lit walls will define vertical boundaries, whilst grazing light will emphasize individual parts and elucidate form and texture. Grazing light can also cause highly three-dimensional features to cast strong shadows.

The difficulty arises when designing a lighting plan to be true to the design concept whilst still fulfilling the technical and economic aspects. The best schemes manage to overcome this hurdle well, but as Alexander points out: 'If the places the light falls are not the places you are meant to go toward, or if the light is uniform, the environment is giving information which contradicts its own meaning' (1977: 646).

Lighting is one of the more difficult aspects of an interior to convey to a client, particularly in terms of its qualitative characteristics. The use of models, or hand drawn and computer renderings will help to explain, but the use of 'mood shots' or even better, field trips to see comparable installations will be of great benefit in explaining concepts.

Light Sources

Daylight   The use of daylight presents the designer with the possibility of forming an effectively lit space whilst at the same time reducing energy consumption. In many cases, the existing building will dictate the degree of daylight that can enter the interior spaces, as the layout of windows (including skylights and saw tooth windows) – their size, glass type and orientation – will affect the amount of daylight entering. However, daylight also enters a space via light wells, courtyards, atria and roof monitors. Clearly the climate, and especially the sky conditions, will have an impact on the quantity and quality of light, so its use needs planning in conjunction with artificial light sources.

Artificial Light   Artificial light is constant in quantity, colour and direction but is often static. It needs translation, reflection and careful control. Designer and artist Constanze Kreiser, in a discussion about the mediating effects of light and the attempts to usurp natural light and dark rhythms, points out that: 'Human manipulations of sunlight aim solely at creating inside space. They erect areas of darkness, and then mitigate them by openings in the confining surfaces' (in Taylor and Preston 2006: 181).

On hitting a dense surface, light, whether sunlight or artificial light, is directly reflected, diffusely reflected, absorbed or transmitted in some combination thereof. These phenomena are important when considering the effects of lighting. Lighting designer Gary Gordon points out 'a common mistake when providing light for buildings is to select the lighting equipment first. Selecting luminaires is the last step in the process. What is important is not what makes the light, but which objects and surfaces receive it. The key to successful lighting design is to decide *what* you want to light first, and then work backwards to determine the solution' (2003: 1).

Writing in 1914, not long after the commercial development of the electric lighting system, interior decorator Elsie de Wolfe was fully aware of the need to plan lighting schemes. She said: 'my first thought in laying out a room is the placing of the electric light openings. How rarely does one find the lights in the right place in our over-magnificent hotels and residences!' (1913: 17). Nearly one hundred years later we may have come a long way, but lighting is still a mystery to many, particularly when planning.

Establish the Lighting Design Concept and Criteria

Initially, an exploration of the particular properties that the lighting scheme should possess are generalized in relation to the tasks and other aspects, through an analysis of the space and the needs of the owners/users. The nature of the space and its condition, location and character will clearly have a major influence. Increasingly, specific computer programs that provide examples of light rendering and quantitative calculations can aid lighting design. By combining direct and reflected artificial light with daylight, the programs can provide luminance guides for specific geographic locations.

A quantitative design plan has to consider the industry standards that will determine particular aspects of the plan, such as the quantity of light, the degree of glare limitation, and the source and colour of the light. The degrees of stimulation needed to perform tasks in a space will affect this planning. To relate activities to stimuli, an analysis of brightness contrast is required.

Brightness Contrast As the sense of sight is contrast-sensitive, so the degree of brightness contrast in a space will stimulate the user in proportion to the levels found. Environmental psychologists define high-load and low-load stimulation levels. In the context of spaces, high-load levels are those that are difficult, multi-faceted, or just different. Those that are unchallenging, open, symmetrical or ordinary are low-load.

The degree of brightness contrast therefore sets the stimulation levels, which will then assist or interfere with the planned action or activity. High levels of contrast encourage participation and increase enjoyment, whereas lower levels create feelings of comfort, relaxation and contentment. The lower the task stimulation, the greater the need for strong brightness contrasts. This process of establishing concepts and criteria should also record any architectural constraints and conditions so that the designer can form the sub-space in response to identified architectural constraints and conditions, in relation to the overall scheme.

Activities and Lighting The next step suggests guidelines for illumination that stipulate individual solutions to the particular aspects of the lighting plan, i.e. ambient, task, general. Again, other factors such as penetrations into other spaces, accesses, spatial flow, the entrance of daylight and the orientation to sunlight will affect it.

Generalized approaches include ways of responding to the spaces. For example, to create an agreeable but unchallenging space, the designer might specify wall lighting in conjunction with a low brightness contrast ratio, as opposed to ceiling-mounted lights. In a public space, more illumination with a consistent level of light supplied from overhead lighting fitments might be more appropriate. To create a sense of space, even distribution of the overall lighting is a useful approach. For specific task-orientated work, levels of light should support the activity/task areas but also with support from secondary illumination.

Considerations that are more specific would include thinking about architectural features and how to deal with them. In other words, do we hide them or highlight them? In addition to the architectural features, the relationship between the lighting plan and the furnishings needs consideration. A distinction between the permanent and the moveable needs to be made, including partitions, counters and workstations, for example. All of this relates to the nature of the role of the interior and are important for a satisfactory result. In this regard, lighting designers plan in relation to circulation paths. In addition to these aspects, the influence of colour selection, the textures and brightness of finishing materials and the identification of focal points are part of the process.

Specification   Only at this stage will designers make the actual specification of light sources, based on practical, economic and energy-efficient controls systems, all considered in relation to the pre-conceived layers. During this stage, decisions are made regarding the particular types and models of equipment that will be utilized, how and where the fixtures will be located and connected, and with what appropriate control methods and systems (Figure 5.17).

CASE STUDY 8.1 Barajas Airport, Madrid, 2006

Lighting large, enclosed public spaces poses a particular challenge. This award-wining airport (the eleventh RIBA Stirling Prize), by Richard Rogers Partnership/Estudio Lamela, has an interesting lighting scheme designed by Speirs and Major Associates for the lower-level baggage reclaim areas (Plate 23). It uses a circular ceiling luminaire, in a shape that has become known as 'the wok'. These large-scale (1.5 metres diameter) fittings meant that a suspended ceiling across all the area was unnecessary, thus saving a considerable cost. However, the effect is of a complete roof of light. This arrangement means that reflected light lights the 'woks'. This has the effect of drawing the eye to the fitting rather than to the bare ceiling above. The designer developed the fittings so that they would provide direct downlighting and some reflected light bouncing from a reflector ring fitted below the downlight.

CASE STUDY 8.2 Lighting in Austin Reed, Regent Street, London, 1929

The menswear store Austin Reed of Regent Street was redeveloped in the 1920s by Percy J. Westwood and Joseph Emberton. In 1929, they installed the amazing 'snake-like' architectural light fitting in the barber's shop in the basement (Figure 8.3). Like many other Art Deco lighting installations, the effect was both decorative and functional. The scale of the fitting dominates the space, which not only reflects light onto the chrome, marble and frosted glass interior, but also acts as task lighting for the barber's work. This space, sometimes called a 'tonsorial Taj Mahal', demonstrates that there is little doubt that the light fitting is as responsible for the luxury ambience and effects as the sumptuous materials employed elsewhere in the interior.

Figure 8.3 Austin Reed Barber's shop, London, Joseph Emberton and Percy Westwood, 1920s.

CASE STUDY 8.3 Alessi Flagship Store, New York, 2008

The renovated loft building, with a narrow 4-metre frontage that only widens slightly to 6.5 metres at the rear, was a challenge for designers Asymptote Architecture (Plate 24). They used a pale blue and cloud-white palette to allow the deep space to become light, airy and delicate. The use of lighting techniques linked to stage design methods were planned to draw customers into the deep space. The angular 'proscenium arches' that graduate down the space are highlighted by 46-centimetre-wide light bars that emphasize the shaped arches, and continue down to highlight the small displays in the wall. The angles vary as the eye moves into the space. Specialist lighting designers Tillotson Design Associates designed these 'light boxes' to help distinguish the functions of each part of the space. The designers explain:

Constructed from medium-density fiberboard (MDF) and stretched Barrisol fabric, the boxes conceal T5 fluorescent fixtures, three per vertical wall element and three per horizontal ceiling element. Rather than use dimmers, which would have exceeded the project's budget, the lighting designers set each fixture on an individual switch. Standard 37W halogen MR16 recessed downlights with custom snoots, arranged in clusters of five, four, and two, make up the remainder of the store's general illumination. (*Architectural Light. Mag.*)

chapter 9

human needs and factors

CHAPTER OVERVIEW

This chapter deals with the needs of clients and users of interior spaces. An understanding of human needs and body-centred factors are crucial tools in the interior designers' kit. Starting with Abraham Maslow's hierarchy of needs, which discusses the needs of humans in an ascending scale from physiological needs, safety needs, affection needs and esteem to self-actualization, the chapter analyses the basic and crucial safety needs of humans, in relation to interiors and well-being. A somewhat neglected aspect of interiors – the sensory needs of people – follows this. Linked to this is an examination of the role of emotions in relation to interiors. Finally, the chapter examines the importance of inclusive design, which embraces 'design for all', and 'universal design'. Two particular examples are then discussed, office spaces and healthcare interiors, followed by a feature on health and the built environment.

introduction

Although human needs and factors have always been a part of the agenda for designers, there has been an increased awareness of these factors over the last fifty years. The impacts of ergonomics, developments in health and safety practices, occupational therapy, accessible design, and barrier-free planning and design, have all improved designed responses to human needs. In addition, much work has been undertaken on the psychological and emotional needs of humans, including the evaluation of mixed user groups, consideration of special demographic groups, the psychology of individuals, and the sociology of groups, to name but a few. Architects Kent Bloomer and Charles Moore have suggested that 'architecture to the extent it is considered an art, is characterised in its design stages as an abstract visual art and not as body-centred art' (1977: x). In that sense, interior design is the opposite of this, in that the interior designer has a greater responsibility for the addressing of 'body-centred' or human needs within the shell of the built environment, as their focus is often as much on these as it is on the aesthetic or 'visual art' of the interior.

The nature of human needs and body-centred factors are wide and demanding. Some are relatively straightforward to deal with, as they relate to functional and physical resources, while others are more elusive. These elusive demands include, for example, attention to orientation and movement as well as sensory needs, but also the subtler concepts such as identity and status; meaning and symbolism of interior spaces; the personalization of space; the 'quality of life'; and issues around territoriality. Consideration of the 'life cycle stages', accepted norms in particular cultures, and issues around social interaction, behaviour and performance, are also important in relating environments to human needs. Therefore, an understanding of concepts such as 'human-centred design', 'universal design' and the needs of special users' groups are crucial for twenty-first century designers.

These concepts, which have connections with values and ethics, generally comprise the issues of inclusiveness (equitable use), choice (flexibility in use), clarity (simple and intuitive use; percep-tible information), safety (tolerance for error) and comfort (low physical effort; size and space for approach and use). Analysis of the various levels of needs is a useful tool for trying to appreciate people's requirements over a range of levels.

maslow's hierarchy of human needs

According to psychologist Abraham Maslow, human beings have a 'hierarchy of needs', ranging from basic survival and safety needs to higher-level needs that strive for intellectual stimulation and self-realization (Maslow 1943). The hierarchy works on the basis that only when the lower-level needs (survival, safety, belonging and self-esteem) are satisfied can the higher-level needs (intellectual success, aesthetic enjoyment and self-actualization) be addressed. People's strongest need usually determines their behaviour at any particular moment. The application of this to the work of interior designers is evident in that they need to consider the complete inter-relationship between the physical, emotional and spiritual needs of their clients, thus connecting to the hierarchy at all levels.

Physiological Needs

These are the biological needs. They are the strongest needs, as they will come first in the person's search for satisfaction.

Safety Needs

Once all the physiological needs are satisfied to an acceptable degree, the security needs become active. Although adults are not usually directly aware of their own security needs other than in emergencies or stressed situations, chil-dren frequently show the need to be secure.

Need for Love, Affection and Belongingness

People reach this level when they begin to seek to conquer feelings of loneliness and estrangement. This requires the giving and receiving of love, caring for self and others and having a sense of belonging.

Need for Esteem

When the three basic needs are satisfied, the esteem need can become foremost. By having a high level of self-respect, as well as respect from others, people will feel self-confident and valued as an individual within society. When this is missing, they will be frustrated and suffer from feelings of inferiority and worthlessness.

Need for Self-actualization

When all of the previous needs are properly satisfied, the needs for self-actualization arise. Maslow describes self-actualization as a person's need to be and do that which the person was 'born to do'. These needs make themselves felt in signs of restlessness. Whilst it is easy to see when the first four needs are missing, it is not always clear when self-actualization is missing in someone's life. Understanding the basis of these needs can give the designer an insight into human nature,

a valuable asset when assessing reasons why particular designs succeed, where others fail.

Fifty years after Maslow, the development of a variation of the hierarchy of needs, by Chilean economist Manfred Max-Neef, provides particular interest for interior designers, as it focusses on needs rather than wants (Figure 9.1). Space is one of the four states that satisfy needs (Elkins and Max-Neef: 1992: 206–207). The difference between this approach and that of Maslow is that there is no order of preference above subsistence, and that the basis of the scheme relates the needs to particular satisfiers. For interior designers, the correspondence between needs, actions and spaces is instructive.

Fundamental Human Needs	Being Qualities	Having Things	Doing Actions	Interacting Spaces
Subsistence	Physical and mental health	Food, shelter, work	Feed, clothes, work	Living environment, social settings
Protection	Care, adaptability and autonomy	Social security, health systems, work	Co-operate, plan, take care	Social environment, dwelling
Affection	Respect, sense of humour, generosity, sensuality	Friendships, family	Share, take care of, express emotions	Privacy, intimate spaces for togetherness
Understanding	Critical capacity, curiosity, intuition	Literature, teachers, education	Analyse, study, investigate	Schools, universities, communities
Participation	Receptiveness, dedication	Responsibilities, duties, work, rights	Co-operate, dissent, express opinions	Associations, parties, churches, neighbourhoods
Leisure	Imagination, tranquillity, spontaneity	Games, parties, peace of mind	Dream, remember, relax, have fun	Landscapes, place to be together/alone
Creation	Imagination, inventiveness, curiosity	Abilities, skills, work, techniques	Invent, build, design, compose, interpret	Spaces for expression, workshops, audiences
Identity	Sense of belonging, self-esteem, consistency	Language, religion, work, customs, values	Get to know oneself, grow, commit oneself	Places one belongs to, everyday settings
Freedom	Autonomy, passion, open-mindedness	Equal rights	Dissent, choose, run risks, develop awareness	Anywhere

Figure 9.1 Manfred Max-Neef's scheme of human needs.

Rudolf Arnheim adds an interior-specific comment to this analysis when he reminds us that the priorities of human needs are by no means self-evident: 'Dignity, a sense of pride, congeniality, a feeling of ease – these are primary needs. … And since they are requirements of the mind, they are satisfied not only by good plumbing, heating and insulation, but equally by light, congenial colours, visual order, well-proportioned space, and so forth' (1977: 3). It is clear then, that the interior designer has a degree of responsibility to help achieve these harmonious states.

health and safety

The basic human need for safety is manifest in interiors in many ways. An interior space may be a place of refuge for the individual, or a social or working environment that is free from interference. Designers have not only to consider human values here, but also performance and legal issues, especially in the areas of ergonomics and environmental control.

Ergonomics, for example, aims to improve safety, efficiency, economy and usability for consumers, through product development and use-analysis. Ergonomics uses objective and wide-ranging standards for designed products and spaces that appear to relate well to human-centred design. Originally, the nature of much ergonomics related to military, workplace or procedural work-study applications, thus ignoring individual emotions, performance abilities and choices.

Environmental controls affect the health and safety of users of spaces in various degrees. For example, a major issue arising from the enclosed spaces in which people operate is the concentration of certain airborne compounds (VOCs or Volatile Organic Compounds), which could, if not dealt with, cause health problems. Pollution of indoor air due to lack of exchange between interiors and exteriors is the main culprit. The so-called sick building syndrome is partly a result of this. Multiple chemical sensitivity (MCS) is another name for it. It is important to recognize that this is not just a workplace phenomenon; it is probably more likely to occur in unregulated spaces such as the domestic home.

Poor indoor air quality (IAQ) is created not so much by the particular organic or inorganic matter itself, but rather by the interactions between them, although clearly some particular problems, such as tobacco smoke, are irritants in their own right. Designers have a responsibility to understand and avoid off-gassing contaminants such as formaldehyde, VOCs, dust traps, radon, carbon monoxide, etc. To partially alleviate the problem, designers can employ natural materials and products such as planting, as well as specifying more mechanical means such as ventilation and humidity, in locations that are under the control of an individual.

the sensory element

Our needs clearly relate to the sensory aspects that link our internal responses to external stimuli. Although we usually give the visual a high priority, other responses are equally valid. The auditory response to sounds and noise; the haptic or tactile that responds to material qualities; taste and smell (air); temperature/humidity; and basic orientation alignments (NSEW) – all affect our response to an environment.

Architect Juhani Pallasmaa, in his *Architecture of the Seven Senses*, is concerned with the apparent over-emphasis on the visual to the detriment of our other senses. He suggests that more consideration be given to aspects of the design that have a bearing on, for example, acoustics, tranquillity, scents, touch, muscle and bone, bodily identification and visual taste. He says: 'A building is encountered—it is approached, confronted, related to one's body, moved about, utilized as a condition for other things, etc. ... We are in constant dialogue and interaction with the environment, to the degree that it is impossible to detach the image of the self from its spatial and situational existence' (1994: 30). As an example, he considers the symbolism of the staircase:

Visual System	Color, material pattern, size of staircase, location of staircase in space and whether in an enclosed or open space
Auditory System	Tread made of material that emits tone when stepped on or tapped with a cane
Taste-Smell System	Venting to include whiff of fragrance to indicate stair room or beginning and end of stair run
Basic Orienting System	Continuous run or changes in direction Rectangular or spiral
Haptic System Touch	Treads – material texture gradient, and change of degree of hardness; selection of material for its thermal conductivity to facilitate temperature transfer when walking barefoot Railings – material texture gradient (rough vs. smooth) and change in degrees of hardness (rubber vs. steel), thermal conductivity (copper vs. wood), drag (leather vs. marble) Vibration transfer between treads and railing or mechanical system and railing
Kinesthesia	Change in tread to riser ratio to decrease or increase exertion and speed of person (take into consideration stair typically thought of as going below ground level or up into attic or loft space) Landings to provide moments of rest
Temperature and Humidity	Heating and air-conditioning vent located at ankle, hand, or head height to indicate first and last treads Air vents located at top and bottom of stair to coincide with direction of main movement on stair Distinct air velocity, temperature and/or humidity change at top and bottom of stair

Figure 9.2 Sensorially designed staircase proposal. (Table created by Joy Malnar and Frank Vodvarka. Used with permission.)

The qualitative differences of ascending and descending derive from the images of Heaven and Hell. Stairs appear frequently in literature, cinema and painting due to their extraordinary image power. The staircase is simultaneously a stage and an auditorium. It is also a vertical configuration of the labyrinth with consequent associations of vertigo, and getting lost. Our human reality has become threateningly concrete and one-dimensional, as the environment has lost its symbolic dimension. (2000: 7–18)

The 'sensory stairs' devised by Joy Malnar and Frank Vodvarka demonstrate a practical example that involves the senses (Figure 9.2).

the emotional element

The factors of affection, esteem and self-actualization all link to emotions. The expression of emotional responses in general are as 'short and reflexive', where the response is to a particular aspect or element, or as 'sustained and reflective' responses that are dependent upon the environment (mood). It is clear that interiors are prime sites for emotional responses of both kinds. As emotional experiences are individual, environments should provide 'stimuli for new experiences, extenders for current experiences and proxies for past experiences' (DiSalvo, Hanington and Forlizzi, in McDonagh et al. 2004: 253–254.), as related to the individual user.

Features including actions/interactions, sensory stimulation, enjoyment, physical attributes, style, symbolism and utility, sense of place, preference and attitude all trigger emotional responses. People process environmental information to increase their chances of 'survival' and to improve their welfare. People need to make sense of, and acquire additional information about, their environment to predict what might occur, then plan their actions accordingly. In this sense, most people prefer environments that are engaging rather than dull.

Environmental psychologists Rachel and Stephen Kaplan have identified four dimensions of information that they organized into a 'preference matrix' or framework. It seems clear that certain attributes of interiors will add to people's preference for an environment. The Kaplans' four dimensions were coherence, legibility, complexity and mystery. Coherence refers to the degree to which a scene 'hangs together'. The more coherent, the greater the preference. Legibility refers to how we make sense of the environment in which we find ourselves. The greater the legibility or degree of distinctiveness that enables one to understand the context of a scene, the greater the preference will be. The third dimension is complexity or involvement, where an increase in the number and variation of elements involved creates a greater preference. Finally, the fourth dimension is mystery, or the promise of involvement or hidden information suggested or implied in order to draw one in to find out (in Bell, Greene et al. 2001 :43–45). These would all appear to be necessary for comfort, function and stimulation. The lack of any of these factors may lead to dissatisfaction, stress or even illness. On the other hand, too much complexity can over-stimulate and confuse people, causing decreased preference and discomfort.

Both external and internal triggers cause human stress. External ones include impacts from the environment such as noise, crowding, temperature extremes and under- or over-stimulation. Internal symptoms relate to interpersonal conflict, low self-esteem, disorganization and worry. Interior designers can help to alleviate these symptoms by addressing the sources over which people have some control. We can restore equilibrium by using noise-reduction techniques, through materials choice, by offering visual escape in the form of interesting interior landscapes, and by allowing individual control over air quality and ambient temperatures.

inclusive design

Inclusive design has the same general meaning as other terms such as 'Design for All' and 'Universal Design'. It is probably a more useful term, as it does not indicate some universal solution that deals with all eventualities. It is also important to distinguish inclusive design from accessibility. The latter refers to the minimum legal compliance levels for access to internal spaces. In practice, inclusive or universal design means providing design solutions that will empower the widest possible groups throughout their lives. Imrie and Hall suggest that inclusive design 'is part of a lineage of ideas which seek to prioritise building users' views and values and to challenge the social and institutional, as well as the technical relations of design and building processes' (2001: 18).

Design for All
Design for All is an approach to design in which all involved parties make sure that their products and environments address all users, irrespective of their age or ability. The European Institute for Design and Disability defined design for all in its Stockholm declaration of 2004:

> Design for All uses the concept of inclusion as its goal to ensure that mainstream design practices are not excluding the needs of potentially marginalized people. To achieve this, designers and other parties will join with particular user groups to ensure they take into account the diversity of users.
>
> Design for All is design for human diversity, social inclusion and equality. This holistic and innovative approach constitutes a creative and ethical challenge for all planners, designers, entrepreneurs, administrators and political leaders.
>
> Design for All aims to enable all people to have equal opportunities to participate in every aspect of society. To achieve this, the built environment, everyday objects, services, culture and information – in short, everything that is designed and made by people to be used by people – must be accessible, convenient for everyone in society to use, and responsive to evolving human diversity.
>
> The practice of Design for All makes conscious use of the analysis of human needs and aspirations and requires the involvement of end users at every stage in the design process. (© Declaration of the European Institute for Design Disability, Stockholm, 2004)

Universal Design
Universal design is a term based on seven principles laid down by architect and designer Ron Mace. The Center for Universal Design

at North Carolina State University states that universal design is the design of products and environments to be usable by all people, to the greatest extent possible, without the need for adaptation or specialized design. The intent of universal design is to simplify life for everyone by making products, communications and the built environment more usable by as many people as possible at little or no extra cost. The Center for Universal Design at NC State University has identified seven principles for defining Universal Design:

PRINCIPLE ONE: Equitable Use
The design is useful and marketable to people with diverse abilities.

PRINCIPLE TWO: Flexibility in Use
The design accommodates a wide range of individual preferences and abilities.

PRINCIPLE THREE: Simple and Intuitive Use
Use of the design is easy to understand, regardless of the user's experience, knowledge, language skills, or current concentration level.

PRINCIPLE FOUR: Perceptible Information
The design communicates necessary information effectively to the user, regardless of ambient conditions or the user's sensory abilities.

PRINCIPLE FIVE: Tolerance for Error
The design minimizes hazards and the adverse consequences of accidental or unintended actions.

PRINCIPLE SIX: Low Physical Effort
The design can be used efficiently and comfortably and with a minimum of fatigue.

PRINCIPLE SEVEN: Size and Space for Approach and Use
Appropriate size and space is provided for approach, reach, manipulation, and use regardless of user's body size, posture, or mobility.

(©1997 NC State University,
The Center for Universal Design)

Inclusive/Universal Design in Relation to Interiors

Interior designers must not only express a concern with the meaning and context of the spaces to the client and user (if different), but also act upon them. This allows for a participative, human-oriented design approach. This may mean educating users in new design attitudes relating to cost, appropriate technology and sustainability.

ANALYSIS An Office Environment

Various issues come together in an analysis of the human needs within a work environment. Broadly, these needs are physical and functional, socio-psychological and aesthetic.

The physical and functional needs relate to task-performance issues and range from bodily comfort to the ambient 'feel' of the environment. Addressing the ease of access to other people and appropriate equipment, the opportunities for open and effective communication, and the ergonomics of equipment will influence the functional efficiency of the environment. Part of the address to the physical needs of the space-users include ensuring freedom from excessive noise, appropriate light quality and levels, the freshness and movement of clean air, an appropriate temperature and humidity controls.

The socio-psychological needs connect to the functional needs at one level, since the opportunity to have discretion and control over the immediate physical environment is important to people. In office situations, it is essential to offer workers opportunities for privacy and the ability to control access to spaces. A well-known aspect of psychological needs in offices is the desire for individuality and personalization. This manifests itself through personally adapted spaces to establish identity through particular markers such as furnishings, photos and personal objects in a workplace. In conjunction with this is the need for status recognition. This may be quite subtle or blatant. For example, the particular office location (for example a corner with two windows) or the selection of chair type may indicate particular status (Hermann Miller Co.).

It may seem obvious, but attractive working surroundings that contribute to a pleasant and enjoyable work setting will improve productivity and satisfy a number of needs. Aesthetics is associated with the colour, forms and textures of a space, along with the arrangement of furniture and other features. In one experiment, symbolism had no effect on employee efficiency or satisfaction, but may have had an effect on non-employed users, for e.g. visitors and clients (Vilnai-Yavetz, Rafaeli and Yaacov 2005: 533–551).

The influence of age on the design requirements of a workspace has been analysed by Virginia Kupritz. Her research has found that age differences were enough to warrant changes in office planning to ensure equal opportunities for efficient performance. This is particularly relevant in the twenty-first century as the mean age of workers rises. Kupritz's results show some expected similarities between the two observed groups of office staff with some supervisory roles (one of 60 years plus; the other 35–50 years). Both groups rated a large personal office as number one, but the older group considered floor to ceiling solid walls as their third choice, as opposed to the younger group who rated it eighth. Other significant variations in ratings referred to space to spread out work for the younger group (second feature) and having up-to-date IT facilities for the older group (second feature) (Kupritz 2004: 110–121).

All these examples seem to point to the need for flexibility in the design, layout and arrangement of office spaces.

ANALYSIS Healthcare Design

Traditionally based on the needs of the staff, healthcare facilities now acknowledge the patients' perspectives on healthcare environments and their interior design, as being of considerable importance in the healing process. A number of studies have evaluated the issues that patients found most important. An understanding of these needs will clearly assist in the interior design planning processes. The work of the American Picker Institute and the Center for Health Design identified eight areas of experience of healthcare facilities that they deem important. They may appear self-evident but the obvious lack of these in use identified room for improvement. The important factors are that the spaces:

* Offer a connection with staff which allowed speedy visual and physical access;
* A sense of well being that assists the management of and recovery from illness;
* Convenience and accessibility including parking, wayfinding, and movement around spaces;

Figure 9.3 Spartanburg Regional Gibbs Cancer Center, South Carolina, LeVino Jones Medical Interiors Inc., 2000.

Figure 9.4 Spartanburg Regional Gibbs Cancer Center, South Carolina, LeVino Jones Medical Interiors Inc., 2000.

- Confidentiality and privacy;
- Caring for the family's needs when attending patients;
- Consideration of impairments and issues relating to universal design;
- A connection with the outside world, through windows, for example;
- Safety and security to reduce vulnerability issues.

(Stern et al. 2003: 20–21)

More specifically, there exists a range of issues facing designers of hospital spaces. These include issues around efficiency and cost effectiveness of the services offered including, for example, no redundant spaces, visual contact between patient and nurses and reduced travel distance between frequently used spaces and functional adjacencies. There is also a clear need for flexibility and expandability, often achieved by modular planning. Environments are never neutral and can create effects that may be either positive or negative. It is clear that the use of natural light, familiar natural materials and textures, where possible, and the display of artworks all make the medical environment more comfortable. The interior designer also needs to ensure that proportions, colour, scale and detail of spaces are appropriate. For example, generously scaled, bright, open public spaces compared with more domestic and intimately scaled patient rooms, day rooms, consultation rooms and offices.

The example of the Spartanburg Regional Gibbs Cancer Center in Spartanburg, South Carolina, by LeVino Jones Medical Interiors Inc. and F.A. Hunter, demonstrates a contemporary approach to hospital care design (Figures 9.3 and 9.4). The designer combined the treatment facilities, medical offices, education and conference centre, and an oncology retail area into a set of spaces that provide a comprehensive and linked facility for patients. However, the overall effect makes reference to leisure facility and hotel spaces. The designers integrated all architectural detailing, finishes, furnishings, artwork and signage.

ANALYSIS The Built Environment and Health

Unless designers and architects address the underlying issues, it is clear that buildings and environments will contribute to ill health. Gary Evans and Janetta McCoy identify five identifiable environmental dimensions that inter-relate with health, and in particularly to stress. These are stimulation, coherence, affordance, control and restoration. The researchers have posited that 'each of these dimensions, in turn, consist of explicit interior design elements' (1998: 85–94). Stimulation relates to the quantity of information received from an interior; too much creates overload; too little, boredom. Coherence relates to the idea of readability, certainty and orientation; the lack of any will cause varying degrees of stress. Affordance relates to the functional reading of spaces and relates to the 'distance' between the design concept and the user's needs and abilities. Control offers choice, privacy and feedback from the spaces. Again, negativity in this field will cause stress. Finally, the restorative element suggests the therapeutic qualities to help reduce stress and uplift the spirit.

The importance of improving life for people was one of the guiding ideals behind the Modern Movement of the 1930s. The example of the Finsbury Health Centre in London, designed by Lubetkin and Tecton, was an important landmark. Figure 9.5 shows one of a set of explanatory drawings prepared for an exhibition in Finsbury Town hall explaining features of the design. The Finsbury Health Centre was an attempt to rationalize the borough's health provision by providing, on a single site, a wide range of facilities, the needs of some of which could alter radically with time. Architectural and medical critics alike hailed Lubetkin and Tecton's solution as a prototype and an important and radical break with traditional health provision. Although the style has changed in contemporary work, the sentiments remain the same.

Figure 9.5 Explanatory drawing depicting the 'cheerful atmosphere' of the Finsbury Health Centre, London, 1938.

chapter 10

decoration and ornament

CHAPTER OVERVIEW

Decoration has been part of human surroundings for thousands of years. This chapter considers what decoration and ornament are in terms of interiors and why they are important. These issues are analysed through a discussion of the functions of ornament, which will help to explain their use and need in interiors. We can divide the functions of ornament into four sections: the symbolic function, the qualifying function, the ordering function and the decorative function. The symbolic refers to significations that have resonance with society or culture. The qualifying function considers ornament as an expression of identity, while the ordering function reflects aspects of design thinking. The decorative function of ornament considers the aesthetic or sensual aspects of a space and its relations with its users. Decoration and its associated symbolism, which offers a personal reading of an interior, introduce the question of collections and roomscapes. Finally, the chapter introduces the role of crafts as an important element in contemporary design, as innovative technologies combine with traditional skills to create new and exciting possibilities for individual decorative works.

introduction

From the caves of Lascaux through to the excesses of the Baroque, from Loos's considerations of 'ornament and crime' to the contemporary re-evaluation of the role of ornament in design, decoration and ornament remain crucially important elements in interiors.

In one definition, decoration is the 'furnishing or adorning of a space with fashionable or beautiful things' (Pitrowski 2004: 4). This is fine as far as it goes, but the nature and role of decoration and ornament within interiors is much more than the arrangement of 'things'. Decoration represents, it defines, it illustrates, it symbolizes, and it creates atmosphere and identity! Perhaps David Brett's pithy description of decoration as 'a family of practices devoted to visual pleasure' (2005) is broad enough to encompass the many aspects, as opposed to one particular definition.

If decoration simply performs aesthetic functions, ornament marks the addition of content through motifs. Ornament is also a linguistic form whereby it communicates and delineates what a thing is. Its function and its identity is part of the communication, which works both ways when the viewer responds through their senses. Ornament is therefore dependent upon the object and has a mediating function that is to provide completeness and thus identity. Indeed, German philosopher Emmanuel Kant (1790) went so far as to suggest that ornament and beautiful form enhance the aesthetic appreciation, but merely attached decoration does not. His examples include the frame on a painting, drapery on a statue and a colonnade on a temple (Kant 1987 [1790]: 72).

During the nineteenth century, design reformers considered the role of ornament and its apparent impact. For John Ruskin, for example, 'architecture is the art which so disposes and adorns the edifices raised by man for whatsoever uses, that the sight of them may contribute to his mental health, power and pleasure' (1859: 7). If we take Ruskin's term 'architecture' in a broad sense, we can see that the decoration or adornment of the interior is in his view crucial.

Christopher Dresser takes this point further: 'Ornament is that which, superadded to utility, renders the object more acceptable through bestowing upon it an amount of beauty that it would not otherwise possess … [however] the application of ornament to objects cannot be said to be absolutely necessary'. He goes on to say: 'for the most part ornament is superadded to utility, a wall is a wall,

---

John Ruskin (1819–1900)

John Ruskin, an English writer and artist, is most famous for his work as an art critic. Ruskin's writings were influential among contemporary architects and artists. His *Seven Lamps of Architecture* and *The Stones of Venice* champion the Gothic and the religious spirit, and the importance of craftsmanship in design. His criticism of contemporary architecture and design decried the growing emphasis on function in architectural works. In conjunction, his social criticism moved towards an anti-industrialization that suggested looking to the past to create a future. Although sometimes dismissed as an irrelevant romantic, Ruskin deplored the reduction of people to machine operators, which inspired William Morris and the Arts and Crafts ideal.

Adolf Loos (1870–1933)

Ironically, Adolf Loos's influence came from a few interior designs and a body of controversial essays. Adolf Loos's buildings were rigorous examples of austere beauty, ranging from conventional country cottages to planar compositions for storefronts and residences. His built compositions, although little known outside his native Austria initially, created an impact as his ideas travelled across Europe. His main development was in the aesthetic puritanism that followed from his disavowal of ornament. In his controversial essay *Ornament and Crime*, he argued that the shedding of ornament was a measure of human progress. However, he espoused high-quality craftsmanship and mastery of materials in his own works.

Figure 10.1 Attic interior roof, house near Lake Orta, Italy, 2003.

whether decorated or not; and a tube will convey gas equally well whether it has chased upon it beautiful devices or is without enrichment'. For Dresser, the important point was that ornament be the 'quality of an object which causes delight, gladsomeness, or satisfaction to spring up within the beholder' (1977 [1862]: 1, 4, 3). Both these critics recognized the valuable role that ornament plays in human life. The example of the exposed construction of a ceiling in an Italian house built in 2003 demonstrates how decoration can simply result from the construction process (Figure 10.1).

Some influential twentieth-century designers seem to have had a problem with ornament. Adolf Loos's *Ornament and Crime* is the classic text that takes a stand against ornament. Loos maintained that: 'The evolution of culture marches with the elimination of ornament from useful objects' (1998: 167). However, Joseph Rykwert points out that:

Wherever he could, Loos used semi-precious materials on walls and ceilings: metal plaques, leather, veined marbles or highly veneered woods, even facing built-in pieces of furniture. But unlike his contemporaries, Loos never used these materials as pieces to be framed, but always as integral, continuous surfaces, always as plain as possible, always displaying their proper texture: almost as if they were a kind of ornament, an ornament which showed the pleasure providence took in making them, as the more obvious type of ornament would display the pleasure experienced by his fellow-men. (1973: 21)

The work of numerous twentieth-century designers who appeared to eschew decoration reflects the notion of integral ornament. On close analysis, it can be located in many supposedly Modernist ornament-free zones. The discussions around Mies van der Rohe's 'I-section beams', which are inherently decorative, are one example; another is his use of onyx walls in his Barcelona pavilion (see also Nierhaus, in Sparke et al. 2009, and Chapter 12). Of course, decoration never really went away in popular culture, art and design. The Art Deco headquarters building for Martins Bank Limited, Water Street, Liverpool, built in 1932, illustrates the use of luxury travertine walls and coloured glass uplighters to create decorative effects (Figure 10.2).

More recently, Kent Bloomer has made the distinctions between cerebral decoration and visual ornament: 'Decoration is a pleasurable arrangement of elements that articulate societal values, order and beauty, while ornament is constituted by motifs that are repetitively distributed about structural and decorative elements to evoke natural cycles, efflorescence and transformation' (in Abruzzo and Solomon 2006: 49).

why is decoration important?

Art historian Ernst Gombrich explored the role of decoration in his *Sense of Order*, where he linked decoration and ornament to the process of making sense of our surroundings. He suggests that the careful establishment of a balance between monotony and complexity is part of our understanding of the built environment (1979). We achieve this in many ways, through decoration that includes patterning, the defining of edges, borders, rims and surfaces, and the creation of focal points in spaces. Kent Bloomer's contemporary framework for describing decorative applications takes this a little further. It includes notions of line work to reinforce a focal point; rhythm to reflect recurring elements that refer to progression or duration; statics that create a balance of composition or placement between ornament and form; and utility that links the object's function with the ornament to create a cohesive meaning (2000).

Apart from the physical aspects, decoration can assist in creating meaning. Kent Bloomer identifies three familiar aspects of an interior whereby a coherent link is made between an object's function and its ornament; between liminal transitions and connections, which are enhanced by ornament; and transformations that use ornament to express imagination, fancy and fantasy. For example, the Paris Opera House's

grand staircase exemplifies this transformation of an ordinary staircase into the entrance to 'another world' (see also the Morris Lapidus stairs example, Chapter 6).

Another example that taps into the viewers' consciousness is the full-size reconstruction of part of the interior of the lounge gazebo on the American steamboat *Mississippi Queen*. Displayed at the Design Centre, London, in December 1975, this setting touched on a number of visual stimuli that are associated in the mind with steamboat interiors (Figure 10.3).

the functions of ornament

It is clear from the above that ornament has a number of functions in the built environment including (a) representing collective identity, (b) signifying place, (c) creating distinction, (d) being a symbol of society, group, etc., (e) personalizing space and (f) aiding orientation.

Mihaela Criticos has usefully analysed ornament into four major functions – the symbolic, the qualifying, the ordering and the decorative (2004: 185–219).

Symbolic Function of Ornament

The symbolic function of ornament reflects the physical manifestation of significations based in ritual, society or culture and reflects an already established system of order. For example, in 1836, Pugin wrote of Egyptian ornament: 'in them every ornament, every detail had a mystical import. The pyramid and obelisk of Egyptian architecture, its lotus capitals, its gigantic sphinxes and multiplied hieroglyphics were not mere fanciful architectural

combinations and ornaments, but emblems of the philosophy and mythology of that nation' (1973: 2). The taxonomy of ornament is a major referencing system in art and design history.

According to Theodor Adorno, 'there is barely a practical form which, along with its appropriateness for use, would not therefore also be a symbol. … According to Freud, symbolic intention quickly allies itself to technical forms, like the airplane … [and] to the car. Thus purposeful forms are the language of their own purposes.' He continues by pointing out that people admired a decoration not for its intrinsic beauty, but for its connection to a building, object or person entitled to it. 'What began as symbol becomes ornament and finally appears superfluous' (in Leach 1997: 10).'

If ornament or decoration is the expression of the ideas of a culture by giving and showing meaning, it is representational. For the German philosopher Hans-Georg Gadamer, 'ornament is not primarily something by itself that is then applied to something else, but belongs to the self-presentation of its wearer. Ornament is part of the presentation. But presentation is an ontological event; it is representation' (in Leach 1997: 136).

This function of symbolic representation suggests that meaning is found not just in the actual ornament, but in its particular context. The understanding of the representation is often developed piecemeal until an overall picture is understood. It is possible that through the Gestalt process of closure, meanings may be ascribed to ornament that is at odds with the intentions of the maker/designer.

Qualifying Function of Ornament

This function relates to the idea of ornament as an adjective in the language of design. Ornament

Figure 10.3 Full-size reconstruction of part of interior of lounge gazebo on the steamboat Mississippi Queen, by Conwy Evans, Sevant & Freeman. From the exhibition 'Mississippi Queen: A New Steamboat for America' at the Design Centre, London, December 1975.

in this case acts as an expression of identity and individual expression – see, for example, Eltham Palace dining room (Figure 2.5). However, for Modernists like Le Corbusier, styles 'are no more than an accidental surface modality, superadded to facilitate composition, stuck on to disguise faults, or duplicated for the sake of display'. As if this was not enough, he protests that: 'Ornament is sick … this surface elaboration, if extended without discernment over absolutely everything, becomes repugnant and scandalous; it smells of pretence' (1987 [1925]: 115 and 89). Criticos reminds us that the lack of this qualifying function is well illustrated in the 'failure of the modernist project … at Pessac (1926), a residential complex near Bordeaux, where Le Corbusier's standard-ized houses, designed as perfect objets-types meant to satisfy essential and typical human requirements, totally ignored the equally hu-man need for expressing cultural and individual meanings'. To relieve the situation the residents transformed the buildings into 'homes' by adding ornament such as 'pitched roofs with wooden gables, stepped cornices, colored window shut-ters, hanging flower-stands, beveled corners for the openings' (Criticos 2004: 197). In other words, ornament can give meaning and identity.

Ordering Function of Ornament

Ornament as an ordering function may represent the reflection of the whole of a design in a part or, conversely, as a structuring factor, which is possibly disordered or amorphous. Gombrich, in his *Sense of Order*, described this function: 'I believe that in the struggle for existence organ-isms developed a sense of order not because their environment was generally orderly but rather because perception requires a framework against which to plot deviations from regularity' (1979: xii).

The French essayist and art theorist Jacques Soulillou reinforces the idea in his *Ornament and Order*, where he suggests that ornament, rather than being simply embellishment, is a 'catalyst for cultural upheaval and perpetual reordering'. This occurs through the process of selection and exclusion, whereas decoration is 'the eternal double of ornament, which the latter [i.e. orna-ment] agrees at regular intervals to denounce, to prevent it threatening order' (in Taylor and Preston 2006: 320). The role of pattern repetition in this ordering is part of the process. The order-ing principle contained in ornament refers both to a formal and to a social order. Soulillou also suggests that: 'One of the formal means of pre-venting ornamental display from degenerating into chaos is by containing it in a more or less defined grid system. Without such a system … the display would run off in all directions' (in Taylor and Preston 2006: 315). The combination of curves played against rectangles in the coffee shop example demonstrates this idea of repeti-tion (Plate 25).

The concept of the interior as a 'total work of art', or *Gesamtkunstwerk*, might be a good ex-ample. For Walter Gropius there was no argument about decoration and design: 'the composite but inseparable work of art, in which the old dividing line between monumental and decora-tive elements will have disappeared for ever' (in Collins 1965: 127). For example, Charles Rennie Mackintosh's interiors have decorative symbols of organic growth or geometric frameworks ex-pressed in a range of objects and patterns, in the textiles, furniture, lighting and the expression of volumes and spaces, but the integrated scheme controls them (Plate 5).

Decorative Function of Ornament

The decorative function of ornament is its playful and hedonistic ability, and its capacity to turn something ordinary or mundane into an aesthetic object that connects to people. Ornament appeals to the senses, contributes significantly to the creation of a sympathetic relationship between people and their surroundings, and can help to create a meaningful location.

Henri Focillon begins to grapple with this idea in *The Life of Forms in Art*. He proposed that: 'Ornament shapes, straightens and stabilizes the bare arid field on which it is inscribed. Not only does it exist in and of itself, but it also shapes its own environment – to which it imparts form.' Focillon continued: 'Even before it [ornament] becomes formal rhythm and combination, the simplest ornamental theme, such as a curve or *rinceau* whose flexions betoken all manner of future symmetries, alternating movements, divisions and returns, has already given accent to the void in which it occurs, and has conferred upon it a new and original existence' (1948: 18).

This appeal to the senses was developed by Gadamer, who proposed that: 'The nature of decoration consists in performing that two-sided mediation; namely to draw the attention of the viewer to itself, to satisfy his taste, and then to redirect it away from itself, to the greater whole of the context of life, which it accompanies' (in Leach 1977: 135).

These four functions of ornament always have a double aspect of communication. One relates to the object, the other to the viewer. Ornament is not self-referential; it enhances the meaning of an object or space with a particular cultural system. The role of the designer and their relationship with ornament is then to speak to the viewer, to explain and enhance the communication between the object and the viewer, and thus enhance the experience of looking or being. In this sense ornament is part of the critical reflection on art and design, called aesthetics.

the role of ornament

The actual use of ornament links aesthetic theory with practice. An interesting analysis of how ornament might work in relation to a building was given by the architect Robert Kerr in his 1869 RIBA lecture, entitled 'The Architecturesque'. Here he identified four approaches to ornament. He discussed 'structure ornamentalized (or rendered in itself ornamental)', whereby structural elements create a self-referential ornamental effect; 'ornament structuralized (or rendered in itself structure)', whereby the ornament or detail is the first step in design; 'structure ornamented', or applied surface decoration; and 'ornament constructed', where the building and its spaces have become integrated ornament (in Culler 1965: 125). Although these may be a little artificial, they do demonstrate something of a framework when evaluating design approaches. They also represent particular approaches to actual practice.

More recently, architect Thomas Beeby has elaborated on how ornament can work as practice. He considers that 'ornament is based on a unit and the finite number of different geometric manipulations that can be enacted upon it to produce the various types of symmetry and rhythm which lie at the heart of ornament. In ornament, symmetry results from a proportional relation of part to whole, and rhythm is produced by the dynamic repetition of proportional parts to a uniform beat' (Beeby/Kiernan 1977: 12). He then suggests that designers can manipulate this unit in four different ways to create ornament. These are translation, rotation, reflection and inversion (see further Chapter 5).

We can consider ornament and decoration as languages, applied either in a scholarly or in an eclectic sense. These uses reflect more widely particular styles or approaches to design. Of course, overuse of ornament can be destructive and it is useful to consider Marcel Breuer's comments on decoration, which reflect a degree of common sense: 'The decorations in … rooms are the tools of daily life, man himself – and the best ornament of all: plants' (in Wilk 1981: 186).

the role of detail

Underlying much of this discussion is the issue of the role and nature of detail. This may be in the build or the furnishing. In terms of build, architectural theorist Marco Frascari says: 'The art of detailing is really the joining of materials, elements, components and building parts in a functional and aesthetic manner' (in Malnar and Vodvarka 2004: 166). In terms of ornament, the term 'accessories' may be pejorative, but we should not dismiss the concept. Indeed, Le Corbusier wrote in 1929 of the value of collected but de-contextualized decorative objects or ornaments for the interior to prompt contemplation.

He wrote:

> Life is full of opportunities for collecting ornaments, which can serve to promote thought:
> This pebble from the seaside
> this admirable pine cone
> these butterflies, these beetles
> this polished steel machine component
> or this piece of ore.
>
> (In Benton, Benton and Sharp 1975: 238)

This passage neatly links the concepts of collecting, memory and decoration.

An example of the attention to detail as decoration is in the design work of Charles and Ray Eames. In their own home, their careful use and

---

Charles (1907–1978) and Ray Eames (1912–1988)

Charles Eames and Ray Kaiser (maiden name) were American designers who married in 1941 and worked together in various areas of design. The Eames's own house and its interiors embodied Charles and Ray's particular approach to interiors. Idiosyncratic, amusing, comfortable and colourful, it demonstrated a blending of the commonplace and the individual. Their concept of functioning decoration 'allowed' personal objects into a modern interior to define the space and the users. Their iconic films and furniture designs, which remain classics, are the enduring legacy of the Eames's studio.

composition of a wide range of decorative objects that they called 'functioning decoration' served to humanize an impersonal, industrially derived shell.[1] Architect Robert Venturi welcomed the Eames's introduction of 'good old Victorian clutter' into the interior but was aware that their 'eclectic assemblages' were a long way from the reality of nineteenth-century interiors (in Kirkham 1995: 167). Venturi's comment that 'old clichés in new settings achieve rich meanings' (1966: 51) may well refer to interiors as well as to architecture. Indeed, Venturi said later of ornament (symbolic rhetoric) 'we like emphasising shelter in architecture, thereby including function in our definition; and we like admitting symbolic rhetoric in our definition which is not integral with shelter, thereby expanding the content of architecture beyond itself and freeing function to take care of itself' (Venturi, Scott Brown, Arnell and Bergart 1984: 62).

the role of crafts

One of the exciting results of the re-evaluation of ornament in interior design and architecture has been the reinvigoration of the crafts and their associated skills. Sandra Alfoldy and Janice Helland explain:

> Like architecture, craft and interior design emphasise the absolute importance of materiality. All three work together to develop perceptions of space. It is the job of decoration to change the way we think about space – not to build spaces but to animate them. Craft contains an undeniable

humanising appeal that continues today despite advances in architectural technology and the contemporary emphasis on economical building. (2008: Introduction)

The important role that craft and its materiality, and thus by extension, ornament, can play in an interior, can help to define particular spaces. This crafted materiality assists the user to understand and use the spaces. Glenn Adamson explains this notion of materiality: 'craft always entails an encounter with the properties of a specific material ... or more than one material in combination' (2007: 39).

This issue of materiality is at the heart of the work of interior designers as it affects structures, cladding and details. In terms of ornament, the role of new construction and manufacturing techniques and materials has made its return both as an economically viable proposition and a desirable one for practitioners. For example, the use of 3D computer modelling can assist 'mass-customization' processes through techniques such as CNC milling, rapid prototyping and laser cutting. The use of stainless steel panels and laser cutting combined with a traditional geometric Islamic design in the work of Natasha Webb (2009), demonstrates a conjunction of craft and design skills that successfully combine tradition and modernity (Figure 10.4). This does not mean that there is a neglect of more traditional crafts, just that the range of possibilities has extended. Indeed, in terms of interior design, the very materiality of craft, in addition to the visual qualities (whether conceptually considered or without critical content), is what makes contemporary crafts so useful and so interesting. Giles Miller's innovative

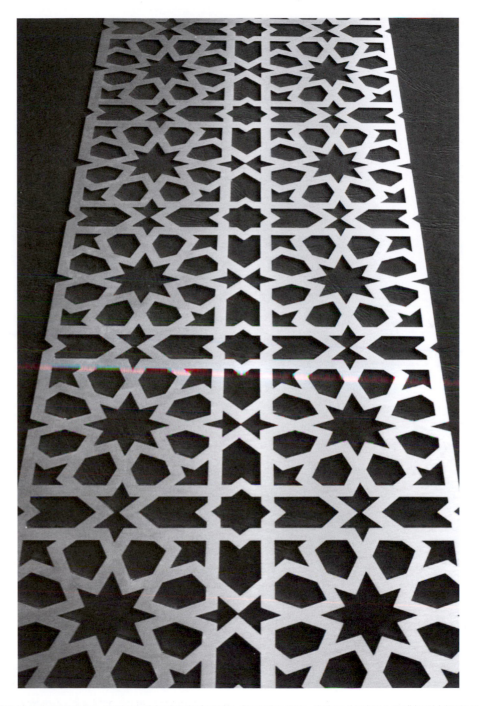

Figure 10.4 Laser-cut stainless steel panel for interior/exterior decorative uses, designed using a traditional Islamic module by Natasha Webb, 2009.

Figure 10.5 Cardboard screen with a damask design by Giles Miller, 2008.

treatment of corrugated cardboard (2008) is just one example of the contemporary combination of sustainable design, craft and technology (Figure 10.5). The role of craft in ornament is therefore a humanizing one. The role of ornament as decoration in the interior will remain important as part of an individual's representation of their identity and personality.

ANALYSIS Islamic (Middle Eastern) Interiors as Decoration

Traditional Islamic interiors have a long tradition of decoration using a variety of patterns. These would include ceramic tiles in varying geometric patterns that covered both floors and walls. Skilled artisans supplied other decorative elements including woodwork such as pierced grilles, carved stonework, and inlay (of both wood and stone), either in naturalistic or geometric designs. The most important elements were often the textiles. These included rugs, cushions and drapes, which were laid upon floors, benches and each other, to create a multiple-patterned effect. In the Barsegh example every surface features applied decoration. The ceiling vaulting, the wall paintings, the inlaid mirror work and, of course, the multiple carpets that overlay floors, walls and furniture (Plate 26).

CASE STUDY 10.1 Baccarat Co., Moscow

In 2008, the luxury French crystal manufacturer, Baccarat, opened a new showroom in Moscow. Set in an historic building dating from the early 1800s, the interior, designed by Philippe Starck, has all the hallmarks of an extravagant showpiece interior. The contrast between the interior architecture and the fittings and displays demonstrates the success of juxtaposition. The intention is that the interior be an experience, with its multiple references to the baroque, to film (Stanley Kubrick) and literature (Lewis Carroll). By concentrating on the mirror and glass themes of the products themselves, contrasted with plain, bare walls, the designer has built up a space that both highlights the products and offers the visitor a visual experience. The illuminated glass floor and the fibre optic lighting inside the display cases set the stage for an exhibition of the crystal work. Overall, the whimsical fantasy effect of palace-museum-boutique works its magic brilliantly (Plate 27).

CASE STUDY 10.2 The Eames's House and Functioning Decoration

Although the collection and display of decorative objects has long been a part of interior design in one form or another, the concept of Charles and Ray Eames's functioning decoration is different. Described by Pat Kirkham (1995) as having the characteristics of addition, accretion, juxtaposition, changing scales, fragmentation, wit and whimsy, cross-cultural references and the de-/recontextualization of objects, it is a great example of the ability to combine Modernism with human touches. Their selection and arrangement of 'crafted' objects combined with natural and found objects, as well as examples of popular culture (especially toys), is distinct from any random accretions that are not deliberately collected, and from contrived tablescapes that are established as a signature. The juxtaposition of these objects, which became pure decoration in a Modernist interior, demonstrates the success of an ideal that was found in the eclectic interiors of artists and designers of the later nineteenth century – namely the creation of individual identity in a space (Plate 28).

CASE STUDY 10.3 Sanderson's London Showroom 1960/2000

In 1960, the fabric and wallpaper retailer Sanderson opened a new, purpose-built showroom for retail and trade customers in the centre of London. From the start, the showroom design laid an emphasis on rich materials and quality finishes: these included sparkling, polished aluminium and brass. The scheme had to complement the colour and patterns of the products on display and the designers incorporated two particular craft-based features. A glass mural of abstract biometric forms, designed by John Piper and executed by Patrick Reyntiens, dominated the main foyer (Figure 10.6). The window acted as a focal point and introduced the visitor to the spectacle found inside. It had no relation to ecclesiastical stained glass and simply purports to represent 'design and colour'.

The other decorative feature was a garden designed by Jupp Dernbach-Mayen. It had a glass and marble mosaic wall as a background, with weeping beech tree, pool and a monolithic fountain, all in an open-air square at the rear of the building. Geoffrey Holroyd wrote that 'Under the controlling architectural influence, the courtyard adds to the urban spectacle, splashing water, lights, sculpture, boulders, trees and plants' (*Architectural Design* 1960: 261). Now a listed building, it has recently (2000) been converted into a lavish 'urban spa' hotel by Philippe Starck.

Figure 10.6 Sanderson House, Berners Street, London. The stained glass panel in the entrance designed by John Piper and executed by Patrick Reyntiens, 1960.

chapter 11

sustainability

CHAPTER OVERVIEW

All the activities of an interior designer need to be as sustainable as possible, therefore this chapter initially considers the question – what is sustainability? It then considers what the principles of sustainability are and what they mean in practice. They cover major ethical issues including the notions of equity and morality, environmental justice for all, inter-generational equity and stewardship or the triple bottom line. We then consider the major issues of sustainability and design practice, with an emphasis on the importance of a firm commitment at all levels to the sustainable design process. The chapter looks next at methods of achieving sustainability and the various approaches made, including life cycle assessment, materials and building assessment, the Natural Step framework and the concept of biomimicry. Finally, the chapter looks at the process of sustainable design from project definition and initial considerations through to post-occupancy evaluation.

introduction

In conjunction with human needs and the factors associated with them, the understanding of environmental issues is crucial to interior designers and their practice (see, for eg, Kang and Guerin 2009: 179–186). Beyond the individual considerations of good social stewardship of our immediate surroundings, the global environmental values of social responsibility, sustainable design and adaptable reuse (sustainability) are ever more important and often have legal requirements attached to them. Daniel Wahl and Seaton Baxter put the issues succinctly: '[There is] a complexity of dynamically interrelated ecological, social, cultural, economic, and psychological (awareness) problems [that] interact and converge in the current crisis of our unsustainable civilization' (2008: 72).

Sustainability has developed into two camps. Ecological sustainability aims to use natural solutions where possible to address the issues of sustainability, whereas technological sustainability looks to using environmentally friendly new technologies to replace the harmful existing ones. David Orr explains: 'Technological sustainability is about stabilizing planetary vital signs, [whereas] ecological sustainability is the task of finding alternatives to the practices that got us into trouble in the first place' (1992: 24).

Sustainability is a process rather than an outcome, a direction rather than a destination. Sustainability is 'development that meets the needs of the present without compromising the ability of future generations to meet their own needs' (Gro Bruntland 1987, in Edwards 2005). Sustainable design is a holistic approach to the environment, and to the associated social and economic issues in relation to individuals and to communities. Sustainable design minimizes the use of non-renewable resources, reduces environmental impact and works closely with the broader sustainability agendas. Therefore, the impact of designers' work is not usually neutral. For example, designers' choices and attitudes to resource conservation, the local and wider environmental issues, waste minimization, and the reduction of operating and maintenance costs, will all be influential.

environmental matters

Sustainability has to operate at individual, local, regional and global levels of vision and co-operation. It cannot be top–down and it needs a holistic approach that involves everyone as a 'designer'. For individuals, these issues include the topics of air quality, availability of light, thermal comfort, and physical and visual connections to nature. Interior designers can influence all of these. Organizing space so that individuals have personal control of access to these is also important. For localities, the issues are around building use, energy use, waste management and pollution control. At the regional level, transportation systems, supply services and waste management are among the key issues. Lewis Mumford's perceptive comments from 1941 are still pertinent to this concept of regionalism:

> Regionalism is not a matter of using the most available local material, or of copying some simple form of construction that our ancestors used, for want of anything better, a century or two ago. Regional forms are those which most closely meet the actual conditions of life and which most fully succeed in making a people feel at home in their environment: they do not merely utilize the soil but they reflect the current conditions of culture in the region. (Mumford 1941)

At the global level, the issues include, for example, global warming, deforestation, aquatic preservation and acid rain. Worldwide developments and applications in environmental controls, new or revised approaches to all aspects of lifestyles and a commitment to sustainability will address these concerns.

Simon Guy and Graham Farmer have recognized alternative logics of ecological design, which have their roots in competing conceptions of environmentalism. In their approach they have identified six approaches to eco-design, which although having a certain fluidity in their boundaries, do offer a framework for consideration:

- Firstly they consider the eco-technic approach, which tends to use technology to deal with environmental problems, often with hi-tech solutions.

- Secondly is the eco-centric approach, which emphasizes the spiritual relationship between humans and nature. This necessarily holistic approach encourages the use of renewable technology and materials.
- Thirdly is the eco-aesthetic approach, which expresses eco credentials through metaphor and meaning. Organic modelling and a fusion of forms is linked to this approach.
- Fourthly comes the eco-cultural approach that is, like Mumford above, locally orientated and tends to use vernacular solutions and relative cultural practices as the basis of any designing.
- Fifthly, they consider the eco-medical, which addresses issues such as sick building syndrome and the problems of VOCs (Volatile Organic Compounds). In this case, designers tend to attempt to provide healthy living environments using passive design and sustainable and harmless products.
- Lastly, there is the eco-social approach, which considers the natural world as well as its users and workers through democratic and locally managed decisions. A simple example would be the involvement of tenants in the decisions around the establishment of a housing project.

(Guy and Farmer 2001: 140–148)

principles of sustainability

The Organization for Economic Co-operation and Development (OECD) has defined four principles that underpin sustainable development. These are Equity Today, Environmental Justice, Inter-gener-ational Equity and Stewardship. Understanding these principles is crucial to a perception of how the individual (and, by extension, a business and a community) must fit into the sustainable world.

Equity Today

The equity principle makes the point that we should ensure equality of resources for all, and not undermine the infrastructure of one community to the advantage of another. The ethicist John Rawls developed the idea of the 'original position', which posits the question: if at the beginning of life you were in complete ignorance of what your own position or location within society would be, what moral principles would you hope would inform that society (1971: 12).

Environmental Justice

Environmental justice is 'equal access to a clean environment and equal protection from possible environmental harm, irrespective of race, income or class or any other differentiating feature of socio-economic status' (Cutter 1995: 111–122). Although this principle often refers to injustices between groups of people, it now includes issues that designers might impact upon, such as the quality of life, neighbourhood unity, freedom from crime and the fear of crime, civic pride and environmental education.

Inter-generational Equity

This principle refers to today's people not interfering with the ability of future generations to meet their own needs. It refers to our dealing with our own unsustainable production and consumption cycles that will degrade the world's ecological and social base.

Stewardship

The concept of stewardship refers to the taking of personal responsibility for the rest of life on Earth. Sustainability depends on recognizing that natural systems underpin all human systems (see, for example, biomimicry below). Human society cannot function without them, and there are clear limits as to the ways in which we exploit natural systems. In addition to the moral case, this concept is in our own self-interest.

The term Triple Bottom Line sometimes defines these principles. Here social equality, environmental quality and economic prosperity come together through sustainability. The economic bottom line is familiar but needs considering in terms of economic sustainability over a long and changing period. The environmental bottom line is crucial, as we cannot continue to function without full consideration of use of implications for resources, emissions, waste, etc. The social bottom line that ensures justice for all will affect the economic, political and ethical aspects of an organization or community (see McDonough/Hannover).

sustainability and design practice: the interior designer's role

There is a clear need for interior designers to take a lead in sustainable practice, particularly as many clients and users are often unaware of the issues and possible solutions. The sustainability issues are in the everyday world and are not simply options. This means that interior designers will have to increase their engagement with what it means to be environmentally sustainable. This can be achieved initially by ensuring that their own practice is environmentally responsible, that they foster and educate environmentally appropriate attitudes in all the stakeholders they come into contact with (i.e. students, staff, clients, suppliers and contractors) and that they maintain and develop their own knowledge base through continuing professional education.

It is clear that one must believe in the needs of the environment and not merely pay lip service (aka 'greenwashing'). Authors of the 'cradle to cradle' concept, environmental campaigners William McDonough and Michael Braungart, point out that: 'Even as architects and industrial designers began to embrace recycled or sustainable materials, they still dealt primarily with surfaces – with, what looked good, what was easy to get, what they could afford' (2002: 9). As a practising interior designer, Cathy Stieg advocates the need for interior designers to develop an emotional connection with the environment: 'Continually reinforcing our natural connection to the environment helps us to support what we believe to be right and forces us to seek information that sustains our beliefs' (2006: x). This holistic approach is part of the value set discussed earlier.

Cathy Stieg further suggests that 'the development of a sustainable design practice can be separated into five unique phases: connection, knowledge, process, practice, and commitment' (vii–xxi). The development of 'sustainable designers' starts with making connections to nature and the environment on a personal level. Designers have to demonstrate to themselves that they are aware of the relationships between humans and the environment and then place themselves accordingly.

The design practices and processes must integrate sustainability issues at all levels, whether related to energy choices, materials selection or the impact on an environment of a particular plan. Continuing evaluation and critical assessment of every stage of the process is essential. The commitment to sustainability is not just part of a business ethic. As Stieg says, it is 'as much an issue of lifestyle, as it is of design practice' (xx).

It should be clear by now that sustainability must come from the individual's commitment to change. Any sustainability policy that simply responds to regulation will limit the possibilities. McDonough and Braungart sum it up well: 'since regulations often require one-size-fits-all end-of-pipe solutions rather than a deeper design response, they do not directly encourage creative problem solving. Ultimately a regulation is a signal of a design failure' (2002: 61).

methods for sustainability

Putting the values introduced above into practice requires that the employment of methods for ensuring the issues of sustainability be at the heart of every project undertaken by interior designers. The following tools will assist in developing and maintaining this approach:

Life Cycle Assessment (LCA)
This is a process of analysing the environmental impact of all aspects of a project 'from cradle to grave'.[1] LCA has four basic stages: a goal and scope definition phase, the inventory analysis stage (extraction, refining, manufacturing, conserving and disposing), the impact assessment

stage, and the interpretation phase.[2] Life cycle costing explains the value of considering the complete costs of acquisition, operation, service and disposal of a product or service. New sustainable materials, lighting technologies, energy choice and delivery systems are planned to reduce the life cycle costs of a building, its equipment and interiors.

Materials and Building Assessment
The need to evaluate and set benchmarks for sustainability and environmental control is well understood through environmental assessment methods. Increasingly, customers are demanding that any work undertaken conforms to these assessments. In the United Kingdom, the BREEAM (Building Research Establishment Environmental Assessment Method) organization is involved in the assessment of buildings at design, post-construction and use stages, as well as evaluating existing buildings.[3] In North America, the LEED (Leadership in Energy and Environmental Design)[4] organization was created to achieve the following goals for green building:

- Define 'green building' by establishing a consensual common standard of measurement.
- Promote integrated, whole-building design practices.
- Recognize environmental leadership in the building industry.
- Stimulate green competition.
- Raise consumer awareness of green building benefits.
- Transform the building market.

The LEED rating system addresses six key aspects of environmental matters. These are sustainable sites, water efficiency, energy and atmosphere, materials and resources, indoor environmental quality, and innovation and the design process. Similar initiatives are the Green Star system in Australia and CASBEE (Comprehensive Assessment System for Built Environment Efficiency) in Japan.

ISO 14000

The ISO 14000 series of environmental management standards assist organizations to minimize the negative effects on the environment that their operations might cause, and to assist with legal compliance. ISO 14001 is an internationally accepted standard that sets out a framework of essential elements for putting an effective Environmental Management System (EMS) in place. The standard addresses the delicate balance between maintaining profitability and reducing environmental impact. The standard specifies requirements for creating an environmental policy; determining and defining environmental aspects and impacts of products/activities/services; planning environmentally related objectives and measurable targets; implementation and operation of programmes to meet objectives and targets; implementing checking and corrective action; and management review.

Natural Step Framework

This scientific system is based on fundamental scientific principles that reflect the limiting conditions for life on Earth. The framework is based on an ABCD approach where A is Awareness, B is Baseline Mapping, C is Creating a Vision and D is Down to Action.

The first phase (A) involves aligning a business around an agreed understanding of sustainability and the 'whole-systems' context for an organization. Secondly, the (B) baseline mapping procedure consists of performing a Sustainability Gap Analysis of the important flows and impacts of the business, to identify any practices or procedures that run counter to the principles of sustainability. This includes the impacts of a business's complete supply chain and an assessment of the products and services, energy, capital and human resources, from cradle to cradle.

Thirdly, creating a vision (C) imagines what the business or service will look like in a sustainable society when based upon full sustainability. Fourthly, down to action (D) is simply getting on with it, and relies on a series of set priorities and goals, based on the vision established above. Businesses including Interface and IKEA have implemented the Natural Step and have become more sustainable (and profitable) as a result. Changes have embraced all their processes including purchase of materials, manufacturing, transportation, construction of facilities, maintenance and waste management. One advantage of adopting the Natural Step is that it provides principles that are grounded in science, and thus measurable (see Natural Step). This approach is suitable for the businesses of both the interior designer and the client.

Biomimicry

Biomimicry is a recent science-based study system that explores the natural world in terms of its organization, processing, systems and design. Biomimicry design then imitates or takes creative inspiration from these natural processes or materials to attempt to solve human issues in a sustainable way.

The science of biomimicry provides designers with a framework. Janine Benyus offers the following nine basic laws of the circle of life, all of which resonate throughout her work and that of other biomimics:

- Nature runs on sunlight
- Nature uses only the energy it needs
- Nature fits form to function
- Nature recycles everything
- Nature rewards cooperation
- Nature banks on diversity
- Nature demands local expertise
- Nature curbs excesses from within
- Nature taps the power of limits

(Benyus 2002: 7)

The design spiral (Figure 11.1) uses biomimicry to consider a design challenge in terms of biology. It then questions the natural world for inspiration, and then evaluates the results to ensure that the final design mimics nature at all levels, i.e. in form, process and ecosystem. It is not hard to see how interior designers can adapt these ideas to their own working practices.

the sustainable design process

Putting these principles into action requires a processing framework. The following generic outline suggests just such a possible framework (see further Mendler, Odell and Lazarus: 2005).

Project Definition and Initial Considerations

In planning for sustainable design, designers must embed the concept in the whole process from the start. As with any project, goals and objectives need establishing to consider ideals and subsequent best practice. Indeed, the issue of the space and building are the first concern. Is reuse, rehabilitation, restoration or reconstruction an option, and if so, is it viable? In any event, some consideration of local vernacular examples that are environmentally aware will sometimes assist. Sustainable design approaches for businesses will offer profitability rewards through proper actions. The planned outcomes should be measurable against recognized standards (LEED etc.), so it is important to 'design out' any criteria that work against integrated solutions.

Integration of Design into Community and Environment

Whatever the project, it is necessary to apply green values and principles from the outset. Examples of this might be to try to avoid functional specificity, to maximize access to daylight and ventilation, and design for simplicity of operation and long life by using, where possible, renewable energy.

Team Assembly (Dependent on Project Size)

For all sustainability issues it is important to assemble a design-and-build team of people that includes specialists and champions. This collaborative approach of a team of experts will be vital to the successful completion of the work.

Site Evaluation

An examination of the constraints and opportunities that the location and site provide includes assessment of the micro- and macroclimates, natural habitats, building history location and existing functionality.

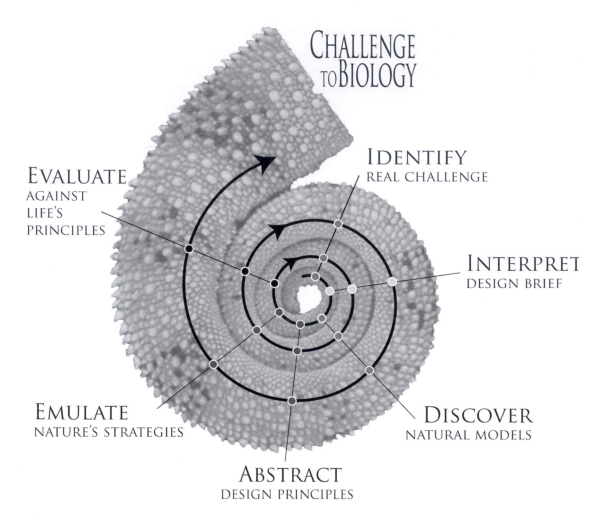

Figure 11.1 Biomimicry design spiral.

Baseline Analysis

An analysis of the supply and delivery of energy, water, etc., based on budgets, specific requirements and established benchmarks.

Concept and Design

This stage will reflect the sustainable strategies that are rooted in the overall concepts and plans. The established team of multi-disciplinary skills will enable solutions to be found that fit closely with the three aspects of design concepts, budgets and environmental objectives.

Optimization

To develop synergies between systems and materials, it is crucial to investigate the range of options in all facets of the project to identify those with the greatest potential.

Specification

The selection of materials that meet sustainable criteria are: 'materials and construction products which are healthy, durable, resource efficient and manufactured with regard to minimizing environmental impact and maximizing recycling' (in Edwards 2005). For many products, the impact on IEQ (Indoor Environmental Quality) is a specifying issue. It is crucial to be alert to the effect of constituent elements such as adhesives, paint, coatings, plastic foams, flooring, furniture components and cleaning materials. Ideally, strategies for enhancing venti-

lation, reducing VOCs, offering personal environmental control, and also creating opportunities for accessing daylight and certain views and outlooks, will be valuable in the longer run. Specification for sustainable design means considering all components, furnishings and installations, with the broad aim of reduction in all aspects (see also Chapter 12).

Operational Phase

It is imperative that consistent monitoring of the contract and materials occurs to ensure the correct specification of products and to verify the installation methods. Any contract documentation must include detailed specifications of the sustainability requirements, detailed instructions for sourcing and installation, and confirmation of monitoring arrangements.

Post-Occupancy Evaluation (POE)

This involves considerations of the final installation from a range of points of view that will identify issues and provide lessons for the future.

ANALYSIS Building Reuse and Adaptive Remodelling

The reuse and adaptation of existing buildings is a crucial method of making better use of the environment. There are a number of approaches to this subject. These include preservation, which maintains the building as found; restoration that attempts to return the building and its spaces to a near-original state; and renovation, which renews aspects of the building and upgrades the overall efficiency and image. Remodelling (also known as adaptive reuse or reworking), which can potentially change the function of the building, alter its internal spaces and circulation, and add or remove parts to adapt it to its new function, also fits here. An early example is the conversion of Spencer House, Greenwich, London, in 1966, which remodelled a 1670s residence (Plate 29).

Brooker and Stone, in their *Rereadings*, offer a useful framework for assessing these activities that follows the process of analysis, strategy and tactics in the reuse of older buildings (2004). The analysis considers issues of existing form and structure, its current or last function, context and environment, and the compatibility with the proposed new function. Designers often undertake this procedure in conjunction with other specialist professionals. The strategy explores relationships between the existing and the new in terms of approach. These might be (a) interventions, which create a narrative with the existing forms; (b) insertions, which are independent and thus create an interesting tension or ambiguity; or (c) installation, which combines existing and new in a symbiotic relationship. The scale of the relationship between old and new is the key issue.

Intervention occurs when the existing building is transformed so that it can no longer viably exist independently, and the nature of the remodelling is such that the old and new are completely intertwined. If a new autonomous element is built to fit within the confines of the existing build, then the system is *insertion.* The final system is *installation*, which includes examples in which the old and the new exist independently. The new elements are placed within the boundaries of the building (Brooker and Stone 2004: 14). The reuse of Santa Marta church in Venice is a good example. This fourteenth-century church, deconsecrated in 1811, is located on the westernmost boundary of Venice. It was later used as a warehouse. Its 2004 restoration by architect Vittorio de Feo was part of a pilot project to upgrade Venice's port waterfront. The interior, fitted with a metal structure and clad with pear wood panels, now serves as a conference and exhibition venue, which includes a projection room, shops and a cafeteria (Plate 30).

Finally, to fulfil the strategy, actions should include the following elements: plans to organize space; objects to provide focus; lighting to illuminate; material surfaces to create meanings; openings to create relationships between spaces; and movement or circulation options to ensure accessibility. It is clear that interior designers have a lot to offer in these circumstances.

CASE STUDY 11.1 'Sweet Water' Student Project for Environmentally Sustainable House in New Orleans

The brief for this project was to devise a home – named 'Sweet Water' – for a location in New Orleans that could withstand rains and hurricane-force winds whilst at the same time meeting LEED gold standards. Indigenous cultures and customs, with particular reference to local architecture, influence the overall design concept. The building is orientated to take advantage of the Earth's movement in relation to the sun and to wind patterns. Building the walls with the recycled material Composite Insulating Concrete Forms enhances the environmental standards. Solar panels and ground-source heat pumps supply heating. Water systems employ rainwater and grey water processing. The interior finishes employ zero VOC products and use recycled or natural materials, wherever possible (Figures 11.2–11.5).

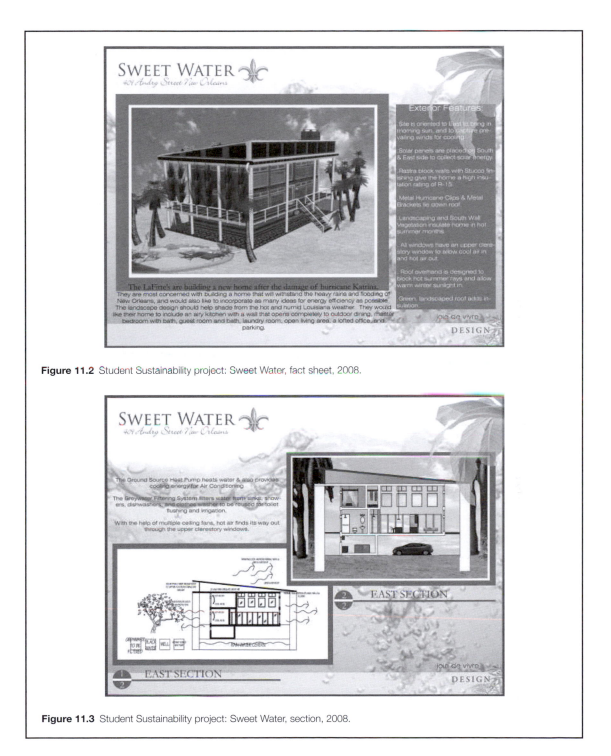

Figure 11.2 Student Sustainability project: Sweet Water, fact sheet, 2008.

Figure 11.3 Student Sustainability project: Sweet Water, section, 2008.

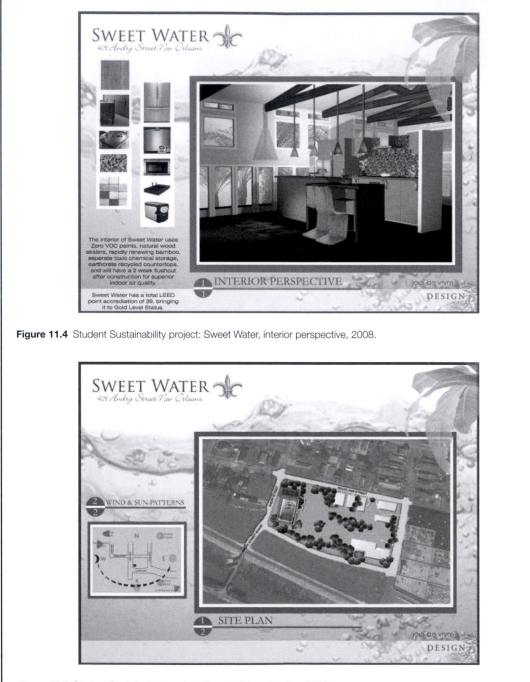

Figure 11.4 Student Sustainability project: Sweet Water, interior perspective, 2008.

Figure 11.5 Student Sustainability project: Sweet Water, site plan, 2008.

chapter 12

interior elements, materials and furnishings

CHAPTER OVERVIEW

One of the key roles of interior designers is the selection of interior elements, materials and furnishings. Not only is this one of the most important aspects of the work but it can also be amongst the most rewarding. Although each project will have its own particular considerations, there are a number of generic criteria that designers use to assist in the selection process. These criteria include intention, where the selection relates directly and indirectly to the functional needs of the particular users. Also included are human factors, which make connections to the emotive aspects of being in particular spaces. The aesthetic criteria, which refer to the power of materials to engage with people on a range of sense levels, are also relevant. The design/function criteria, relating to the practical aspects of a material choice across a range of particular parameters, is obviously key. Other factors include budgetary criteria, and the all-important sustainability and environmental criteria. Finally, we briefly explore the nature of furniture and furnishings in interiors.

---

introduction

English author and diplomat Sir Henry Wooton's well-known phrase, from his *Elements of Architecture* of 1624, can still provide insights when considering the material elements of interiors. He wrote that 'Well building hath three conditions: firmness, commodity, and delight'. Firmness (*firmitas*; Wooton quoting Vitruvius) refers to the suitability, strength and function of material in particular locations. Commodity (*utilitas*) refers to the appropriateness of material in use, in a context, and for a purpose. Thirdly, the delight (*venustas*) was originally referred to as a sense of proportion and order, but now also refers to the aesthetic and sensual appreciation of the materials and their use, i.e. how their physical properties emit a sense of place and offer tactile experiences and associational connections. Nowadays, we add a fourth dimension, that of sustainability.

There are no particular selection methods that can be applied mechanically to material choices, but the process can essentially be divided into four approaches, most of which are usually combined in one form or another. The first is inspiration, which is dependent upon random and directed searching, sketching or thinking until something seems right and will meet the criteria. Following this is the idea of selection by comparison. This looks at existing material solutions in similar situations and replicates them without particular consideration of the deeper meanings associated with the choices. More sophisticated are the approaches around analysis and synthesis. The analytical approach matches precisely specified requirements to known solutions found in, for example, databases of materials and their properties. Synthesis, in this model, uses our own experience, so that we match the desired features of a material to meet the needs of the brief. Other criteria will of course temper this apparently mechanistic approach.

selection criteria

The selection criteria of elements and materials include intentions, human factors, aesthetics, function and design, budgetary issues and environmental considerations. Architect Eva Jiricna has a take on the crucial role of materials right at the beginning of the conceptual process of designing: 'In a way material dictates the concept … and materials are not interchangeable … to me the material really is the starting point of the story' (in Lawson 2005: 171). (See also Mies van der Rohe, quoted below.)

Intention

This simply relates to the priorities of the designer, commissioner and user and the intended purpose of the finished space. Different spaces require differing material specifications: e.g., for spaces used by children to those used by seniors; spaces used for passing through, to those that are permanently in use; private spaces to public spaces, and so on. Materials selection also has some connections to their semiotics (see below) and any sensory perceptions of them, whatever the apparent functional priority of the choice.

Human Factors and Material Selection

Apart from the obvious functional relationships with human use, there needs to be consideration of the 'meaning' of materials to the people who will be in contact with the spaces. For semioticians, materials and objects provide signs that stand for other things. Baudrillard suggests that 'these materials, though disparate in themselves, are nevertheless homogeneous as cultural signs, and thus susceptible of organization into a coherent system' (1996 [1968]: 39). Baudrillard's example is wood: 'Wood draws its substance from the earth, it lives and breathes and "labours". It has latent warmth, it does not merely reflect, like glass, but burns from within. Time is embedded in its very fibres. … Wood has its own odour, it ages, it even has its own parasites, and so on. In short, it is a material that has being' (38).

For other materials/objects, meanings are often simply a set of possibilities located in the mind of the beholder and are not particularly intrinsic to the material. This is a difficult aspect since it relates to perceived attributes of materials, which will vary with cultures, age groups and prevailing tastes and fashions. Nevertheless, all material carries cultural values and semiotic meanings and suggests sensory responses. This human-centred approach allows for variable interpretations and is important to bear in mind, especially when dealing with a culturally diverse clientele.

Aesthetic Criteria

There is an element of intuition and an apparent understanding of when 'something looks or feels right' that often influences aesthetic choices in design. This sensory response may indicate that aesthetic reactions to visual, tactile, acoustic and olfactory stimuli equate to a highly developed process of environmental assessment relating ultimately to fundamental human needs.

However, part of the role of the interior designer is to use skills and understanding of the visual world to provide appropriate schemes that work aesthetically through colour, texture and pattern. Mark Humphrey's use of solid illuminated onyx to create vanity basins in a London club not only demonstrates the luxury and aesthetic of the material itself, but also the mirrors and lighting create a dramatic sense of excitement in the whole space (Plate 31).

Phenomenology suggests that, because of sensori-emotional experiences, we can relate directly to materials through textures, colours and patterns. J.-K. Huysmans gives a fascinating example of the power of materials in his 1884 novel *Against Nature*. The hero considered how he could renounce his dandyish ways by using magnificent materials that would create an imitation of a modest monkish interior:

He set about it in the following way: to imitate the yellow distemper ... he had the walls hung with saffron silk; to represent the chocolate brown dado ... he covered the lower part of the walls with kingwood, a dark brown wood with a purple sheen. ... The ceiling was similarly covered with white Holland, which had the appearance of plaster without its bright shiny look; as for the cold tiles of the floor, he managed to hit them off quite well, thanks to a carpet patterned in red squares. (2003 [1884]: 61–62)

Frank Lloyd Wright commented upon aesthetic criteria: 'good "alive" colour, soft textures, textural materials, beauty of all materials and methods revealed and utilized in the building scheme itself – these are the means of "decoration" so called, although not considered, as such by myself' (1910, in Malnar and Vodvarka 2004: 35). Additionally, all humans tend to respond to universal aesthetic elements such as form, symmetry and rhythm.

Wright also fully understood the sensory nature of materials. In 1928, he considered 'The Logic of the Plan'. Wright's idea of the plan was not based on the formal organization of spaces, rather that the plan's actual character should be expressed through choice of materials: 'A wood plan is slender: light in texture, narrower spacing. A stone or brick plan is heavy: black in masses, wider in spacing. Combination of materials: lightness combined with massiveness. A cast block building: such massing as is felt to be adequate to the sense of block and box and slab, more freedom in spacing' (in Etlin 1994: 56).

Figure 12.1 Living room in Avisfield house, Edinburgh, by Morris and Steedman, architects, 1958.

Evidence of the influence of Frank Lloyd Wright's thinking can be seen in a Modern Movement interior from Avisfield House in Edinburgh. This house, built in 1958 by architects Morris and Steedman, demonstrates the use of natural materials (wood and stone) in conjunction with an idea of the centrality of the hearth in a home (Figure 12.1).

Materials tell us not only about place but also about time: Finnish architect Juhani Pallasmaa is lyrical about materials in this passage: 'Natural material expresses its age and history as well as the tale of its birth and human use. The patina of wear adds the enriching experience of time; matter exists in the continuum of time' (1994: 27). An understanding of all these culturally manifest ideas is valuable to the designer.

Design/Function Criteria

The main criteria here must relate to the suitability of the material to the central purpose of its use. Related to this are issues around durability, ease of maintenance, resistance to damage and vandalism, and health and safety characteristics. For each material, consideration should be made of the following:

- Its history and image
- Features and properties; chemical composition
- Natural resources used in production
- Manufacturing process and energy consumption
- Testing methods; commercial dimensions; waste production
- Available colours and shapes
- Installation methods
- Impact on users' health
- Research findings that relate to sustainability issues
- Conflicting evaluations
- Environmental and safety concerns

Furthermore, and especially in relation to universal design matters, sensorial qualities should be considered as part of the criteria, including weight, elasticity, texture (roughness-smoothness), temperature, light reflection, colour, acoustical performance and odour.

In some circumstances, particular material choices may seem inevitable, and be the starting point of a design. For example, Mies van der Rohe, when discussing the choice of onyx for a wall in the 1929 Barcelona Pavilion, said: 'Eventfully I found an onyx block of certain size and since I only had the possibility of that block, I made the pavilion twice that height and then we developed the plan' (in Frampton 1995: 171).

Budgetary Criteria

The initial costs of materials and their relation to the budget is the major consideration here and each project will differ. However, the lifetime cost of particular materials, calculated on the anticipated durability, the degree of maintenance and repair and the replacement cost, etc., would give a truer picture of the value for money. In general, the cost of interior finishing materials in the service life of a building is much higher than the cost of other building materials. In the end, maintenance costs are the ones that often have a major impact in the total life cycle cost of interior building materials.

Environmental Criteria

Materials knowledge not only includes the products themselves, but also an understanding of the source and ecological soundness of the material, the cost, and the methods of installation and maintenance. The environmental credentials of a material are as important as issues of aesthetics and price. A preference for products based on renewable natural resources (linoleum, bamboo, cork and rubber) or on biodegradable or recyclable material, and an avoidance of polluting materials, should be self-evident. In some cases, the adaptive reuse or recycling of materials will be appropriate.

A useful and rigorous questionnaire for the evaluation of materials in relation to environmental criteria asks the following questions:

- Do we need it?
- Can it be sourced as recycled, adapted, second-hand?
- Does it minimize waste possibilities?
- Is it durable?
- Is it multi-functional?

- Is it toxic in any way?
- Has it been produced with renewable re-sources?
- Has it been produced with minimal pack-aging?
- Has it been produced with recycled material?
- Is the supplier and the supply chain eco-friendly?
- Is it sourced locally where possible?

If the material meets satisfactory responses to most of these questions, is aesthetically and functionally appropriate, and comes in on budget, it is a good solution.

environmental impacts of various materials

Assessment of the environmental impact when selecting products is crucial. One particularly important issue for interior designers is the impact on Indoor Environmental Quality (IEQ). Pollution caused by materials such as asbestos, carbon monoxide, cleaning solvents, formaldehyde, nitrogen dioxide, ozone, pesticides, radon and VOCs in a building, or the furnishing products used therein, affects IEQ. The aim of avoiding these hazardous contents by developing and using mainstream products that are biodegradable, renewable or recyclable is one major aspect of sustainability.

The American *Whole Building Design Guide* points out that: 'it is easy to forget that the ultimate success or failure of a project rests on its indoor environmental quality (IEQ). Healthy, comfortable employees are invariably more satisfied and productive. Unfortunately, this simple,

compelling truth is often lost, for it is simpler to focus on the first-cost of a project than it is to determine the value of increased user productivity and health' (NIBS). The Guide lists the following considerations for successful IEQ:

- Facilitate quality IEQ through good design, construction, and operating and maintenance practices;
- Value aesthetic decisions, such as the importance of views and the integration of natural and man-made elements;
- Provide thermal comfort with a maximum degree of personal control over temperature and airflow;
- Supply adequate levels of ventilation and outside air to ensure indoor air quality;
- Prevent airborne bacteria, mold, and other fungi through heating, ventilating, air-conditioning (HVAC) system designs that are effective at controlling indoor humidity, and building envelope design that prevents the intrusion of moisture;
- Avoid the use of materials high in pollutants, such as volatile organic compounds (VOCs) or toxins;
- Assure acoustic privacy and comfort through the use of sound-absorbing material and equipment isolation;
- Control disturbing odors through contaminant isolation and careful selection of cleaning products;
- Create a high performance luminous environment through the careful integration of natural and artificial light sources; and
- Provide quality water.

(NIBS/'Enhance ...' feature)

These targets, though demanding, are essential to the health of the planet.

In this next section, there are some examples of generic products and their associated sustainability issues relating to interiors.

Composite Boards

Designers employ composite boards such as fibreboards, MDF, plywood and particleboards for structural efficiency and value, but there are concerns about the sourcing of the raw materials and the toxicity of their binding agents. Many composite boards still use toxic resins, although alternatives are available. Additionally, large quantities of the original timber content derive from non-sustainable sources, since FSC (Forest Stewardship Council) products are not widely employed. Composite boards are common in the furniture industry as well as for internal construction purposes, so great care needs to be taken with selection.

Joinery Paints and Stains

The major sustainability factor relating to paints for woodwork is the issue of VOCs (Volatile Organic Compounds). Often employed as rapidly evaporating solvents, they carry the pigment and binder. 'Natural' paints with a water base and natural ingredients are increasingly available, as are zero-VOC paints. Specifying zero-rated products for interior and exterior use is good practice.

Smooth Flooring

The market for smooth or hard flooring has long been associated with vinyl or PVC products, although there has also long been a place for less processed materials, such as linoleum, cork and

rubber. In fact, the so-called 'natural materials' such as linoleum, cork, FSC-sourced wood and locally sourced stone are all sustainable in relation to synthetic alternatives. Manufacturers produce a range of products made from natural or recycled rubber, ceramic or stone. If 'plastic' type materials are required, then it is good practice to specify polyolefins such as polyethylene and polypropylene in place of PVC.

Carpets and Matting

Synthetic fibres or synthetic–wool blends still make up the majority of carpets. Nylon is still popular, as is polypropylene. The use of traditional wool fibres occurs in smaller quantities, while we see other natural fibres, such as sisal and grasses, in speciality materials.

Apart from the pile yarns, there is a problem with waste carpet. Recycling, or alternatives such as carpet tiles, address this problem. Recycled carpet is made from recovered textile fibres or from recycled polyethylene terephthalate (PET). Carpets made with recycled materials possess the same qualities as virgin material, though often have the added benefits of increased stain resistance and improved indoor air quality through the reduction of volatile organic compounds (VOCs). To facilitate recycling, some manufacturers are initiating programmes to recover used carpet at the end of its planned life (see GreenSpec).

These few examples from the many thousands of choices available indicate the importance of careful negotiation through the 'minefield' of specifying and selection.

Finally, appropriate product and material selections and specifications involve compliance with codes, life safety, building standards, bidding processes, sustainability guidelines and human needs such as accessibility and ergonomic considerations. Like all other products, life cycle, cost analysis and recycling or disposability need careful consideration. Other practical aspects include particular specifications and installations: finishes (selection, cost, schedules); fixtures (location and specifications); supplier/vendor requirements (information, installation plans, shipping instructions); product attributes (selection, cost, application, properties and performance criteria); and installation methods and costs.

practice and process

Some familiarity with other issues is useful when working with materials. All materials have contexts, whether they are historical, cultural or spatial, and these contexts will vary over time, location and culture. Materials will have specific aesthetic qualities that may or may not make them particularly suitable for interior applications. The artificial distinction between natural and apparently unnatural materials, in both surface and hidden materials, is also worth considering. Baudrillard claims that 'objectively, substances are simply what they are: there is no such thing as a true or a false, a natural or an artificial substance. How could concrete be somehow less "authentic" than stone?' (1996 [1968]: 38). Nevertheless, they do have different cultural identities and references.

Beyond these general points, an understanding of the particular properties, characteristics and types of selected materials is valuable, as are understandings of sources, manufacturing and fabrication methods, to enable informed assessments of any environmental and health impacts. A more detailed knowledge of technical issues such as jointing methods, finishing processes and installation and maintenance methods will be advantageous in explaining materials selection. The issue of choice of finish is also useful to consider: should the material be exposed, enhanced and protected but otherwise exposed, coated but allowed to reflect the material character, or be covered completely to hide it?

furniture and furnishings

Apart from the interior space arrangements, the next major issue for interior designers is often the selection and placement of furniture and furnishings. In most interiors, furniture is a key element in making the scheme and therefore has some significance in the planning process. In addition to the functional aspects, furniture and furnishings often have important social and emotional purposes.

It is becoming increasingly apparent that clients assume functionality and reliability to be a 'given', therefore successful design will meet other higher-level needs. The formula devised by the Frog design team, 'Form Follows Emotion', recognizes that:

Product design should always include something extra; no matter how elegant and functional a design, it will not win a place in our lives unless it can appeal at a deeper level, to our emotions. ... The emotional element can be present in any number of ways: it may appeal to our desire for enhanced nostalgia. ... Or it might be a tactile ergonomic experience … or it could be reinventing the familiar. (in McDonagh et al. 2004: 377)

Mark Kingwell points out that furniture has various functions, enabling humans to complete tasks, and at this level all furniture types are equal. However, he also reinforces the role of furniture to meet higher-level human needs. He says 'a "good" table, a table worth having, isn't just a handy surface or prop; it must also be striking, beautiful, elegant, witty – or some combination thereof' (2002: 239). He takes this further by noting how 'furniture structures space, making what is otherwise undifferentiated into something meaningful. I place a couch in an empty room and it acquires new significance: the air now shimmers with the possibilities of conversation or napping or seduction' (243). Stanley Abercrombie suggests that furniture can be categorized in three basic types: 'those that serve our bodies, those that serve our possessions and those that serve only our senses' (1990: 80). If interior designers seriously consider furniture in something like these terms, it will be beneficial to the whole scheme.

The relationship between the available space and the furniture required is analysed through the Furniture Footprint. Designers draw up this plan of the size, type and clearance of furniture and equipment in co-ordination with the architectural and associated components (Plate 32). The furniture footprint plan, whilst not considered a final layout, will demonstrate the designer's ability to comprehend and plan for the various planned functions in the facility, and at the same time provide the user with a good indication of the adequacy of each space from a size and shape standpoint. The designer should use standard furniture sizes at this point since the final solution may utilize various combinations of new and used furniture.[1]

We can demonstrate the example of the role of furniture and furnishings in office spaces through various factors.

Physical and Task Needs

Furnishings have to relate to the particular location and overall scheme employed, the specified functions and the ergonomic and other needs of the users. These will vary between the user groups, and considerations regarding children's furniture, for example, will be radically different from those for seniors. In other situations, such as public spaces and healthcare facilities, issues of hygiene will affect choices and specifications. Furniture should relate to the space plan, though may also be required to be flexible in relation to tasks. All specifications will have to take into account codes, trading standards and fitness for purpose.

Health, Safety and Environment

These aspects are an essential and often legal requirement relating to the elements of an interior, and will affect performance. Apart from compliance issues, consideration of the ergonomics of furniture, the siting and use of VDUs and other equipment, and matters such as IAQ and a sustainable agenda, are all crucial.

Productivity

Clearly a priority for all commercial customers, productivity is influenced by furnishing processes that consider areas such as universal access to furniture and equipment, the needs of cross performance by staff, issues with storage and retrieval, lighting and physical comfort.

Privacy Needs

In specifying furniture for this aspect, the designer has to consider the shape and height of partitions, the degree of enclosure, the need for low noise levels and the appropriate size of the workstation.

Need for Recognition

This is a sensitive issue but is important to the occupants of an office space. Status and recognition include the ability to display personal items and the employment of furnishings and equipment that is suited to the user's status.

The simple example of an office space that has just been given demonstrates something of the complex issues surrounding the design of spaces and the furnishing selections required to meet the client's needs.

ANALYSIS Chairs

A chair certainly can be somewhere to sit down, but this is only the beginning. Chairs offer a view of collective ideas about authority and status, self-definition and identity, discipline, domination and behaviour, and comfort and relaxation. They also act as aesthetic manifestos and statements of intent. In any event, a chair is not neutral. A chair is a social construct: it need not be called a chair and we do not necessarily have to use chairs, but we continue to do so to the point where we seem obliged to make use of them. Western society is so organized that sitting and using chairs appears to be completely natural. Chairs organize our relations with one another, and many of us have come to believe that sitting in chairs is correct and natural and the only way we can live. Therefore, chairs embedded with social, political, philosophical, historical and cultural meanings that have varied over time reflect how particular cultures have related with and to them. Some chairs become icons. For example, the bentwood products of Thonet are well known. The contemporary Japanese lifestyle company Muji proposed a reinterpretation of the No. 14 chair (now 150 years old). The Thonet/Muji chair is the result of taking a nineteenth-century model and simplifying it. Reinterpreted by James Irvine, it was introduced in 2008 (Figure 12.2).

Of course, in some cultures the chair is, or has been, irrelevant, and the range of differing postures used throughout the world indicates that 'sitting on a chair' is only one of many possible states (Hewes 1955: 231–244). It is just these cultural issues that designers need to be aware of in the global economy.

The Herman Miller Embody chair is a good example of contemporary design that addresses many of the criteria above, including sustainability. Made from non-toxic and sustainable materials with 42 per cent recycled content, at the end of use it is 95 per cent recyclable. The chair addresses the human need criterion through its adjustable back, which reflects the form of the human spine and adjusts with movement. Herman Miller explains how this works: 'a matrix of pixels creates dynamic seat-and-back surfaces that automatically conform to your every movement and distribute your weight evenly' (see Herman Miller). The seat comprises four separate layers. The bottom layer provides suspension; the second provides support; the third is a system of hexagonal rings that adjust in relation to your weight as you move; and the final layer is a mesh for air circulation (Figure 12.3).

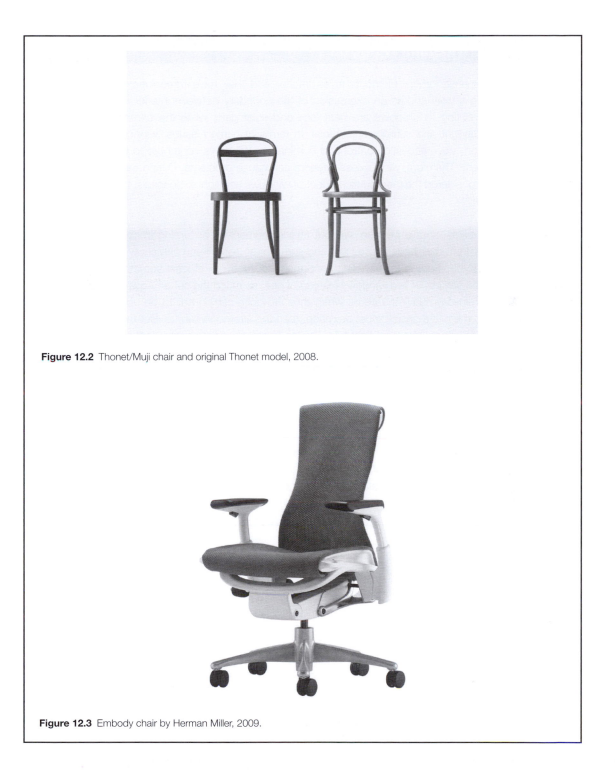

Figure 12.2 Thonet/Muji chair and original Thonet model, 2008.

Figure 12.3 Embody chair by Herman Miller, 2009.

ANALYSIS Hospital Windows

Windows are generally crucial elements in an interior and they have three functions: admittance of light, capturing a view and as an expression of the boundary between interior and exterior. The physical issues relating to windows are heat loss and solar gain, while the benefits of ventilation and access to daylight and sunlight are crucial. In terms of human issues, windows offer thermal comfort/discomfort, view, acoustic control and illumination. Windows contribute to the quality of the indoor environment. Therefore, windowless interiors can cause problems. During the mid-nineteenth century, nurses considered the therapeutic aspect of windows and light in hospitals. In 1860, Florence Nightingale wrote:

> Therefore, [patients] should be able, without raising themselves or turning in bed, to see out of the window from their beds, to see sky and sun-light at least, if you can show them nothing else, I assert to be, if not of the very first importance for recovery, at least something very near it. … If they can see out of two windows instead of one, so much the better. Again, the morning sun and the mid-day sun – the hours when they are quite certain not to be up, are of more importance to them, if a choice must be made, than the afternoon sun. … But the best rule is, if possible, to give them direct sunlight from the moment he rises till the moment he sets. (84)

Modern hospital planning takes the provision of light as an important part of the healing process and in some cases mimics Nightingale's ideas. Many studies have found that wards or rooms with windows with a view (especially of nature) improve a patient's recovery. For example, research in the USA found that 'patients in intensive care units (ITU) with no view to the outside will occupy ITU beds for longer than patients who can see out of a window. The USA has taken this finding so seriously that in many states it is compulsory to have windows and views from all ITU beds. Where this is not possible, specially designed computer-controlled false windows that mimic the passing of the day are fitted, where lighting comes up at the beginning of the day, clouds pass and the sun sets in the evening' (Biley 1996: 110–115).

ANALYSIS Smart Materials

The developments of smart, intelligent materials are having an increasing impact on architecture and interiors. The physics and chemistry of these can be complex as many work at the 'nano' level; however, some understanding of type and capabilities is useful. These materials fall into two groups: those that change properties and those that change energy. The property-changing materials include: thermochronic, whereby heat alters the molecular structure – to change the perceived colour, for example; magnetorheological, whereby magnetic or electric fields change the viscosity of a material; thermotropic, where inputs of thermal energy change phases (i.e. from liquid to gas), thus demonstrating differing properties; and shape memory, where thermal energy changes structures through crystalline phase change.

The energy-change systems include photovoltaic, where light energy produces electric current; thermoelectric, where the electric current creates temperature differences; piezoelectric, where 'strain energy' produces electric current; photoluminescence, where UV radiation energy changes to radiation energy in the visible spectrum; and electrostrictive, where the current alters the energy of molecules to deform shape.

These abstract examples can be better understood when seen as applications for tasks such as the control of solar radiation, conductive heat transfer, interior heat generation in relation to optimizing energy delivery, lighting systems and HVAC systems. Particular materials such as glass, coatings/paints and fabrics are all involved in adapting and developing with smart material applications. The role of smart materials in sensors, detectors, activators and control systems will grow in importance, especially with developments in MEMS (Micro-Electro-Mechanical Systems). Designers find that the benefits of employing smart materials include their immediacy, transience, self-actuation, selectivity and directness (see Addington and Schodek 2005).

Randomly selected examples include woven, hard-surface materials made from polyethylene textiles and polyester resin material, resulting in hard, tactile and easy to maintain surfaces. These may be opaque or translucent and may be draped into forms and heat-manipulated to form shapes. They may be sculptural aluminium sheets that fold longitudinally for applications such as cladding, display, lighting and signage. They may be chromatic fabrics with light interference pigments that change colour with the light and viewing angle, which can be used for upholstery, wall coverings, etc. Recycled polyethylene used as laminate or solid surfacing material has unique colour combinations and may be used flat or curved.

CASE STUDY 12.1 Domestic Interior

This case study of a small-scale interior decorating project is a good, typical example of working with issues around materials. The images (Figures 12.4 and 12.5) show the 'before' and 'after' results. Note the emphasis on the role and nature of the materials used. Here the decorator, Susan Ginesi, explains her working practices and how the elements went together:

I was called in to update this, an existing space, by a very active couple. I saw he loved tennis, as she loved her golf. Their clothing exemplified their life style … casual & tailored. Yet they lived but 30 minutes from NYC & had an appreciation for the arts. By the end of our initial consultation we were all in agreement that the largest room in the home need not be a living room to look at only, and that the smallest room in the house currently utilized as a den, would become their exercise room.

This being said, design boards for the open space area, which included the living room, dining room & kitchen began taking form centred around the attached art. I wanted to de-clutter & simplify the environment, and the menswear movement in the home textiles market inspired me.

Today their walls are partially papered in natural linen. As we crown molded, we wainscotted some walls too … which added interest without confusion. I chose a tweed sectional contrast welted with a very dark brown suede, with just a bit of shine, to help it pop off the matt textured neutral rug. The case goods selected remained traditional but with cleaner lines … more transitional. Large key art pieces replaced smaller collections filling the previous shelving units. Swags & jabots were replaced with striped silk stationary Romans, and textured solid panels banded in suede. The chairs flanking the console are also adorned with metallic threads. The shape of the custom floral arrangements mirrors the chair fabric pattern. The fireplace plaster applied is also glazed with a copper wash. (Susan Ginesi, Morristown, NJ)

Figure 12.4 Domestic decoration: Before room by Susan Ginesi, 2008.

Figure 12.5 Domestic decoration: After room by Susan Ginesi, 2008.

chapter 13

the business of interior design

CHAPTER OVERVIEW

This chapter briefly introduces some of the business elements of an interior design practice. They are general pointers for those considering a career in interior design, and anyone intending to set up a practice should seek professional advice. One of the most important factors of business is responsibility. This responsibility extends to staff, clients, contractors and the wider social world.

Sets of ethics and values are the basis for this corporate social responsibility. The actual planning and successful practice of a business relies upon a number of aspects including: the type of business organization that will be used; a clear understanding of issues relating to insurance, personnel and staff (HR); and financial and marketing considerations. Successful practices have sound management at all levels and in all aspects of the work of the business. These include office management, individual time management and project management. Project management itself is introduced with an overview of the various stages that a project goes through from conception to completion.

introduction

Interior design is a major design discipline and a broad area of work that covers a diverse range of practices and specializations. For example, Mary Knackstedt notes over 100 speciality subdivisions of the interior design profession from adaptive reuse to wayfinding specialists (2008).

The challenges and constraints that affect a business grow every day. It is only by constant vigilance, attention to detail and an updated understanding of both the wider world around us and the more local conditions of business that designers will survive satisfactorily. As with any successful business, there must be a professional attitude and practice, which is not distracted by short-term gains. Corporate social responsibility underlines the triple bottom line of people, planet and profit.

corporate social responsibility

Corporate social responsibility reflects a company's involvement in, and attitude towards, all stakeholders and the environment. A frequently cited definition by the World Business Council for Sustainable Development states that 'Corporate social responsibility is the continuing commitment by business to behave ethically and contribute to economic development while improving the quality of life of the workforce and their families, as well as the local community and society at large' (WBCSD).

Ethics

In Chapter 4 there was some discussion of the role of ethics, morality and values in relation to design and designing. These are also important in commercial activities. The maintenance of a code of ethics is based on strategies that support staff and client relations through careful and considered approaches to business practice. In reality, protection is given to clients and the public through health and safety legislation, accounting procedures, contracts and so on; it is the actual ethical dimension of a business that underpins its whole approach. There are a number of examples of companies that have a commitment to, for example, fair trade, sustainability, the welfare of the 'family' constituted by their staff and relations with the wider community, all reflecting their ethical approach.

Ethical standpoints also relate to issues around intellectual property and the recognition of others' contributions, the declaration of conflicts of interest and an acknowledgement of wider social responsibilities, particularly as a result of work undertaken. In other words, there should be a high level of integrity in relation to the physiological, aesthetic, social and moral aspects of working practices. At the very least, compliance with industry codes of conduct should be a minimally acceptable level of ethical activity.

establishing an interior design business

There are several essential foundation blocks to understand when starting an interior design business.

Planning and Practice

Establishing a design consultancy could begin with an honest assessment of the individual(s) involved. The completion of a SWOT analysis will reveal potential difficulties as well as potential strengths. In this way, the apparent 'gaps' are filled through working with other people, in various ways. The establishment of personal goals, business goals and plans, a profitability plan and a staffing plan, if required, will all be part of the initial planning cycle. In addition, the issue of membership of professional design organizations, professional certification, licensing and/or registration requirements will warrant assessment. A useful maxim is to act within the limits of your competence and authority and to know what they are.

Business Organization

The establishment of a business will require a particular form of organization to ensure that it functions correctly and legally within a particular jurisdiction.[1] Business formats include:

Sole Trader: The basic format of a business organization whereby an individual trader has responsibility for all the profits and all the risks.

Partnerships: These operate in much the same way as sole traders but involve two or more people working together. It is good practice to have a partnership agreement drawn up to define issues such as responsibilities and profit-sharing (usually equally); if losses are incurred, each partner is liable for all the trading losses of a partnership. The agreement is also a basis for settling disputes among partners.

Limited Liability Companies (Private and Public): By following a registration procedure, one or more directors can establish a company. This should be done through a lawyer to ensure compliance with company law. Crucially, the directors register the limit of their personal liability and can share profits as they so choose. There are demands on companies including annual filing of accounts, holding minuted meetings and issues of corporate identity, which must include the registration number and place of registration together with the words Limited or Ltd. after the name. Directors must ensure that they conduct the business in such a manner as to avoid trading unlawfully or insolvently. In public limited companies, shares may be traded, shareholders may vote and there are a number of particular considerations that vary, depending on jurisdiction and location.

Insurance

The legal responsibility for public liability relating to goods, services, interiors and structures requires designers to ensure that goods meet the requirements of the market in which they are sold and used. Insurance against public liability is an essential but necessary charge on the business. Professional negligence is also an issue in terms of advice offered, and insurance is available against claims relating to damages that may arise from reliance on bad advice. Liability also extends to the health and safety of employees and visitors. Indeed, the impact of health and safety regulations, as well as sustainability criteria and minimum standards as to materials and construction, are often built into contracts.

Legal Issues

Avoid legal disputes by:

- Understanding the legal frameworks in which designers operate.
- Recording all meetings, agreements, negotiations and agreed changes.
- Identifying your work with company details, names and dates.
- Keeping duplicate copies of all correspondence and photographically recording art and design works.
- Negotiating the use of written checklists.
- Working to the level of your own competence.
- Following codes of practice.
- Using industry standard software and agreement forms if appropriate.

Financial Planning

A successful business needs an array of financial tools for planning, reporting and responding to changes in income and expenditure. Amongst the most important tools are the budgets. These work on assumptions for income, any growth or shrinkage of the market, changes in fixed and variable costs, any inflation or deflation of prices, or any planned expansion or contraction of work undertaken. Budgets will also make assumptions about profit margins, and their levels will be based on pricing polices.

Issues surrounding cash flows, profit forecasts, credit management, overheads, fee structure and pricing, as well as, for example, how to deal with banks, tax authorities and accountants, are essential to a healthy and profitable business.

Personnel and Staff

Interior designers may be sole traders working from their own homes/studios with irregular hours and income, or may work in large design firms, with regular hours, in an office/studio situation. Like other groups working to provide a service, interior designers may suffer stress in their efforts to achieve deadlines, stick to budgets and satisfy clients' demands. Designers may work with colleagues and clients over a wide geographical base, and they will certainly use electronic systems to research products and make purchases on-line.

Whatever the particular role of the employee, the importance of knowing the objectives, whether it is task-, project- or company-related, along with an honest assessment of people's strengths and weaknesses, will assist the manager or team leader to deliver satisfactorily. To motivate others, or get things done through other people, is a key skill. Setting goals and standards that are specific, attainable, measurable and supported is one key aspect of motivation and achievement. The combination of individual and team needs is a challenge, though when correctly addressed, can work very well. Through example, delegation, counselling and feedback, the benefits of the approaches taken will be evident in the outcomes produced.

management

Discussing personnel, task-setting and motivation brings us on to discuss project management in more depth, and then to explore some other management categories:

Project Management

Five aspects underlie successful project management. These are: (a) that all the responsibilities and roles are clearly defined; (b) that there is a clear and well-designed brief; (c) that thorough planning arrangements exist; (d) that communication channels always remain open; and (e) that there is effective monitoring and control.[2] As well as offering interior design services, the designer may also: act as lead consultant or as an agent; procure furnishings, fittings and equipment (FF&E) or supply goods as a principal (retailer); undertake detached oversight of the execution of building work as contract administrator; or assume responsibility for simple building works and/or decorations.

Time Management

Individual and group time is expensive and easily wasted, so proper time management is a valuable skill. Over-commitment, lack of concentration and poor delegation can lead to time wasting. Design studios are busy places, therefore to assist in time management it is essential to define goals and aims, understand the objectives required to achieve those aims, establish priorities and be decisive.

Attention to how well organized the space is for working, the use of a diary and a planner and sensible controls over access to your phone line and over internal interruptions, e-mails, meetings, etc., will all add to the good planning of time: a skill that is only learnt with practice in relation to your method of working.

Office Management

At any level of business, competent management systems need to be in place, not only for legal reporting, taxation and so on, but also to ensure efficiency in dealing with projects, clients, finances, etc. We discussed some ways of using management tools in Chapter 4, but other more generic issues arise. Record-keeping, for example, is key to controlling all aspects of the business.

marketing

The marketing of interior design services, like that of many other creative works, has to tread a line between a number of conflicting demands. For example, many clients think they know what 'bad design' is, but have difficulty articulating what they want.

Marketing an interior design business essentially entails promoting a service. This begins with positioning the business in relation to its skills base, experience, objectives, resources and so on. The market needs to be understood in relation to the competition, market segments, possible client base and, of course, where the product or service is offered.

To achieve some of these goals, the role of desk-based and field-based market research of existing and new markets is important. Understanding the message aimed at the market place is crucial and should relate to the aims of the business. PR and advertising are the bases of implementation of this aspect of the marketing programme.

Selling

The business of an interior design consultancy is not necessarily to sell goods (although this may be part of the package), but to sell themselves. Hence skills in interviewing, presentation and negotiation are important. Knowledge is power, and in this context, knowing the detail, knowing yourself and your strengths/weaknesses and knowing how to negotiate are very valuable tools.

Skills such as effective personal interaction, direct communication, listening and having the patience to analyse issues and adjusting to compromises can all be acquired through training and experience. Selling interior design concepts is based on an exciting mix of oral, visual and written communication.

operational methods

We now turn in more depth to working methods. Once there is an acceptance by the client of the general processes needed to go ahead and develop an agreed project, then a project-specific agreement, based on the outline brief already given, is established. This will be in addition to the general terms of business. This agreement should include the contract and general terms and conditions; the brief; how the issue of changes will be dealt with; termination matters; costing, prices and quotations; and environmental issues. The progress management of the work will often follow a generally standard pattern, as outlined below.

The Brief

- Review brief to ensure understanding and agreement of all parties.
- Research and understand the client and their needs; ensure feedback from research in appropriate form and time.
- Finalize the brief so that it provides a benchmark that all have signed up to, and ensure that all parties are aware of what constitutes the basis of the objectives, constraints and scope of the project.

Agreements

- Agree responsibilities and establish channels of communication with other professionals and the client.
- Consider issues of confidentiality.

Planning

- Team composition agreed.
- Time and budget allocations tentatively made and costed.
- Schedule planning based on CPA (Critical Path Analysis) or similar.

Concept Design

- Agree concepts for development and review.
- Design a development-based detailed analysis of conceptual ideas.

- Undertake design refinements developed from comparisons with research, the initial brief and any interim meetings.
- Final presentation, which is a serious selling situation for which detailed planning is essential.

General Costings

- Establish total design time and time required for each component of the job.
- Establish amount of work to be done in-house and how much outside.
- Establish management costs.
- Consider payment basis, credit terms, etc.
- Method of charging for bought-in goods and services.
- Method of charging for disbursements.

Pricing

Fees, rechargeables and disbursements are the major cost components of a project. Fees are often based on a fixed basis, on hourly or daily rates, or as a retainer. Fixed fees allow the client to know the expenditure charge for the whole project or parts as appropriate. Hourly and daily rates have risks of uncertainty attached though may be appropriate for particular job types or for experimental work. Extra work charging is a difficult area but must be negotiated and agreed to avoid later problems. Rejection fees are also an important matter, as being paid for work undertaken, even if not eventually progressed, is crucial.

- Calculate cost for design time based on current charging rates.

- Calculate charges for sub-contractors, rechargeable labour items and any other external labour costs.
- Calculate charges for materials based on costs and added mark-up.
- Calculate charges for any production costs based on suppliers' quotes and added mark-up.
- Calculate charges for disbursements (and any mark-up if added).
- Adjust final price in line with market/projects demands if necessary.

Upon Acceptance of Contract Terms and Pricing

- Letters of confirmation of acceptance.
- Standard form of contracts may be agreed and exchanged.
- Contract administration develops contracts based fully on usual business practices.
- Any consultants' work fully integrated into the planning.

Measuring and Controlling

- Job numbering and sheets.
- Ordering systems and expense control.
- Authorizations to be established.
- Only authorized signatories on official order forms to place orders for goods or services.
- Accurate recording of time spent on particular projects.

Design Development

- Final presentations show how the agreed design will be developed and completed.

- Working drawings are developed and maintained in drawing registers.
- Tendering for particular aspects of the project begins.
- Shop drawings are sets of drawings produced by a manufacturer or contractor to provide information for fabricators and installers.

At about this stage a 'design freeze' occurs whereby the detailed designs have been agreed and any further changes will incur extra costs to the client and may delay completion.

Installation Supervision

At this stage, the designer is effectively a quality controller and supervisor. It is here that the designer's knowledge base needs to be broad enough to deal with a wide range of situations relating to materials, techniques, technologies, etc.

- Pilot fit out and evaluation to test plans and ideas (if appropriate).
- Problem review and evaluation during alteration and construction.
- Observation and preparation of punch list, snagging or to-do lists/deficiency reports.
- Further refinement.
- Fit out, installations, decorations, etc.
- Hand-over and sign-off by both client and designer.

Getting Paid

Timely and accurate billing to clients is essential for the health of the business. Check the client credit worthiness before any engagement begins, so chasing of invoices and potential default will be minimal.

After Completion

- Post-Occupancy Evaluation (POE).
- Public relations. The publication of a project in the media may be something to embrace or to avoid. It depends on how the outcome is viewed, where and by whom. Any PR activity needs to be agreed and cleared with the client involved.

research

An ongoing aspect of the planning and progression process is research, to develop databases of information and approaches to project management. This is especially important in areas of sustainability. Research topics might include:

- Selection of contractors and suppliers.
- Role of design centres.
- Buying methods.
- Working with contractors.

- Continuing professional development. The importance of continuing professional development cannot be underestimated in a fast-changing world.

in conclusion

These introductory remarks on the nature of the interior design business indicate not only the similarities with other business types but also some of the specific issues that will need to be confronted, whether the business is a sole trader or a corporation. The key issues then relate to the initial setting of objectives; the identification of your particular 'products'; the preparation of financial forecasts and business plan; the raising of finance and employment of staff (if appropriate); and the marketing of your business and development of a client base. In all cases, the use of professionals such as lawyers, accountants, bankers and public agencies will be essential to the establishment and development of the business, as will associations with allied professional bodies and individual consultants.

glossary

A

Accent Lighting – Controlled and focused light used to accent interior elements or architectural details.

Accessible – A design consideration to ensure that the approach and use of a building or structure by physically handicapped individuals is simple and easy.

Accessible Design – Dwelling that meets the prescribed requirements enabling the access and egress of handicapped individuals.

Accessory – Decorative objects of art, lighting, plants, area rugs and wall hangings added to an interior space to enhance and reinforce the design style.

Achromatic – A colour scheme that employs shades of white, black and the range of greys between them is called achromatic; the term neutral colours is also used.

Acoustics – Effect of sound produced in an enclosed space. Acoustic specialists advise on sound requirements, avoidance of noise pollution and special equipment as appropriate.

Adaptable Design – Readily adjustable spaces that may be used by a wide range of occupants. Adaptable spaces have accessible features but some items may be omitted or concealed until needed as accessible features can change the original use or appearance of a space. In an adaptable dwelling, it is usual to have wide doors, knee spaces, no steps, appropriate control and switch locations, and other access features.

Adaptive Reuse – The utilization of an existing space or structure for a new purpose.

Aesthetics – The philosophy or theory of taste, or of the perception of the beautiful in nature and art.

Ambient Light – Measurement of the overall illumination of a room from reflected sunlight or overhead lighting applications.

Analogous Colour – Colours adjacent to each other on the colour wheel, i.e. Red next to Orange, Blue next to Green.

Anthropometrics – The measurement of body dimensions and the statistical analysis that comes from the collected data. Anthropometrics play a valuable role in design, ergonomics and architectural planning.

Area Rug – Custom, handmade, loomed rugs in woven textiles such as cotton, wool or silk, in any shape and size; manufactured floor coverings in materials such as nylon or plastic; or other types made of various synthetic fibres; typically available in standard sizes such as 2×3, 3×5, 5×8, 8×10 ft and so on.

Asset-based Design – Asset-based design refers to the social involvement of designers and communities where design-works are made by building on the strengths already present in the community.

Assisted Living – Assisted living residences or assisted living facilities (ALFs) provide supervision or assistance with daily activities; organization of services by external health care providers; and supervision of resident activities to help ensure health, safety and well-being.

Atrium – Originally in Roman buildings, an open central court from which other enclosed rooms led off. In contemporary usage it refers to a several-stories-high interior open space, often with a top-lit glazed roof. They have been associated with impressive hotels, office blocks and malls.

Axis – Single or multiple imaginary or drawn lines bisecting major interior or architectural components of a space.

Axonometric – See ISOMETRIC.

B

Balance – The visual weight of interior components and furnishings that creates a sense of equilibrium in an interior. Balance relates to visual weight and textures, surfaces, shapes and colour, all of which can influence the perception. The axis or fulcrum of a design is therefore often critical, as this is the basis for perceptual and conceptual factors, although balance does not equate to symmetry.

Barrier-free – This refers to spaces with no access or egress limitations for handicapped individuals. It is a process of modifying buildings or facilities so that the physically disadvantaged or disabled can access the spaces. Barrier-free modification may be the most appropriate or only valid approach in existing buildings, but for new-builds, it has largely been superseded by the concept of universal design.

Biodegradable – The process by which organic substances are broken down by the enzymes produced by living organisms.

Budgeting – Financial planning intended to keep control of costs, expenses and potential profits.

C

CAD/CADD – CAD, or Computer-Aided Design, is software that can draft and model a wide range of spaces in two or three dimensions. This can often rotate in three dimensions, so that the space/object can be viewed from multiple angles. Several CAD packages are able to use dynamic mathematical modelling; these are defined as CADD-computer-aided design and drafting.

Change Management – A structured approach to transitioning individuals, teams and organizations from a current state to a desired future state. The process is complex but there are some guides. Objectives need to be inspired via the right guiding team, who will have a vision and the necessary tools to implement change. Involving as many people as possible, and communicating with each other continually, will reduce obstacles and encourage feedback. Setting short-term achievable goals and finishing each stage before a new one starts will keep the process under control. Change is ongoing so it is important to continually reinforce the culture of change.

Charette – Any collaborative gathering in which a group of designers rough out a plan or scheme to solve a design brief. In certain cases, the term may refer to a concentrated phase of working undertaken by the team or individuals, completing work to an established deadline.

CID – Certified Interior Designer, used by some state licensing agencies to identify an interior designer registered with a state; also used by various organizations to indicate that a member meets their standards.

Circulation – Lobby and corridor spaces designated for movement by individuals from one area to another. They are often difficult to manage as they may not have room for spatial alterations, may lack any particular focal point, are often boring in shape, and in some cases have no opportunity to place furniture. On the other hand, they can offer unusual opportunities for exciting treatments that can create great impact.

Classic Orders of Architecture – A formulation by noted scholars of Greek and Roman architectural designs into five distinct orders: i.e. Greek Doric Order, Ionic Order and Corinthian Order, and also the Roman Composite Order and Tuscan Order.

Code of Ethics – A formal statement of agreed values about certain ethical and social topics. Some codes apply general principles about beliefs on matters such as quality, employees or the environment. Others set out the measures to be used in specific ethical situations and define the procedures to determine whether a violation of the code has occurred and, if so, what remedies should be imposed.

Codes and Building Standards – Sets of rules that denote the minimum acceptable level of safety for constructed objects and their outfitting. The main function of the building codes is to protect public health, safety and general welfare in relation to the construction and occupancy of spaces. The building codes are usually legally binding.

Colour Palette – A specific group or range of traits in various colours, which can be contrasting, complementary or monochromatic, utilized in a specific project.

Colour Rendering (Rendition) Index (CRI) – See CRI.

Colour Temperature – A characteristic of visible light, it is an important element in interior lighting plans. For example, a warmer-coloured light (i.e. lower colour temperature) is often used in public areas to promote relaxation, while a cooler, whiter light (of a higher colour temperature) is used in offices. Colour temperature may also refer to the apparently perceived temperature of particular colours in a palette.

Colour Trends – A process of predicting and using particular colour palettes. Although it is a very elusive topic it is likely that colour choices in interiors will be inspired by fashion, excited by emotion and reinforced by cultures.

Composition – The method of arrangement or assembly of the part of an interior according to a design.

Conservation – The act or process of preserving, protecting or maintaining precious resources of all kinds. These may be natural resources, historic resources or others.

Corporate Culture – A set of values devised by an organization that defines relationships with stakeholders, and comprises the attitudes, experiences and beliefs of an organization.

CRI – The Colour Rendering Index (CRI) is a quantitative measure of the capacity of a source of light to replicate colours accurately when compared with a model or natural light source. A reference source, such as black body radiation (as no light is either reflected or transmitted, the object appears black when it is cold), is defined as having a CRI of 100. This is why incandescent lamps have that rating, as they are similar to a black body. The nearer a CRI rating is to 100, the greater its capability to show true colours to the human eye.

Custom Furniture – Bespoke furniture made to specification for individual orders.

D

Daylighting – The system of placing windows in such a way that, during the day, natural light provides effective internal illumination. Within the design of a building, attention should be given to daylighting to maximize visual comfort, increase productivity or to reduce energy use.

Detailing – The process of production of accurate scaled drawings based on the preliminary outline sketches of a design. The design detailing process allows accurate costings to be calculated and the final construction and design drawing to be created for accurate working and finishing.

Diversity – The principle of including people of a range of diverse cultural and religious backgrounds and encouraging tolerance. This is often achieved through educating employees, students, etc., so they understand how they can operate in a diverse and multi-cultural environment.

Dormer Window – A window placed vertically in a roof with its own independent roof. The name derives from an original use as a sleeping space in the roof.

Downlight – A light fixture that is installed into a hollow opening in a ceiling. When lit, there appears to be a concentrated spot or flood of light shining from a hole in the ceiling.

E

Egress – Vertical or horizontal means of escape or exit from a building.

Enfilade – Linear arrangement of interior doors providing a vista when the doors remain open; French term describing a low Provincial buffet (sideboard) with four or more doors.

Environmental Control – The assessment and control of factors in the environment that can potentially affect health. The design of buildings and their interiors requires an understanding of environmental control and systems relating to heating, air quality, humidity, etc. Although these can be passive, i.e. through a building's materials and processes, it is active engagement through mechanical means that will regulate temperature, condition the air, alleviate humidity and adjust lighting, for example. Integrated Environmental Design (IED) used in so-called intelligent buildings controls all the mechanical processes along with external heat-gain, daylighting and so on, to manage the building and its efficient use of energy.

Environmental Health – Those aspects of human health and disease that are determined by factors in the environment. It also refers to the theory and practice of assessing and controlling factors in the environment that can potentially affect health.

Ergonomics – Scientific analysis of human beings and how we function in conjunction with a variety of equipment, products, methods and circumstances, in order to improve our health, safety and welfare.

Evidence-based Design – A process used in the planning, design and construction of commercial buildings. This process bases design decisions on the best contemporary research evidence and careful observation of completed projects. The value of POE is clear here. Decisions are made by the designer and client based on the research and project evaluations. Evidence-based design requires careful analysis and thinking about appropriate solutions that can later be evaluated through perceived improvements in the organization's performance indicators. Originating in healthcare, it is now being used in other public, commercial and industrial situations.

F

Facilities Management – The management of buildings or estates that includes both hard (e.g. air conditioning) and soft (e.g. cleaning) services.

Feng Shui – An ancient Chinese system of space planning and use that is believed to use astronomy and geography to help improve one's life by harmonizing energy flows through the house.

Fider – Foundation for Interior Design Research, now known as the Council for Interior Design Accreditation (CIDA).

Finish Schedule – Documents detailing doors, windows, furniture, room finishes, colours and other components needing clarification for construction purposes.

Focal Point – Specific visual elements such as a spectacular view, home entertainment system, fireplace, art, sculpture or furniture piece that becomes the focus of the room or vignette. The focal point will vary with every commission and there may be primary and secondary versions.

FSC – The Forest Stewardship Council is an international organization established in 1993 to promote responsible management of the world's forests. It sets benchmarks, and offers autonomous certification and classification of forest products. This assures customers that the certified wood products are derived from socially and environmentally managed timber sources.

G

Gender – Gender identity is a person's self-conception as being male or female, as distinguished from their actual biological sex. Although gender is commonly used interchangeably with sex, it often refers to specifically social differences, known as gender roles, that are socially constructed.

Globalization – A process of changing local phenomena into worldwide ones. The term is often used to refer to economic globalization, i.e. integration of national economies into the international economy through trade, foreign direct investment, capital flows, migration and the spread of technology.

Grazing Light – Type of lighting that lands on a surface at a flat angle to highlight and heighten the surface structures.

Green Design – Sustainable design methods that utilize recycled, renewable and environmentally friendly materials and design elements, i.e.

energy-efficient insulation, solar power, water conservation methods, renewable bamboo flooring, etc.

H

Home Automation – Technological innovations and electronics pre-wired or retrofitted into residential applications.

Home Office – A facility to work at home that uses electronic technologies to communicate with colleagues, clients, etc., without the need to commute.

Home Theatre – Electronic equipment system designed to create theatre-quality images and sound in a home.

Hospitality Design – Interior design specialization for individuals with specific knowledge and skills for the professional hotel/motel/convention design market.

Hue – A particular name for a colour, e.g. Red, Blue, Yellow, Green, etc., that is based upon the amount of light and its wavelength across the colour spectrum.

Human Behaviour – The action or reaction of humans in relation to a particular environment. Although human behaviour is studied by psychologists, sociologists, economists and anthropologists, a working knowledge of the basics is very valuable to interior designers.

Human Needs – Fundamental human needs (as opposed to wants) include subsistence, protection, affection, understanding, participation, recreation, creation, identity and freedom. See Maslow's hierarchy of needs in Chapter 9.

HVAC – An acronym for the services of heating, ventilation and air conditioning.

I

Incandescent Light – Light from a conventional bulb, halogen bulb or heat lamp.

Indirect Lighting – Glare-free ambient lighting on ceiling, walls or floors, encased and hidden from view, e.g. sconce, uplight, downlight.

Indoor Air Quality – Quality of indoor air supply measured by the number of contaminates suspended in the air. Ventilation is one of the major methods of ensuring high-quality indoor air.

Interdisciplinary – The qualities of studies that cut across several established disciplines or traditional fields of study.

Isometric – An isometric projection is a form of graphical projection – more specifically, an axonometric projection. It is a method of visually representing three-dimensional objects in two dimensions, in which the three co-ordinate axes appear equally foreshortened and the angles between any two of them are 120°.

L

Laminate – A manufacturing process that sandwiches layers of material and seals them with heat and/or pressure, usually with an adhesive. Laminate also refers to the product of this process, e.g. flooring, worktops, etc.

LED Light Emitting Diode – LEDs are often used as small indicator lights on electronic devices and increasingly in higher power applications such as flashlights and area lighting. The colour of the emitted light depends on the composition and condition of the semi-conducting material used.

Life Cycle Analysis/Costs – Investigation and valuation of the environmental impacts of a given product or service caused or necessitated by its existence. The analysis consists of four factors: goal and scope, inventory, impact assessment and interpretation.

M

Marketing – Business activity that tries to present the products or services supplied by a business in such a way as to make them more attractive than the competition.

MCS – Multiple Chemical Sensitivity is an abnormal sensitivity or allergy-like reaction to various kinds of pollutants including solvents, VOCs (Volatile Organic Compounds), scents, fuel, smoke and other non-specified chemicals.

Mock-up – A complete model that is built to scale.

Module – A regulating set of proportions used in architecture and design. It can also refer to an independent unit that can be combined with others and easily rearranged, replaced or interchanged to create alternative structures.

Multimedia – The use of a range of media in combination. Media include sound, telephone, television, text, video, film, computer programs, etc.

Musculoskeletal Disorders (MSDs) – Musculoskeletal disorders can affect the body's muscles, joints, tendons, ligaments and nerves. Most work-related MSDs develop over time and are caused either by the nature of the work itself or by the particular working environment. MSDs typically affect the back, neck, shoulders and upper limbs. Many MSD problems can be prevented or greatly reduced by complying with existing safety and health law, using equipment and furnishings correctly.

N

NCIDQ – National Council for Interior Design Qualifications.

Noise Reduction Coefficint (NRC) – A scalar representation of the amount of sound energy absorbed upon striking a particular surface. An NRC of zero indicates perfect reflection; an NRC of one indicates perfect absorption.

O

Occupancy Load – The maximum number of people expected to use a space. The occupant load of a space or a building influences the quantity of the exits. It also affects the classification of the spaces, and the number and nature of plumbing, heating and ventilation requirements. Occupant load calculations are essential for new and renovated spaces.

Open Plan – A description of space that has few or no dividing walls. The idea is to minimize the use of private offices and to encourage interaction. Many open-plan schemes now include some form of divider to create a degree of privacy while trying to maintain a degree of openness.

Operating Costs – Costs of doing business such as sales as opposed to any production costs that are incurred.

Orders – A term in classical architecture that refers to a column – base, shaft and capital – and entablature whose form, decoration and proportions reflect one of the five orders: Doric, Tuscan, Ionic, Corinthian, Composite.

Orientation/Wayfinding – The client experience of orientation and path/route selection within a built environment. It also refers to the architectural and/or design factors that are introduced to assist wayfinding. See section on wayfinding in Chapter 6.

P

Personalization – Making a consumer product personal to the individual user. This may be done remotely, based on supplied personal details or characteristics provided, or it may be done locally by the individual.

Perspective – A three-dimensional drawing, with horizon line and single or multiple vanishing points, to illustrate volume and spatial relationships. In a visual context, perspective refers to how objects appear to the viewer. Perspective effects are usually produced by the situation of the eye in relation to the viewed location.

Physiology – Branch of biology that deals with the internal workings of living things, including functions such as metabolism, respiration and reproduction, rather than with their shape or structure.

Plan View – Scaled layout, typically drawn at ¼ in to 1 ft, showing all walls, windows, openings, door swings, floor levels, ceiling angles, etc., with supporting documents in larger scale detailing construction specifications.

Post-occupancy Evaluation (POE) – The systematic assessment of the process of delivering buildings or other designed settings or the performance of those settings as they are actually used, or both, as compared to a set of implicit or explicit standards, with the intention of improving the process or settings.

Pre-occupancy Study – The study of existing conditions, work practices, layouts, etc., to be fed into the planning of a new concept. In a workplace environment, surveys might measure staff evaluations of management quality, compensation quality, environment quality and workstation quality, for example. The study will then consider the current physical environment and the associated control systems, etc. Then an analysis of the two aspects of the interior can be made in an attempt to improve both.

Presentation – The maintenance of a building or site in its currently found state. See also ADAPTIVE REUSE, CONSERVATION, RENOVATION and RESTORATION.

Professional Development – The continuing education and training of practitioners in their field. Lifelong learning as well as updating is now considered an essential part of a career. Sometimes referred to as CPD (Continuing Professional Development) or CPE (Continuing Professional Education).

R

Remodelling – Adaptive reuse or reworking of a space or spaces including changes of function, circulation, spatial relations; additions and removal of interior and/or exterior structures.

Renovation – An important aspect of an interior designer's work that impacts on environmental issues and encourages building reuse and refurbishment based on renewal and upgrading of the spaces in a building.

Restoration – A programme of repair and replacement directed to the reinstatement of historic buildings or spaces to a near-original state.

Retrofit – The installation or fitting of a device or system, for example for use in or on an existing structure, especially an older dwelling. This may be related to energy efficiency, environmental management or even building safety.

Risk Management – Process that covers all the processes involved in identifying, assessing and reviewing risks, assigning ownership, taking actions to alleviate or foresee them, and monitoring and reviewing progress.

S

Saturation – The purity of a HUE based on the amount of grey (i.e. the proportion of black and white in it). In the Munsell system, the strongest saturations are farthest away from the grey scale.

Scale – Drafting instrument used to measure and establish distances or relationships between a specific volume of space and the architectural or interior elements.

Schematic Design – A process of design that attempts to arrive at a clearly defined, feasible concept of spatial definitions, etc., in conjunction with the client.

Sense of Place – A social experience that exists independently of any one individual's perceptions or experiences yet is reliant on human engagement for its existence. Sense of place is often derived from the natural environment, but is often found in a combination of natural and cultural features in the landscape, and generally includes the people who occupy the place.

Sensory Responses – The way individuals react to their surroundings through the sense of smell, sight, hearing, touch and taste. See Chapter 9.

Sick Building Syndrome (SBS) – A combination of ailments (a syndrome) associated with an individual's place of work (office building) or residence and often related to poor indoor air quality. Causes of sick building syndrome include flaws in HVAC systems or contaminants produced by volatile organic compounds, moulds or inadequate air filtration.

Space Planning – Arranging the fixtures, furnishings and equipment within a given space taking into account traffic flow, furniture scale, use of occupants, handicap requirements, electrical fittings, etc. This is increasingly a particularly expert specialism.

Special Populations – A term that defines population-groupings based on common features such as pregnancy, age, locomotive ability, mental health or particular activity.

Specification – Detailed outline including all important and necessary criteria for the construction or implementation of a designed scheme.

Strategic Planning – The planning of all the activities of a business to ensure competitive advantage and profitability. Strategic planning defines an organization's strategy and decision-making in terms of all of its resources. Tools such as SWOT analysis (Strengths, Weaknesses, Opportunities and Threats) and STEER analysis (Socio-cultural, Technological, Economic, Ecological and Regulatory factors) can assist in the process, although contingency and amendment processes must be built in.

Sustainable Design – Sustainable design (also known as 'green design', 'eco-design', or 'design for environment'/DfE) is the designing of objects and the built environment so they observe the philosophy and practice of economic, social and ecological sustainability. Sustainable design minimizes the use of non-renewable resources, reduces environmental impact and works closely with the broader sustainability agendas. These agendas include approaches such as life cycle assessment and life cycle energy analysis, to evaluate the environmental impact of various design choices.

T

Task Lighting – Lighting required for visually intensive activities or a work surface, e.g. a reading lamp.

Teamwork – Co-operative approach to working with the view to better thinking and subsequent results. See also CHARETTE.

Telecommuting – See HOME OFFICE.

U

Universal Design – Items and spaces that can be accessed and utilized by individuals regardless of their age, size or disabilities. It is intended for everyone, so is more inclusive than accessible design, for example.

Uplight – Light source fixed so it shines upwards, often originating at the floor.

V

Vaastu – The Indian 'Vaastu Shastra' considers various aspects of the creation of living environments that are in harmony with physical and metaphysical forces. The Vaastu is conceptually similar to FENG SHUI, although it differs in detail.

Value – A reference to the amount of greyness in a HUE on a scale from white to black, which affects its degree of light or darkness.

Vernacular – A building and its interior created by a series of local conventions that rely on precedent rather than fashion. Locally sourced materials are employed and often reflect the character of the region.

Volatile Organic Compounds (VOCs) – Volatile Organic Compounds are specific materials that evaporate readily and are found in the atmosphere from vehicle exhausts, cleaning agents, furniture polish and fabric softener, for example. Legislation controls the production of VOCs as they can contribute to the pollution of the atmosphere.

W

Wall Washer – Light fitting that is designed and fitted to flood a wall with light so as to highlight it. When entering a space, we are often aware of the vertical surfaces first. Lighting designers therefore use wall washing to create the appearance of lighter or brighter spaces.

Water Conservation – The reduction in the use of fresh water and the recycling of grey water for different purposes.

Wayfinding – See ORIENTATION.

Well-being – The physical and psychological quality of life for an individual. It is not the same as standard of living. Well-being includes measures relating to general life experiences and job-related experiences as well as more specific considerations related to individuals.

notes

2 the development of the interior

1. See for example, Charlotte Gere, *Nineteenth Century Decoration* (London: Weidenfeld and Nicolson, 1989).

4 the processes of design

1. For professional business activity ethics see Chapter 13. See also the ASID and IIDA Codes of Practice.
2. In this case, the brief has a meaning distinct from the brief supplied by a client.
3. See Kang, M., 2007.
4. See also Environmental Design Research Assoc. at http://www.edra.org/

7 colour and colour systems

1. Henry Munsell developed his system from 1898 onwards with the creation of his colour sphere, or tree, which was finally published as *A Color Notation*, in 1905.
2. Complementary colours are found on opposite sides of the colour wheel.
3. The circumplex is a two-dimensional model that describes expected relationships among a number of variables (Guttman 1954). The relationship among variables is said to be circular, implying an ordering of variables that is without beginning or end, in which similar variables are closer to one another on the circle, variables that are semantic or behavioural opposites are located directly across the circle (i.e. through the origin) and variables that are unrelated or orthogonal are separated by angles of ninety degrees. http://www.interpersonalcircle.com/overview.htm; accessed 27 February 2009.
4. Other primary colour sets include the additive (based on light) version of red, green and blue and the subtractive version (based on reflected light) of yellow, magenta and cyan.

10 decoration and ornament

1. Functioning decoration describes objects that 'were taken out of their usual contexts for visual effect and "extra-cultural surprise"' (see Kirkham 1995: 143).

11 sustainability

1. Software for Life Cycle Analysis includes GaBi, LCAiT, Life-Cycle Advantage TM, KCL-ECO, SimaPro and Team 3.0.
2. See ISO 14040 (2006): Environmental management – Life cycle assessment – International Organization for Standardization (ISO), Geneva.
3. *The Environmental Assessment Method For Buildings Around The World* http://www.breeam.org/index.jsp Accessed 29 July 2009.
4. See U.S. Green Building Council http://www.usgbc.org/ Accessed 29 July 2009.

12 interior elements, materials and furnishings

1. See, for a comprehensive example: http://www. swt.usace.army.mil/library/Architectural%20and%20 Engineering%20Instructions%20Manual/Chapter11. pdf Accessed 30 July 2009.

13 the business of interior design

1. These general comments reflect UK usage. In any event, specialist advice should be sought.
2. In the UK, the RIBA/BIDA Form of Appointment for Interior Design Services has been developed specifically for professionals undertaking interior design projects.

bibliography

Aalto, A., Fleig, K., 1963, *Alvar Aalto*, Scarsdale: Wittenborn.

Abel, C., 1980, 'The Language Analogy in Architectural Theory and Criticism', *Architectural Association Quarterly* 12 (3), pp. 39–47.

Abercrombie, S., 2003, *A Century of Interior Design, 1900–2000: a Timetable of the Design, the Designers, the Products, and the Profession*, New York: Rizzoli.

Abercrombie, S., 1990, *A Philosophy of Interior Design*, Boulder, CO: Westview Press.

Abruzzo, E., and Solomon, J., 2006, *Decoration 306090*, Princeton: Princeton Architectural Press.

Adamson G., 2007, *Thinking Through Craft*, Oxford: Berg.

Addington M. and Schodek, D., 2005, *Smart Materials and Technologies for the Architecture and Design Professions*, Architectural Press: Oxford.

Adorno, A., 'Functionalism Today', in Neil Leach (ed.), *Rethinking Architecture*, 1997, London: Routledge, p. 10.

Ainley, R. (ed), 1998, *New Frontiers of Space, Body and Gender*, London: Routledge.

Albers, J., 1963, *Interaction of Color*, New Haven: Yale University Press.

Alberti, L.B., *On Painting* [1435–36], Translated with Introduction and Notes by John R. Spencer, 1970 [first printed 1956], New Haven: Yale University Press.

Alberti, L.B., 1991, *On the Art of Building in Ten Books*, Cambridge, MA: MIT Press.

Alexander, C., 1971, *Notes on the Synthesis of Form*, Cambridge, MA: Harvard University Press.

Alexander, C., 1977, *A Pattern Language*, Oxford: Oxford University Press.

Alfoldy, S., and Helland, J. (eds), 2008, *Craft, Space and Interior Design, 1855–2005,* Aldershot: Ashgate.

Altman, J., 1975, *The Environment and Social Behaviour*, Monterey: Brooks/Cole.

Altman J. and Low, S., 1992, *Place Attachment*, New York: Plenum.

Anderzhon, J.W., Fraley, I.L. and Green, M., 2007, *Design for Aging: Post-Occupancy Evaluations,* New York: Wiley.

Archer, B., 1973, 'The Need for Design Education', London: Royal College of Art (Article, unpaginated).

Architectural Design, 30 July 1960.

Architectural Lighting Magazine, 1 July 2007.

'The Architecture of the Estate: Modern Times', 1977; Survey of London: Volume 39: The Grosvenor Estate in Mayfair, Part 1 (General History) (1977), pp. 161–170. URL: http://www.british-history.ac.uk/report.aspx?compid=41849 Accessed 25 March 2009.

Ardener, S., 1984, *Women and Space: Ground Rules and Social Maps*, New York: St. Martin's Press.

Arnheim, R., 1974, *Art and Visual Perception*, Berkeley and Los Angeles: University of California Press.

Arnheim, R., 1977, *Dynamics of Architectural Form,* Berkeley and Los Angeles: University of California Press.

Arnheim, R., 'Sketching and the Psychology of Design', in V. Margolin and R. Buchanan (eds), *The Idea of Design: A Design Issues Reader*, 2000, Cambridge, MA: MIT Press, 2000.

Arrowsmith, H.W. and A., 1840, *The House Decorator and Painter's Guide; Containing a Series of Designs for Decorating Apartments Suited to the Various Styles of Architecture*, London: Thomas Kelly.

Associates III, Foster, K., Stelmack, A., Hindman D., 2006, *Sustainable Residential Interiors*, New York: Wiley.

Attiwill, S., 2003, 'Di-vision/Double Vision', *IDEA*, pp. 3–10.

Attiwill, S., 2004, 'Towards an Interior History', *IDEA*, pp. 1–8.

Bachelard, G., 1995 [1959], *The Poetics of Space*, trans. Maria Jolas, Boston: Beacon Press.

Bafna, S., 2003, 'Space Syntax: A Brief Introduction to Its Logic and Analytical Techniques, *Environment and Behavior* 35: 1, pp. 17–29.

Baillie Scott, H., 1895, *The Studio* magazine, p. 131.

Bal, M., 2002, *Travelling Concepts in the Humanities,* Toronto: University of Toronto Press.

Baldwin, B., 1972, *Billy Baldwin Decorates*, New York: Holt, Rinehart and Winston.

Baljeu, J., 1974, *Theo van Doesburg*, London: Macmillan.

Ballantyne, A. (ed.), 2002, *What is Architecture?* London: Routledge.

Banham, J. (ed), 1997, *Encyclopaedia of Interior Design*, 2 Vols, Chicago and London: Fitzroy Dearborn.

Barthes, R., 1989, 'On Reading', in *The Rustle of Language*, trans. Richard Howard, Berkeley and Los Angeles: University of California Press.

Baudrillard, J., 1996 [1968], *The System of Objects*, trans J. Benedict, London: Verso.

Baxandall, M., 1985, *Patterns of Intention,* New Haven: Yale University Press.

Bechtel, R. B., and Churchman, A., eds, 2002, *Handbook of Environmental Psychology,* New York: Wiley.

Beder, S., 1996, *The Nature of Sustainable Development*, Newham,Victoria: Scribe Publications.

Beeby, T., 1977, 'The Grammar of Ornament/Ornament as Grammar' *VIA III Ornament*, ed. Stephen Kiernan, Philadelphia: Falcon Press.

Bell, P.A., Greene, T., Fisher, J.D., Baum, A., 2001, *Environmental Psychology*, Fifth Edition, New York: Harcourt.

Bell, V.B., and Rand, P., 2006, *Materials for Architectural Design*, London: Laurence King.

Benjamin, W., 1999, *The Arcades Project*, trans. Howard Eiland and Kevin McLaughlin, prepared on the basis of the German volume edited by Rolf Tiedemann, Cambridge, MA and London: Belknap/Harvard University Press.

Benton, T., Benton, C., and Sharp, D., eds, 1975, *Form and Function: a Source Book for the History of Architecture and Design 1890–1939,* London: Granada Publishing.

Benyus, J., 2002, *Biomimicry: Innovation Inspired by Nature*, London: Harper Perennial.

Benzel, K.F., 1998, *The Room in Context: Design Beyond Boundaries*, New York: McGraw-Hill.

Berleant, A., 2003, 'The Aesthetic in Place', in S. Menin (ed.), *Constructing Place: Mind and Matter*, London: Routledge.

Berleant, A. and Carlson, A. (eds), 2007, *The Aesthetics of Human Environments*, Guelph, Ontario: Broadview.

Best, K., 2006, *Design Management: Managing Design Strategy, Process and Implementation*, Lausanne: AVA.

Bevlin, M. E., 1994, *Design Through Discovery: an Introduction to Art and Design*, Fort Worth: Harcourt Brace College Publishers.

Biley, F., 1996, 'Hospitals: Healing Environments?' *Complementary Therapies in Nursing and Midwifery* 2: 4, August, pp. 110–115.

Binggeli, C., 2003, *Building Systems for Interior Designers*, New York: John Wiley & Sons, Inc.

Binggeli, C., 2007, *Materials for Interior Environments*, New York: Wiley.

Birren, F., 1950/1982, *Color Psychology and Color Therapy*, New York: McGraw-Hill.

Blonsky, M., 1985, *On Signs*, Baltimore: Johns Hopkinson University Press.

Bloomer, K., 2000, *The Nature of Ornament: Rhythm and Metamorphosis in Architecture*, New York: Norton.

Bloomer K., 2006, 'Critical Distinction Between Decoration and Ornament', in E. Abruzzo and J. Solomon, *Decoration 306090*, Princeton: Princeton Architectural Press.

Bloomer, K., and Moore, C., 1977, *Body, Memory and Architecture*, New Haven: Yale University Press.

Boudon, P., 1972, *Lived-in Architecture,* Cambridge MA, MIT Press.

Brandi, U., 2006, *Lighting Design: Principles, Implementation, Case Studies*, Basel: Birkhauser.

Brett, D., 1992, *On Decoration,* Cambridge: Lutterworth Press.

Brett, D., 2005, *Rethinking Decoration: Pleasure and Ideology in the Visual Arts*, Cambridge: Cambridge University Press.

Brooker, G. and Stone, S., 2004, *Rereadings*, *Interior Architecture and the Design Principles of Remodelling Existing Buildings*, London: RIBA Enterprises.

Brooker, G., and Stone, S., 2007a, *Basic Interior Architecture: Form and Structure*, Lausanne: AVA Publishing SA.

Brooker, G., and Stone, S., 2007b, 'From Organisation to Decoration', *Thinking Inside the Box*, London: Middlesex University Press.

Brown, N.C., 2004, 'Aesthetic Composition and the Language of Light', *Journal of Interior Design* 30:3, pp. 8–22.

Bruton, D., 2007, 'Fusing Horizons – A Grammatical Design Approach for the Arts and Humanities', *Arts and Humanities in Higher Education* 6, pp 309–327.

Buchanan, P., 2005, *Ten Shades of Green: Architecture and the Natural World*, New York: Architectural League of New York/W.W. Norton.

Bureau of Vocational Information, 1924, *Training for the Professions and Allied Occupations: Facilities Available to Women in the United States*, New York.

Busch, A., 2004, *Geography of Home: Writings on Where We Live*, New York: Princeton Architectural, London: Hi Marketing.

Caan, S., 2007, 'Consensus or Confusion' in *Thinking Inside the Box*, London: Middlesex University Press.

Cache, B., 1995, 'Body and Soul', in *Earth Moves, The Furnishing of Territories*, Cambridge, MA: MIT Press.

Caedmon Records [i.e. audio recording], Spring 1955, TC 1064, interview with Wright. http://www.oprf.com/unity/tour/index.html Accessed 28 July 2009.

Cairns, S., 'Notes For an Alternative History of the Primitive Hut,' in J. Odgers, F. Samuel and A. Sharr (eds), 2006, *Primitive: Original Matters in Architecture*, London: Routledge.

Cairns S. and Jacobs, J., 2006, 'The Modern Touch: Interior Design and Modernisation in Post-independence Singapore', Institute of Geography Online Paper Series: GEO-0242006 University of Edinburgh. http://www.era.lib.ed.ac.uk/bitstream/1842/1434/1/jjacobs004.pdf Accessed 5 February 2010.

Calloway, S., 1988, *Twentieth Century Decoration*, London: Weidenfeld and Nicolson.

Canestaro, N.C. and Carter, E.H., 1992, 'Survey of Teaching Innovations in Interior Design Classes', *Journal of Interior Design* 17: 2, pp. 25–34.

Cantor, D., 1974, *Psychology for Architects*, London: Applied Science.

Caplan, R., 2005, *By Design*, New York: Fairchild.

Carpman, J. and Myron Grant, M., 'Wayfinding a Broad View' in R. Bechtel and A. Churchman (eds), 2002, *Handbook of Environmental Psychology*, New York: Wiley, p. 427.

Carr, W., and Kemmis, S., 1986, *Becoming Critical*, London: The Falmer Press.

Caruso St John Architects: 'The Structuralist Office: http://www.carusostjohn.com/media/artscouncil/history/structuralist/index.html

Casson, H., 1968, *Inscape: The Design of Interiors*, Architectural Press: London.

The Center for Universal Design, 1997, *The Principles of Universal Design,* Version 2.0. Raleigh, NC: North Carolina State University http://design.ncsu.edu/cud/about_ud/udprinciples.htm Accessed 30 July 2009.

Chalmers, L. and Close, S., 2007, 'But is It Interior Design', in *Thinking Inside the Box*, London: Middlesex University Press.

Cheng, H.-L., 2001, 'Consuming a Dream: Homes in Advertisements and Imagination in Contemporary Hong Kong', in G. Mathews and T.L. Lui (eds), *Consuming Hong Kong*, Hong Kong: Hong Kong University Press.

Cherry, E., 1998, *Programming for Design*, New York: Wiley.

Ching, F., 2004, *Interior Design Illustrated*, ed. II, New York: Wiley.

Chu, C., 2003, 'Interior Design in Hong Kong: A Practice in Transition', *Design Issues* 19, pp. 37–47.

Clarkson, J. (ed.), 2003, *Inclusive Design: Design for the Whole Population*, New York: Springer.

Coleman C. (ed.), 2002, *Interior Design Handbook for Professional Practice,* New York: McGraw-Hill.

Collins, P., 1965, *Changing Ideals in Modern Architecture, 1750–1950,* London: Faber and Faber.

Colomina, B., 1992, *Sexuality and Space*, Princeton, NJ: Princeton University Press.

Colomina, B., and Lleó, B., 1998, 'A Machine Was Its Heart: House in Floirac', *Assemblage 37,* MA: MIT Press.

Constanze Kreiser, 1990, 'On the Loss of (Dark) Inside Space', cited in Taylor and Preston (eds), p. 181.

Crabtree, A., 2000, 'Remarks on the Social Organisation of Space and Place', *Journal of Mundane Behavior* 1:1: http://www.mundanebehavior.org/index2.htm Accessed 29th July 2009.

Crane, W., 1911, 'The English Revival in Decorative Art', in *From William Morris to Whistler*. London: G. Bell.

Criticos, M., 2004, 'The Ornamental Dimension: Contributions to a Theory of Ornament', *New Europe College Yearbook*, Special edition, pp. 185–219.

Csikszentmihalyi, M., 1991, 'Design and Order in Everyday Life', *Design Issues,* 8: 1, pp. 26–43.

Culler, J., 1997, *Literary Theory: A Very Short Introduction*, New York: Oxford University Press.

Culler, P., 1965, *Changing Ideals in Modern Architecture 1750–1950*, London: Faber and Faber.

Curtis, W., 1986, *Le Corbusier: Ideas and Forms*, New York: Rizzoli.

Cutter, S.L., 1995, 'Race, Class and Environmental Justice', *Progress in Human Geography* 19, pp. 111–122.

Cwerner, S. B. and Metcalfe A., 2003, 'Storage and Clutter: Discourses and Practices of Order in the Domestic World,' *Journal of Design History* 16, pp. 229–239.

Dalke, H., Little, J., Niemann, E., Camgoz, N., Steadman G., Hill, S., and Stott, L., 2006, 'Colour and Lighting in Hospital Design', 38: 4–6 *Optics & Laser Technology,* pp. 343–365.

Dant, T., 1999, *Material Culture in the Social World: Values, Activities, Lifestyles*, Buckingham: Open University Press.

de Certeau, M., 1984, *The Practice of Everyday Life*, University of California Press: Berkeley.

de Certeau, M., 'Spatial Stories' in A. Ballantyne (ed.), 2002, *What is Architecture?* London: Routledge.

de Wolfe, E., 1913, *The House in Good Taste*, New York: Century.

Declaration of the European Institute for Design and Disability, Stockholm, 2004. http://www.designforalleurope.org/Design-for-All/EIDD-Documents/Stockholm-Declaration/ Accessed 30 July 2009.

Degraff, J., Naylor, T., and Wann, D., 2002, *What is Affluenza?, Introduction to Affluenza: The All Consuming Epidemic*, San Francisco and London: Berrett Koehler; MacGraw Hill.

Deleuze, G., and Guattari, F., 1991, *A Thousand Plateaus*, Minneapolis: University of Minnesota Press.

Dethier, K., 1991, 'The Early American Journals of Interiors: Reflections of an Emerging Profession', *Journal of Interior Design Education and Research* 17: 1, pp. 37–42.

DiSalvo, C., Hanington, B., Forlizzi, J., 'An Accessible Framework of Emotional Experiences', in D. McDonagh, et al (eds), 2004, *Design and Emotion*, London: Taylor and Francis.

Dittmar, H., 1992, *The Social Psychology of Material Possessions: To Have Is to Be,* Hemel Hempstead: Harvester.

Downing, A.J., 1850, *The Architecture of Country Houses*, New York: Appleton and Co.

Dresner, S., 2002, *The Principles of Sustainability*, London: Earthscan.

Dresser, C., 1977 [1862], *The Art of Decorative Design*, New York: Garland.

Dresser, C., *Studies in Design*, 1988 [1879], London: Studio Editions.

Duffy, F. (ed), 1990, *The Responsive Office: People and Change*, Streatley-on-Thames: Steelcase-Polymath.

Duffy, F., 1997, *The New Office*, London: Conran Octopus.

Dunster, D., *Key Buildings of the Twentieth Century* Volume 2: Houses 1945–1989, pp. 16–17. Cited on www.greatbuildings.com/buildings/Eames_House.html Accessed 27 July 2009.

Eastlake, C. 1969 [1868)], *Hints on Household Taste*, Reprint, New York: Dover.

Edwards, B., 2005, *Rough Guide to Sustainability*, London: RIBA.

Elkins, J., 2003, *Visual Studies, A Skeptical Introduction*, London: Routledge.

Elkins P. and Max-Neef, A., 1992, *Real Life Economics*, London: Routledge.

Enquist, P., 2002, 'New Vision for Urban Life Needs to Integrate Planning with Design', *Design Intelligence*, 15 August, http://www.di.net/articles/archive/2106/ Accessed 29 July 2009.

Ellin, R.A., 1994, *Frank Lloyd Wright and Le Corbusier, A Romantic Legacy*, Manchester: Manchester University Press.

Ettema, M., 'The Fashion System in American Furniture', in Gerald Pocius (ed.), 1991, *Living in a Material World*, St. Johns: Memorial University of Newfoundland Press.

European Commission, et al., 1999, 'The Green Building', in *A Green Vitruvius: Principles and Practice of Sustainable Architectural Design*, London: James & James.

Evans G., and J. M. McCoy, 1998, 'When Buildings Don't Work: The Role Of Architecture In Human Health', *Journal of Environmental Psychology*, 18:1, pp. 85–94.

Falke, J. von., 1878, *Art in the House*, Boston, MA: Prang and Co.

Fehrman, K.R., 2004, *Colour: the Secret Influence*, Upper Saddle River, N.J.: Prentice Hall.

Feisner, E.A., 2006, *Color Studies*., 2nd Edition, New York: Fairchild.

Ferry, E., 2003, '"Decorators May be Compared to Doctors": An Analysis of Rhoda and Agnes Garrett's Suggestion for House Decoration in Painting, Woodwork and Furniture [of 1876]', *Journal of Design History*, 16: 1, pp. 15–33.

Finlay, K., Marmurek, H.C., Kanetkar, V., and Londerville, J., 2007, 'Trait and State Emotion Congruence in Simulated Casinos: Effects on At-risk Gambling Intention and Restoration', *Journal of Environmental Psychology*, 27: 2, pp. 166–175.

First Research Inc, June 2009, *Interior Design Services Report*.

Fleischman, D. (ed.), 1928, *An Outline of Careers for Women: a Practical Guide to Achievement*, Garden City, N.Y.: Doubleday, Doran and Co.

Flores C. A. Hrvol, 2006, *Owen Jones: Design, Ornament, Architecture, and Theory in an Age in Transition,* New York: Rizzoli.

Flusser, V., 1999, *The Shape of Things: a Philosophy of Design*, London: Reaktion.

Focillon, H., 1948, *The Life of Forms in Art*, New York: George Wittenborn.

Forty, A., 2004, *Words And Buildings: A Vocabulary of Modern Architecture*, London: Thames & Hudson.

Foster, K., Stelmack, A., and Hindman, D., 2007, *Sustainable Residential Interiors*, Hoboken, N.J.: John Wiley.

Frampton, K., 1995, *Studies in Tectonic Culture*, Cambridge, MA: MIT Press.

Frank, I., 2000, *The Theory of Decorative Art: An Anthology of European and American Writings 1750–1940,* New Haven and London: Yale University Press.

Frankl, P., 1972 [1930], *Form and Re-forms; A Practical Handbook of Modern Interiors,* reprint New York: Hacker Art Books.

Franz, J., 'An Interpretive-Contextual Framework For Research in and Through Design' in H. Giroux, C. Lankshear, P. McLaren and M. Peters (eds), 2000, *Counternarratives: Cultural Studies and Critical Perspectives in Post-modern Spaces*, New York: Routledge.

Franz, J., 2002, 'Fostering Social Responsibility For Interior Design Practice', *IDEA*, pp. 19–34.

Freeman, M., 2005, *India Modern*, Boston, MA: Tuttle Publishing.

Frey, D., 'On the Problem of Symmetry In Art', cited in H. Weyl, 1983, *Symmetry*, Princeton, NJ: Princeton University Press.

Friedman, B., 2000, *Designing Casinos to Dominate the Competition*, Reno Nevada: Institute for the Study of Gambling and Commercial Gaming.

Gadamer, H.G., 'The Ontological Foundation of the Occasional and the Decorative', in Neil Leach (ed.), 1997, *Rethinking Architecture*, London: Routledge.

Gage, J., 1999, *Colour and Meaning*, London: Thames & Hudson.

Ganoe, C., 1999, 'Design As Narrative: A Theory of Inhabiting Interior Space', *Journal of Interior Design* 25: 2, pp. 1–15.

Gelernter, M., 1995, *Sources of Architectural Form*, Manchester: Manchester University Press.

Gere, C., 1989, *Nineteenth Century Decoration*, London: Weidenfeld and Nicolson.

Gibson, J.J., 1968, *The Senses Considered as Perceptual Systems*, London: Allen and Unwin.

Ginthner, D., *Lighting: Its Effect on People and Spaces*, Implications, Vol. 2 no. 2 http://www.informedesign.umn.edu/_news/feb_v02-p.pdf Accessed 4 January 2010.

Glasser, W., 1968, *Choice Theory: A New Psychology of Personal Freedom*, London: Harper Collins.

Godsey, L., 2007, *Interior Design Materials and Specifications*, Oxford: Berg.

Goffman, E., 1959, *The Presentation of Self in Everyday Life*. New York: Doubleday.

Gombrich, E.H., 1979, *The Sense of Order: A Study in the Psychology of Decorative Art*, Ithaca: Cornell University Press.

Gordon, G., 2003, *Interior Lighting for Designers,* 4th edition, New York: Wiley.

Gravagnuolo, B., 1995, *Adolf Loos, Theory and Works,* New York: Art Data.

Gray, S. (ed), 2004, *Designers on Designers*, New York: McGraw Hill.

Greenhalgh, P. (ed.), 1990, *Modernism in Design*, London: Reaktion Books.

Greenhalgh, P. (ed.), 1993, *Quotations and Sources on Design and the Decorative Arts*, Manchester: Manchester University Press.

GreenSpec; http://www.greenspec.co.uk/ Accessed 30 July 2009.

Grier, K., 1988, *Culture & Comfort: People, Parlors and Upholstery 1850–1930*, Rochester: Strong Museum.

Groër, Léon de, 1986, *Decorative Arts in Europe, 1790–1850*, New York: Rizzoli.

Gropius, W., 1962, *Scope of Total Architecture*, New York: Collier.

Gropius, W., 1965 [1935], *New Architecture and the Bauhaus* cited in Peter Collins, *Changing ideals in modern architecture, 1750–1950,* London: Faber and Faber.

Grosz, E., 1995, *Space, Time and Perversion: Essays on the Politics of Bodies*, London: Routledge.

Grube, E., 1978, *Architecture of the Islamic World,* London: Thames & Hudson.

Guerin, D. and Martin, C., 2001, *The Interior Design Profession's Body of Knowledge: Its Definition and Documentation*. An original report prepared for the Association of Registered Interior Designers of Ontario, Toronto, Canada: ARIDO.

Guerin, D.A. and Martin, C.S., 2004, 'The Career Cycle Approach to Defining the Interior Design Profession's Body of Knowledge', *Journal of Interior Design* 30, pp. 1–22.

Guy, S., and Farmer, G., 2001, 'Re-interpreting sustainable architecture', *The Journal of Architectural Education*, 54: 3, pp. 140–148.

Hall, E.T., 1966, *The Hidden Dimension,* New York: Doubleday.

Hamilton, C., 2005, *Affluenza: When Too Much is Never Enough*, Crows Nest, NSW: Allen & Unwin.

Hanson J., 'Morphology and Design Reconciling Intellect, Intuition, and Ethics in the Reflective Practice of Architecture', http://eprints.ucl.ac.uk/1024/ accessed 4 February 2010

Hardy, A., and Teymur, N. (eds), 1996, *Architectural History and the Studio*, London: Question.

Harrigan, J.E., 1987, *Human Factors Research: Methods and Applications for Architects and Interior Designers*, Amsterdam and Oxford: Elsevier.

Harrison-Moore, A. and Rowe, D.C. (eds), 2006, *Architecture and Design in Europe and America 1750–2000*, Oxford: Blackwell.

Hartje, S.C., 2005, 'Universal Design Features and Product Characteristics for Kitchens', *Housing and Society* 32: 2, pp. 101–118.

Hayward, G., 'Psychological Factors in the Use of Light and Lighting in Buildings', in J. Lang, 1974, *Designing For Human Behavior: Architecture and the Behavioral Sciences*, Stroudsburg: Dowden Hutchinson and Ross.

Heidegger, M., 1971, *Poetry, Language and Thought*, trans. A. Hofstader, New York and London: Harper and Row.

Heidegger, M., 'Building, Dwelling, Thinking', in N. Leach ed., 1997, *Rethinking Architecture*, Routledge: London.

Hershberger, R., 'Behavioral-Based Architectural Planning' in R. Bechtel and A. Churchman (eds), 2002, *Handbook of Environmental Psychology*, New York: Wiley.

Herwig, O., 2008, *Universal Design: Solutions For a Barrier Free Living,* Basel: Birkhauser.

Hewes, G.W., 1955, 'World Distribution of Certain Postural Habits', *American Anthropologist*, New Series, 57, April, 2: 1, pp. 231–244.

Heynen, H., 1999, 'Walter Benjamin: The Dream of a Classless Society', in *Architecture and Modernity*, Cambridge, MA: MIT Press.

Heynen, H., 'Leaving Traces: Anonymity in the Modernist House', in Sparke et al. (eds), 2009, *Designing the Modern Interior*, Oxford: Berg.

Hicks, D., 1979, *Living with Design,* London: Weidenfeld and Nicolson.

Hildebrandt, H., 2001, 'The Rise of a Profession: The Evolution of Interior Design', *Perspective: Journal of the IIDA*, pp. 74–81.

Hing, A., 2006, 'Understanding the Plan: A Studio Experience', *Journal of Interior Design*, 31:3, pp. 10–20.

Hölscher, C., Meilinger, T., Vrachliotis, G., Brösamle, M., and Knauff, M., 2006, 'Up the Down Staircase: Next Term Wayfinding Strategies in Multi-Level Buildings', *Journal of Environmental Psychology* 26, 4, pp. 284–299.

Holtzschue, L., 2002, *Understanding Color: an Introduction for Designers,* John Wiley & Sons, Inc., New York.

Howe, S., 1999, 'Untangling the Scandinavian Blonde: Modernity and the IKEA PS Range Catalogue 1995', *Scandinavian Journal of Design History*, p. 99.

Hudson, J., 2007, *Interior Architecture Now,* London: Laurence King.

Hutton, G.H. and Devonal, A.D.G. (eds), 1973, *Value in Building*, London: Applied Science Publishers.

Huysmans, J.-K., 2003 [1884], *Against Nature*, Harmondsworth: Penguin.

IIDA, Definition of Interior Design, http://www.iida.org/i4a/pages/index.cfm?pageid=380; Accessed 2 May 2009.

IIDA, IIDAF and E-lab, 1998, *Study of Interior Design: An Analysis of the Needs of the Practice and Implications for Education*, Chicago: International Interior Design Association and E-lab.

Imrie, R., and Hall, P., 2001, *Inclusive Design: Designing and Developing Accessible Environments,* London: Spon Press.

Isenstadt, S., 2006, *The Modern American House: Spaciousness and Middle-Class Identity*, New York: Cambridge University Press.

Itten, J., 1970, *Elements of Colour*, New York: Wiley.

Itten, J., 1974, *The Art of Color: The Subjective Experience and Objective Rationale of Color*, New York: John Wiley and Sons.

Jenkins K. and Munslow, A., 2002, *Rethinking History*, London: Routledge.

Jennings, J., and Beecher, M.A., 1998, 'Object, Context, Design: the State of Interior Design History, an Introduction to the Thematic Issue; Toward a Critical Approach to the History of Interiors', *Journal of Interior Design* 24: 2, pp. 1–11.

Johnson, P.-A., 1994, *Theory of Architecture, Concepts, Themes and Practices*, New York: Wiley.

Jones, L., 2008, *Environmentally Responsible Interior Design,* New York: Wiley.

Jordan, P.W., 2000, *Designing Pleasurable Products: An Introduction to the New Human Factors*, London: Taylor and Francis.

Juracek, J.A., 2000, *Soft Surface: Visual Research for Artists, Architects and Designers*, London: Thames & Hudson.

Kang, M., 2007, 'A Computer Database of Design Methodological Tool Patterns for Interior Designers', *International Journal of Instructional Technology and Distance Learning*, 4: 3, pp. 45–62.

Kang, M., and Guerin, D., 2009, 'The State of Environmentally Sustainable Interior Design Practice', *American Journal of Environmental Sciences* 5: 2, pp.179–186.

Kant, E., 1987 [1790], *Critique of Judgement*, Indianapolis: Hackett Publishing.

Karlen, M., 2003, *Space Planning Basics*: 2nd Edition. New York: Wiley.

Karlen, M. and Benya, J., 2004, *Lighting Design Basics*, New York: Wiley.

Kelly, R., 1955, 'Lighting's Role in Architecture', published in *Architectural Forum,* February, http://www.iesnyc.org/Documents/RK_works_May07.pdf Accessed 29 July 2009.

Kernaghan, B., 2005, 'Architecture as Space', in *Interiority*, London: Butterworth-Heineman.

Kerr, R., 1864, *The Gentleman's House*, London: John Murray.

Kiernan, S., ed., 1977, *VIA III Ornament*, Philadelphia: Falcon Press.

Kilmer, R., and Kilmer, W.O., 1992, *Designing Interiors*. Fort Worth: Harcourt Brace Jovanovich.

Kingwell, M., 2002, *Practical Judgments: Essays in Culture, Politics, and Interpretation*, Toronto: Toronto University Press.

Kirkham, P., 1995, *Charles and Ray Eames*, Cambridge MA: MIT Press.

Knackstedt, M.V., 1993, *Marketing and Selling Design Services: the Designer Client*, New York: Van Nostrand Reinhold, London: Chapman and Hall.

Knackstedt, M.V., 2008, *The Challenge of Interior Design*, New York: Allworth Press.

Knackstedt, M.V., 2006, *The Interior Design Business Handbook: A Complete Guide to Profitability*, 4th edition. New York: Wiley.

Kopec, D., 2006, *Environmental Psychology for Design*, New York: Fairchild.

Kranes, D., 1995, 'Playgrounds', *Journal of Gambling Studies*, 11, pp. 91–102.

Kreitler, H., and Kreitler, S., 1972, *Psychology of the Arts*, Durham, N.C., Duke University Press.

Kriebel, T. M., C. Birdsong and D.J. Sherman, 1991, 'Defining Interior Design Programming', *Journal of Interior Design*, 17:1, p 29–36.

Krippendorf, K., 'Redesigning Design; An Invitation to a Responsible Future' in Tahkokallio and Vihma (eds), 1995, *Design: Pleasure or Responsibility*, University of Art and Design: Helsinki.

Krippendorf, K., 2006, *The Semantic Turn*, *A New Foundation for Design*, Boca Raton and London: CRC.

Kruft, H.W., 1994, *A History of Architectural Theory from Vitruvius to the Present*, New York: Princeton Architectural Press.

Kubba, S., 2003, *Space Planning for Commercial and Residential Interiors*, New York: McGraw Hill.

Kupritz, V., 2004, 'The Effect of Physical Design on Routine Work Activities', *Journal of Architectural Planning and Research* 20: 2, pp.110–121.

Kurtich, J., 1995, *Interior Architecture,* New York: Wiley.

Kurtich, J., and Eakin, G., 1996, 'Interior Architecture: The Philosophy', in *Interior Architecture*, New York: Van Nostrand Reinhold.

Kwallek, N., 'Color in Office Environments', *Implications*, 5/1, http://www.informedesign.umn.edu/_news/jan_v05r-p.pdf Accessed 25 July 2009.

Lang, J., et al., 1974, *Designing for Human Behavior: Architecture and the Behavioral Sciences*, Stroudsburg, PA; Dowden, Hutchinson and Ross.

Laurel, B. (ed), 2003, *Design Research: Methods and Perspectives*, Cambridge, MA, MIT Press.

Lawson, B., 2001, *The Language of Space*, Oxford: Architectural Press.

Lawson, B., 2005, *How Designers Think*, 4th edition, Oxford: Architectural Press.

Le Corbusier, 1946 [1927], *Towards a New Architecture*, London: Architectural Press.

Le Corbusier, 1961, *The Modulor: A Harmonious Measure to the Human Scale Universally Applicable to Architecture and Mechanics,* London: Faber.

Le Corbusier, 1987 [1925], *The Decorative Art of Today*, translated by J. Dunnett, Oxford: Architectural Press.

Le Corbusier, 'L'aventure du mobilier', *Précisions,* Paris: Crès, cited in 'Documents', *Journal of Design History* 3: 2/3 (1990), pp. 103–124.

Leach, N. (ed.), 1997, *Rethinking Architecture*, London: Routledge.

Le-Duc, E.V., 1875, *Discourses on Architecture*, Boston, Osgood.

Lefebvre, H., 1976, 'Reflections on the Politics of Space', *Antipode* 8:2, pp. 30–37.

Lefebvre, H., 1991, *The Production of Space*, translated by Donald Nicholson-Smith, Oxford: Blackwell.

Lefebvre, H., 'The Everyday and Everydayness', in Harris, S., and Berke, D. (eds), 1997, *The Architecture of the Everyday*, New York: Princeton Architectural Press.

Lidwell, W., Holden K., and Butler, J., 2003, *Universal Principles of Design*, Gloucester, MA: Rockport Publishers.

Lloyd-Wright, F., 1954, *The Natural House*, New York: Horizon.

Lloyd-Wright, F., 'The Cardboard House' (1931), in Benton and Sharp, 1975, *Form and Function*, London: Granada, p. 64.

Loos, A., 1998, *Ornament and Crime: Selected Essays*, Opel, Adolf (ed.), trans. M. Mitchell, Riverside, California: Ariadne Press.

Love, T., 2000, 'Philosophy of Design: a Meta-Theoretical Structure for Design Theory', *Design Studies* 21: 3, pp. 293–313.

Loveday, T., 'Design, the Decoration of Culture?' http://www.idea-edu.com/Journal/2003/Design-the-Decoration-of-Culture Accessed 5 February 2010

Lowe, I., 'Achieving a Sustainable Future', in J. Goldie, Douglas, B. and Furnass, B. (eds), 2005, *In Search of Sustainability*, Collingwood, VIC: CSIRO.

Lynch, K., 1960, *Image of the City*, Cambridge MA MIT Press.

Lyons, A., 2007, *Materials for Architects and Builders*, 3rd edition, Butterworth: Oxford.

Mahnke, F.H., 1996, *Color, Environment, and Human Response: An Interdisciplinary Understanding of Color and Its Use as a Beneficial Element in the Design of the Architectural Environment*, New York: Wiley.

Mahnke, F.H. and Mahnke, R.H., 1987, *Color and Light in Man-Made Environments*, New York: Van Nostrand Reinhold.

Mak, M.Y. and Ng, S.T., 2005, 'The Art and Science of Feng Shui—a Study on Architects' Perception', *Building and Environment* 40: 3, pp. 427–434.

Mallgrave, H.F., and Contandriopoulos, C., 2008, *Architectural Theory*, Vol. II, Oxford: Blackwell.

Malnar, J. M., and Vodvarka, F., 1992, *The Interior Dimension: A Theoretical Approach to Enclosed Space*, New York: Van Nostrand Reinhold.

Malnar, J.M., and Vodvarka, F., 2004, *Sensory Design*, Minnesota University Press: Minneapolis.

Manovich, L., 2000, 'Computer Space', in *The Language of New Media*, Cambridge, MA: MIT Press.

Manuelli, S., 2006, *Design for Shopping: New Retail Interiors*, New York: Abbeville Press.

Manzo, L.C., 2005, 'For Better or Worse: Exploring Multiple Dimensions of Place Meaning', *Journal of Environmental Psychology,* 25: 1, pp. 67–86.

Margolin, V., and Buchanan, R. (eds), 2005, *The Idea of Design: A Design Issues Reader*, Cambridge, MA: MIT Press.

Markus, T. and Arch, M., 'Optimisation by Evaluation in the Appraisal of Buildings' in G.H. Hutton, and A.D.G. Devonal (eds), 1973, *Value in Building*, London: Applied Science Publishers.

Martin, C., 2007, *Interior Design: From Practice to Profession*, Washington, DC: American Society of Interior Designers.

Maslow, A.H., 1943, 'A Theory of Human Motivation', at: http://psychclassics.yorku.ca/Maslow/motivation.htm Accessed 27 July 2009.

Massey, A., 1990, *Interior Design of the 20th Century*, Thames & Hudson.

Massey, D., 1994, *Space Place and Gender*, University of Minnesota Press: Minneapolis.

May, B., 2008, 'Nancy Vincent McClelland 1877–1969: Professionalizing Interior Decoration in the Early Twentieth Century', *Journal of Design History* 21: 1, pp. 59–74.

McCarthy, C., 2005, 'Towards a Definition of Interiority', *Space and Culture* 8: 2, pp. 112–125.

McClelland N.V., 1936, *Furnishing the Colonial and Federal House,* J.B. Lippincott Company.

McClure. W.R., and Bartuska, T.J. (eds), 2007, *The Built Environment: A Collaborative Inquiry Into Design and Planning*, 2nd edition, Wiley.

McCoy, J., and Evans, G., 2002, 'The Potential Role of the Physical Environment in Fostering Creativity', *Creativity Research Journal* 14: 3/4, pp. 409–26.

McCullagh, K. in E. Dudley and S. Mealing (eds), 2000, *Becoming Designers*, Exeter: Intellect.

McDonagh, D., Hekkert, P., van Erp, J., and Gyi, D. (eds), 2004, *Design and Emotion: The Experience of Everyday Things*, London: Taylor and Francis.

McDonough W., and Braungart, M., 2002, *Cradle to Cradle*, New York: North Point Press.

McDonough W., as deviser of the 'Hannover Principles'; at http://www.mcdonough.com/principles.pdf Accessed 29 July 2009.

McFadden, D.R., 1982, *Scandinavian Modern Design, 1880–1980*, New York: Abrams.

McFall, B., and Beacham, C., 2006, 'Ideal Design Programming with Photoethnographic Data and Systems Analysis', *Journal of Interior Design* 3: 3, pp. 21–34.

McGowan, M., 2006, *Specifying Interiors: A Guide to Construction, and FF&E for Residential and Commercial Interiors Projects*, New York: Wiley.

McGuire, C., 'Socio-Cultural Changes Affecting Professions and Professionals', in L. Curry and J. Wergin (eds), 1993, *Educating Professionals*, NY: Wiley.

McKellar, S., and Sparke, P., 2004, *Interior Design and Identity*, Manchester: Manchester University Press.

McLain-Kark, J., S. Dhuru, K. Parrott, R. Lovingood, 1998, 'Client Comparison of Three Design Presentation Methods', *Journal of Interior Design* 24: 1, pp.1–11.

McLuhan, M., *Counterblast,* London: Rapp + Whiting, 1970.

Mcneil, P., 1994, 'Designing Women: Gender, Sexuality and the Interior Decorator, *c.*1890–1940', *Art History* 17: 4, pp. 631–657.

Meerwein, G., 2007, *Color: Communication in Architectural Space,* trans: Laura Bruce with Matthew Gaskins and Paul Cohen, Basel and Boston: Birkhauser Verlag.

Mendler, S., Odell, W., and Lazarus, M., 2005, *The HOK Guidebook to Sustainable Design*, 2nd edition (New York: Wiley). http://www.hoksustainabledesign.com/pdf/10KeySteps.pdf Accessed 30 July 2009.

Miller, Hermann Co., *Office Environments* http://www.hermanmiller.com/hm/content/research_summaries/pdfs/wp_Office_Environ.pdf, p.3 and ASID *Workplace Values How Employees Want to Work* 2001, http://www.asid.org/designknowledge/publications/center/workplacevalues.htm Accessed 5 February 2010. Also Chapter 12: http://www.hermanmiller.co.uk/our-products-test/seating/embody/

Miller, M.C., 1997, *Color for Interior Architecture*, New York: Wiley.

Miller, S., 1995, *Design Process: A Primer for Architectural and Interior Design*, New York: Van Nostrand.

Millett, M.S., 1996, *Light Revealing Architecture*, New York: Van Nostrand Reinhold.

Mitchell, C.T., 1993, *Redefining Designing: From Form to Experience*, New York: Van Nostrand Reinhold.

Mitton, M.C., 2007, *Residential Interior Design: A Guide to Planning Spaces*, New York: Wiley.

Montello, D., 'The Contribution of Space Syntax to a Comprehensive Theory of Environmental Psychology' in Proceedings, 6th International Space Syntax Symposium, İstanbul, (2007), iv-02, http://www.spacesyntaxistanbul.itu.edu.tr/papers%5Cinvitedpapers%5Cdaniel_montello.pdf Accessed 29 July 2009

Moughtin, C., 1995, *Urban Design, Ornament and Decoration*, Oxford: Architectural Press.

Mumford, L., 1941, *The South in Architecture: the Dancy Lectures, Alabama College*, New York: Harcourt, Brace & Co.

Muthesius, S., 2009, *The Poetic Home*, London: Thames and Hudson.

Natural Step, the; http://www.naturalstep.org Accessed 29 July 2009.

Naylor, G., 'Swedish Grace', in Paul Greenhalgh (ed), 1990, *Modernism in Design*, London: Reaktion Books.

NCIDQ interior design process definition, at http://www.ncidq.org/who/definition.htm Accessed 28 July 2009.

NCS website: http://www.ncscolour.com/webbizz/mainPage/main.asp Accessed 29th July 2009.

Newcomb, R., 1927, *The Spanish House for America, Its Design, Furnishing and Garden*, J.B. Lippincott Company.

Newman, O., 1976, *Design Guidelines for Creating Defensible Space,* US Department of Justice, US Government Printing Office: Washington, DC.

NIBS (National Institute of Building Sciences), *Whole Building Design Guide*, including feature 'Enhance Indoor Environmental Quality'; http://www.wbdg.org/design/ieq.php Accessed 11 May–30 July 2009.

Nierhaus, I., 'The Modern Interior as a Geography of Images, Spaces and Subjects …' in Sparke, Massey, Keeble, Martin (eds), 2009, *Designing the Modern Interior* Oxford: Berg.

Nightingale, F., 1860, *Notes on Nursing,* New York, Appleton and Co.

Norberg-Schulz, C., 1965, *Intentions in Architecture*, Cambridge, MA, MIT Press.

Norberg-Schulz, C., 1980, *Genius Loci: Towards a Phenomenology of Architecture*, New York: Rizzoli.

Norberg-Schulz, C., 1996, 'The Phenomenon of Place', in *Theorising a New Agenda for Architecture*, New York: Princeton Architectural Press.

Ojeda, O. R., *Materials*, introduction and captions by Mark Pasnik, Gloucester, MA: Rockport.

Ornstein, S., 1992, 'First Impressions of the Symbolic Meanings Connoted by Reception Area Design', *Environment and Behavior* 24: 1, pp. 85–110.

Orr, D.W., 1992, *Ecological Literacy: Education and the Transition to a Post Modern World*, Albany, NY: State University of New York Press.

Owens, M., 2006, 'Surreal Deal', *New York Times*, 2 April.

Padovan, R., 2002, *Towards Universality*, London: Routledge.

Palladio, A., 2002, *I quattro libri dell'architettura*, translated by Robert Tavernor, Richard Schofield, Cambridge, MA: MIT Press.

Pallasmaa, J., 1994, 'An Architecture of the Seven Senses', Questions of Perception: Phenomenology of Architecture, *A+U Special Issue* (July), Tokyo: A+U Publishers.

Pallasmaa, J., 2000, 'Stairways of the Mind', *International Forum of Psychoanalysis* 9:1, pp. 7–18.

Panero, J., 1979, *Human Dimension & Interior Space: a Source Book of Design Reference Standards,* London: Architectural Press.

Panofsky, E., 1955, *Meaning in the Visual Arts*, New York: Doubleday.

Papanek, V., 1995, *The Green Imperative: Ecology and Ethics in Design and Architecture*, London: Thames & Hudson.

Parsons, F.A., 1920, *Interior Decoration, its Principles and Practice*, New York: Doubleday.

Pawson, J., website: http://www.johnpawson.com/ Accessed 27 July 2009.

Peck, A., and Irish, C., 2001, *Candace Wheeler: The Art and Enterprise of American Design 1875–1900*, New York: Metropolitan Museum/Yale.

Pennartz, P. J., 'The Experience of Atmosphere', in I. Cieraad (ed.), 1999, *At Home: an Anthropology of Domestic Space,* Syracuse: Syracuse University Press.

Peponis, J., and Wineman, J., 'Spatial Structure of Environment and Behavior' in R. Bechtel and A. Churchman (eds), 2002, *Handbook of Environmental Psychology*, New York: Wiley.

Pevsner, N., Richards, J.M., and Sharp, D., 2000, *Anti-Rationalists and Rationalists*, Oxford: Architectural Press.

Phillips, C., 2003, *Sustainable Place: a Place of Sustainable Development*, Chichester & Hoboken, NJ: Wiley.

Phillips, D., 2000, *Lighting Modern Buildings,* Oxford: Architectural Press.

Pile. J., 2006, *A History of Interior Design*, London: Laurence King.

Pitrowski, C.M., 1998, *Designing Commercial Interiors*, New York: Wiley.

Pitrowski, C.M., 2002, *Professional Practice for Interior Designers,* New York: Wiley.

Pitrowski, C.M., 2004, *Becoming an Interior Designer*, New York: Wiley.

Pocius, G. (ed.), 1991, *Living in a Material World*, St. John's, Nfld: Institute of Social and Economic Research, Memorial University of Newfoundland.

Pogue H.R., 2003, 'What is a House?' in *The Dominion of the Dead*, Chicago: The University of Chicago Press.

Pope, R., 2005, *Creativity, Theory, History and Practice*, London: Routledge.

Porteous, C., 2002, *The New Eco-Architecture: Alternatives from the Modern Movement*, New York: Spon Press.

Portoghesi, P., 2000, 'Nature and Architecture', in *Nature and Architecture*, Milan: Skira.

Princen, T., Maniates, M., and Conca, K. (eds), 2002, *Confronting Consumption*, Cambridge MA: MIT Press.

Pugin, A.W.N., 1973, *Contrasts*, Leicester: Leicester University Press.

Rajchman, J., 1998, 'Lightness', in *Constructions*, Cambridge, MA: MIT Press.

Rasmussen, S.E., 1962, *Experiencing Architecture*, Cambridge, MA: MIT Press.

Rawls, J., 1971, *A Theory of Justice*, Oxford: Oxford University Press.

Redclift, M., 1996, *Wasted: Counting the Costs of Global Consumption*, London: Earthscan Publications.

Reed, C., 'Taking Amusement Seriously: Modern Design in the Twenties', in Sparke et al. (eds), 2009, *Designing the Modern Interior,* pp. 79–93.

Rendell, J., Borden; I, Penner, B., 2000, *Gender Space and Architecture, an Interdisciplinary Introduction*, London: Routledge.

Rengel, R., 2003, *Shaping Interior Space*, New York: Fairchild Publications.

Rice, C., 2006, *The Emergence of the Interior*: *Architecture, Modernity, Domesticity,* London: Taylor and Francis.

Rice, C., 2007, 'For a Concept of the Domestic Interior: Some Historical and Theoretical Challenges', in *Thinking Inside the Box*, London: Middlesex University Press.

Riggs, J., 1996/2007, *Materials and Components of Interior Architecture*, Englewood Cliffs, NJ: Prentice Hall.

Rignall, J., 'Benjamin's Flaneur and the Problem of Realism', in A. Benjamin (ed.), 1989, *The Problems of Modernity: Adorno and Benjamin*, London: Routledge.

Riley, C., 1995, *Color Codes*, Hanover, NH: University Press of New England.

Roscoe, T., 2007, 'Immaterial Culture', in *Thinking Inside the Box*, London: Middlesex University Press.

Rosner, V., 2005, *Modernism and the Architecture of Private Life*, New York: Columbia University Press.

Rossotti, H., 1983, *Color: Why the World Isn't Grey*, Princeton: Princeton University Press.

Rothschild, J. (ed.), 1999, *Design and Feminism: Revisioning Spaces, Places and Everyday Things*, Piscataway, NJ: Rutgers University Press.

Rüedi, K., 1996, 'Architectural Education and the Culture of Simulation: History Against the Grain', in Hardy, A., and Teymur, N. (eds), *Architectural History and the Studio*, London: Question Press, pp. 109–125.

Ruskin, J., 1859, *Seven Lamps of Architecture*, New York: J. Wiley and Sons.

Ryder, B., 2006, *Bar and Club Design,* London: Laurence King.

Rykwert, J., 1973, 'Adolf Loos: the New Vision', *Studio International* 186: 957, http://www.studio-international.co.uk/archive/loos_1973_186_957.asp Accessed 4 February 2010.

Sahlins, M., 1976, 'Colours and Cultures', cited in J. Gage, 1999, *Colour and Meaning*, London: Thames & Hudson.

Sassi, P., 2005, *Strategies for Sustainable Architecture*, New York: Taylor & Francis.

Schon, D.A., 1985, *The Reflective Practitioner: How Professionals Think in Action,* New York: Basic Books.

Schon, D.A., 1987, *Educating the Reflective Practitioner: Toward a New Design for Teaching and Learning in the Professions*, San Francisco: Jossey-Bass.

Scruton, R., 1980, *The Aesthetics of Architecture*, London: Princeton.

Serageldin, I., 1995, 'Architecture and Behaviour: The Built Environment of Muslims', *Architecture & Comportement/Architecture & Behaviour*, 11: 3–4, pp. 193–206.

Sharpe, D., 1974, *Psychology of Color and Design,* Chicago: Nelson-Hall.

Snodgrass, A., and Coyne, R., 2006, *Interpretation in Architecture: Design as a Way of Thinking*, London: Routledge.

Sottsass, E., 1989, 'Travel Notes' *Terrazzo*, cited in Malnar and Vodvarka, 2004, *Sensory Design*, p. 207.

Soulillou, J., 2002, *Ornament and Order*, cited in *Intimus*, Taylor and Preston, 2006, p. 320.

'Space Syntax' website: http://www.spacesyntax.com Accessed 29 July 2009.

Spain, D., 1992, *Gendered Spaces,* Chapel Hill: North Carolina University Press.

Spanbroek, N., and Lommerse, M., 1999, *Interior Architecture in Australia and Canada: A Comparative Study of the Development of University Education for Interior Designers/Architects*. http://espace.lis.curtin.edu.au/archive/00001022/02/Microsoft_Word_-_99_IDEAPaper__Part_Two_Spanbroek_Lommerse__2_.pdf Accessed 5 February 2010.

Sparke, P., 2005, *Elsie De Wolfe: the Birth of Modern Interior Decoration*, New York: Acanthus Press.

Sparke, P. and McKellar, S. (eds), 2004, *Interior Design and Identity*, Manchester: Manchester University Press.

Sparke, P., Massey, A., Keeble, T., Martin B. (eds), 2009, *Designing the Modern Interior: From the Victorians to Today*, Oxford: Berg.

Stamps, A., 2000, *Psychology and the Aesthetics of the Built Environment*, Norwell, MA: Kluwer.

Stanton, C.H., 1968, 'What Comes After Carnaby Street', *Design,* February, pp. 42–3.

Steele, J., 2005, *Ecological Architecture: A Critical History*, London: Thames & Hudson.

Stegmeier, D., 2008, *Innovations in Office Design: The Critical Influence Approach to Effective Work Environments,* New York: Wiley.

Steig, C., 2006, 'Sustainability Gap', *Journal of Interior Design,* 32: 1, pp. vii–xxi.

Stern, A.L., et al., 2003, 'Understanding the Consumer Perspective to Improve Design Quality', *Journal of Architectural and Planning Research* 20: 1, pp. 16–28.

Stickley, G,. 1905, *The Craftsman*.

Sutherland, M., 1989, *Lettering for Architects and Designers*, New York: Van Nostrand Reinhold.

Tahkokallio, P. and Vihma S. (eds), 1995, *Design: Pleasure or Responsibility*, Helsinki: Helsinki University of Art and Design.

Tanizaki, J., 1977, *In Praise of Shadows*, Stony Creek, CT: Leete's Island Books, Inc.

The Tao Te Ching, http://www.terebess.hu/english/tao/wrigley.html, XI, Accessed 28 September 2009

Tate, A. and Smith, R., 1986, *Interior Design in the 20th Century*, New York: Harper and Row.

Taylor, C., 'The Person', in Carrithers, M., Colins, S., and Lukes, S. (eds), 1985, *The Category of the Person*, Cambridge and New York: Cambridge University Press.

Taylor, C., 1989, 'Epiphanies of Modernism', in *Sources of the Self: The Making of Modern Identity*, Harvard University Press: Cambridge, MA.

Taylor, M., and Preston, J. (eds), 2006, *Intimus: Interior Design Theory Reader*, New York: Wiley Academy.

Thomas, K.L., 2007, *Material Matters: Architecture and Material Practice*, Abingdon, Oxon: Routledge.

Thompson, E.P., 1988, *William Morris*, Palo Alto, CA: Stanford University Press.

Thornton, P., 1984, *Authentic Decor*, London: Weidenfeld and Nicolson.

Tigerman, B.J., 2007, 'I Am Not a Decorator': Florence Knoll, the Knoll Planning Unit and the Making of the Modern Office', *Journal of Design History* 20, pp. 61–74.

Tilley, C., 2006, 'Theoretical Perspectives' in Tilley, C., et al. (eds), *Handbook of Material Culture*, London: Sage.

Todd, N. and Todd, J., 1994, *From Eco-cities to Living Machines: Principles of Ecological Design*, Berkeley, California: North Atlantic Books.

Tofle, R.B., Schwartz, B., Yoon, S., and Max-Royale, A., 2004, *Color in Healthcare Environments,* for the American Center for Health Design (for summary see Young, J., 2007).

Trilling, J., 2003, *Ornament: A Modern Perspective*, Seattle and London: University of Washington Press.

Tschumi, B., 1996, *Architecture and Disjunction,* Cambridge, MA: MIT Press.

Tuan, Yi-Fu, 1977, *Space and Place: The Perspective of Experience*, Minneapolis: University of Minnesota Press.

Turpin, J., 2001, 'Omitted, Devalued, Ignored: Re-evaluating the Historical Interpretation of Women in the Interior Design Profession', *The Journal of Interior Design* 27:1, pp. 1–11.

Turpin, J., 2007, 'The History of Women in Interior Design: a Review of Literature', *Journal of Interior Design* 33:1, pp. 1–15.

Tversky, B., 2003, 'Structures of Mental Spaces: How People Think About Space', *Environment and Behavior* 35, pp. 66–80.

Ulmer, G., 'Chora', in *Heuretics, The Logic of Invention*, 1994, Baltimore: Johns Hopkins University Press.

Ulrich, R., Zimring, R., et al., 2004, *The Role of the Physical Environment in the Hospital of the 21st Century*, Center for Health Design: Concord CA.

USACE (US Army Corps of Engineers), Southwestern Division, http://www.swd.usace.army.mil/capabilities/SWD_AEIM_Jan_2003.pdf Accessed 28 July 2009.

V & A (Victoria and Albert Museum), Archive of Art and Design, Ref AAD/1988/20 (about Incorporated Institute of British Decorators).

von Meiss, P., 1990, *Elements of Architecture, From Form to Place*, London: Taylor and Francis.

Van Brakel, J., 1990, 'The Coming into Being of Colour Spaces', in Saunders, B., Brakel, J. van (eds), *Theories Technologies Instrumentalities of Colour: Anthropological and Historiographical Perspectives,* Lanham, MD: University of America Press.

Van Onna, E., 2003, *Material World: Innovative Structures and Finishes for Interiors*, Basel: Birkhauser.

Varney, C., 1988, *The Draper Touch: The High Life & High Style of Dorothy Draper,* New York: Prentice-Hall, Inc.

Veitch, J.A., and McColl, S.L., 2001, 'A Critical Examination of Perceptual and Cognitive Effects Attributed to Full-Spectrum Fluorescent Lighting', *Ergonomics* 44: 3, pp. 255–279.

Venturi, R., 1966, *Complexity and Contradiction in Architecture*, New York: The Museum of Modern Art.

Venturi, R., Scott Brown, D., Arnell, P., Bickford, T., Bergart, C., 1984, *A View From the Campidoglio: Selected Essays, 1953–1984*, Harper & Row.

Vilnai-Yavetz, I., Rafaeli, A., Yaacov, C.S., 2005, 'Instrumentality, Aesthetics, and Symbolism of Office Design', *Environment and Behavior* 37: 4, pp. 533–551.

Vining, D., April 2006, 'Why We Think Blue is Calming: Color-Mood Associations as Learned or Innate': http://www.geocities.com/huntgoddis/appendixe.doc

Vitruvius, 1960, *Ten Books of Architecture,* New York: Dover.

Vodvarka, F., *Aspects of Color*, http://www.midwest-facilitators.net/downloads/mfn_19991025_frank_vodvarka.pdf

Vogel, C., 1991 (February 1), 'Eleanor Brown is Dead at 100; Interior Designer Pioneered Field', *New York Times* Obituary.

Voysey, C.F.A., 1911 (27 January), 'The English Home', *British Architect*, LXXXV.

Wagner, C., 1988, *The Wagner Color Response Report*, Chicago, IL: Color Communications, Inc.

Wahl, D.C., and Baxter, S., 2008, 'The Designer's Role in Facilitating Sustainable Solutions', *Design Issues* 24: 2, pp. 72–83.

Walter, E., 1988, *Placeways, a Theory of Human Environment*, cited in Malnar and Vodvarka, 2004, *Sensory Design*, Minneapolis: Minnesota University Press, p. xi.

Ward, L., 'Chintz, Swags and Bows: the Myth of the English Country House Style 1930–90', in Susie McKellar and Penny Sparke, 2004, *Interior Design and Identity*, Manchester: Manchester University Press.

Waxman, L., 2006, 'The Coffee Shop: Social and Physical Factors Influencing Place Attachment', *Journal of Interior Design,* 31: 3, pp. 35–53.

WBCSD/World Business Council for Sustainable Development www.WBCSD.org Accessed 30 July 2009.

Weisman, L., 1992, *Discrimination by Design: A Feminist Critique of the Man Made Environment*, Champaign, IL: University of Illinois.

Westin, A., 1967, *Privacy and Freedom*, New York: Athenaeum.

Weyl, H., 1983, *Symmetry*, Princeton, NJ: Princeton University Press.

Wharton, E., 1934, *A Backward Glance*, New York and London: Appleton-Century.

Wharton, E., and Codman, O., 1978 [1897], *The Decoration of Houses*, New York: Norton.

Wigley, M., 2001, *White Walls, Designer Dresses: The Fashioning of Modern Architecture,* Cambridge, MA: MIT Press.

Wilde, Oscar, 1890 (2 July), Letter to the Editor, *Daily Chronicle*.

Wilk, C., 1981, *Marcel Breuer, Furniture and Interiors*, Oxford: Architectural Press.

Williams, T.S., 1981, *Interior Designers Guide to Pricing, Estimating and Budgeting*, Allworth Press.

Winchip, S., 2007, *Fundamentals of Lighting*, New York: Fairchild.

Winchip, S., 2007, *Sustainable Design for Interior Environments*, New York: Fairchild.

Wood, M., 2005, *Nancy Lancaster, English Country House Style*, London: Frances Lincoln.

Wood, M., 2007, *John Fowler, Prince of Decorators,* London: Frances Lincoln.

World Commission on Environment and Development (WCED), '*From One Earth to One World*', in *WCED, Our Common Future*, 1987, Oxford: Oxford University Press.

Wright, F.L., 1910, *The Sovereignty of the Individual*, cited in Malnar and Vodvarka, *Sensory Design*, p. 35.

Wright, F.L., 1954, *The Natural House*, New York: Horizon Press.

Wright, F.L., 1954b (2 August), *Time Magazine*.

Yeager, J.I., and Teter-Justice, L., 2000, *Textiles for Residential and Commercial Interiors,* New York: Fairchild.

Yencken, D., and Wilkinson, D., 2000, 'The Physical and Global Context', *Resetting the Compass*, Collingwood, Victoria: CSIRO Publishing.

Yildirim, K., Akalin-Baskaya A., Celebi, M., 2007, 'The Effects of Window Proximity, Partition Height, and Gender on Perceptions of Open-plan Offices', *Journal of Environmental Psychology*, 27:2, pp. 154–65.

Young, D.J.B., 2004, 'The Material Value of Color: The Estate Agents Tale', *Home Cultures* 1:1 (March), pp. 6–10.

Young, J., 2007 (September), 'A Summary of Color in Healthcare Environments: A Critical Review of the Research Literature', *Healthcare Design* Sept. 2007.

Zimring, C., 'Postoccupancy Evaluation: Issues and Implementation', in Bechtel and Churchman (eds), 2002, *Handbook of Environmental Psychology*, New York: Wiley.

Unpublished

Holm, I., 2006, *Ideas and Beliefs in Architecture and Design*, Oslo School of Architecture and Design, PhD Thesis.

Index